METAVERSE:

The Visionary Guide for Beginners to Discover and Invest in Virtual Lands, Blockchain Gaming, Digital art of NFTs and the Fascinating technologies of VR, AR and AI

Table of Contents

1 INTO THE METAVERSE..1

   1.1   What is the Metaverse? 1

   1.2   The History of the Metaverse...........................5

   1.3   Other Metaverses..13

   1.4   What to Do in a Digital Universe 15

   1.5   Conclusion...16

2 BASICS OF THE METAVERSE 18

   2.1   The Data Needs of a Digital Universe...........18

   2.2   The Tools to Create the Metaverse Domain..............27

   2.3   Ethical Considerations of the Digital Realms...........43

   2.4   The Need for Protocol Requirements 48

   2.5   Innovations of the Metaverse.........................50

   2.6   Conclusion...52

3 WHEN REALITY GOES VIRTUAL 54

   3.1   The Definition of Virtual Reality 54

   3.2   A Glossary of Common VR Terms 56

      3.2.1   Virtuality...56

      3.2.2   Virtual Object/Image.............................56

      3.2.3   Virtual World/Environment...................57

3.2.4   Presence..58

3.2.5   Telepresence 59

3.3   Other Virtual Worlds 60

3.4   Equipment and Key Players in the VR World...........67

3.5   Conclusion..75

4   AUGMENT REALITY 77

4.1   What Augmented Reality is all about............................79

4.2   Types of Augmented Reality 81

4.3   The Realization of Augmented Reality 85

4.4   Key Players of Augmented Reality................................90

4.5   Utility of Augmented Reality...103

4.6   Mixed Realities 104

4.7   Extended   Realities: Advantages   and
Disadvantages..105

4.8   Conclusion...105

5   NON-FUNGIBLE TOKENS 107

5.1   NON-FUNGIBLE TOKEN - MEANING...................110

5.1.1   What is NFTs...113

5.1.2   Fungibility in NFTs.......................................114

5.1.3   Fungible and non-fungible 115

5.1.4   Characteristics of NFTs 115

5.1.5   The Future of Art Market in the Blockchain
industry   120

5.1.6   Hype for art 121

5.1.7   Key function 122

5.1.8   Benefit of NFT 123

5.2   ASSET FOR COLLECTIBLES 125

5.2.1   Main characteristics 125

5.2.2   Complementary features 127

5.3   HISTORY OF NON-FUNGIBLE TOKENS 129

5.3.1   Non-Fungible Tokens Myths 131

5.3.2   Problems or Controversies 133

5.3.3   Make enlightened business decisions 134

5.4   CASES OF USE OF NON-FUNGIBLE TOKEN 136

5.4.1   What are ERC-721 tokens? 137

5.4.2   Important information 138

5.4.3   What are the Cryptokitties? 140

5.4.4   What Are CryptoPunks? 141

5.4.5   CoinMarketcap X the Sandbox: CMC Heroes 141

5.4.6   What else can be converted into an NFT? 142

5.5 POPULAR PROJECTS 143

5.5.1 Top NFT Projects 144

5.5.2 Latest Sells of NFTs 146

5.5.2.1 NFT sold a column from 'The New York Times' for 475,000 euros................................. 146

5.5.3 Expensive NFTs 148

5.5.3.1 Beeple's Digital Art Collection - $ 3.5 million 148

5.5.3.2 Rick and Morty ($ 2.3 million)....................... 148

5.5.3.3 Axie Infinity Lands- $ 1.5 million 149

5.5.3.4 The Crypto Punks 149

5.5.3.5 One F1 Delta Time track....................... 150

5.5.3.6 Finance Insurance for NFT 150

5.5.3.7 Virtual lands in Decentraland 151

5.5.3.8 Land at 22.2 in Decentraland is available for purchase for 345 ETH. 151

5.5.3.9 CryptoSpaceCommanders Battlecruiser - 250 ETH 151

5.5.3.10 Gods Unchained (Atlas) -210 ETH 152

5.5.3.11 Gods Unchained (Prometheus) -235 ETH . 153

5.6 SECURITY AND NON-FUNGIBLE TOKEN 155

5.6.1 Standards for Non-Fungible Token...................155

5.6.1.1 Non-Fungible Tokens Metadata 158

5.6.2 Be smart about copyright 159

5.6.3 Keeping your information safe 160

5.15.3.3   Key players..251

5.15.3.4   When will the project launch?......................252

5.15.3.5   Do you want to partecipate to AirDrop?...252

6   CRYPTOCURRENCY...253

6.1   What are Cryptocurrencies?...............................255

6.2   How does Crypto work in the Metaverse? Why Choose Cryptocurrency?...256

6.3   Make the most of the Metaverse with Crypto Investments...261

6.4   Conclusion..268

7   INVESTMENTS IN THE METAVERSE 269

7.1   Business Areas of the Metaverse 270

7.2   Metaverse Marketing 274

7.3   Best Means to Invest in the Metaverse 278

7.4   The Key Players of the Metaverse Domain 280

7.5   Where you should invest your money?................284

7.6   Other methods to earn in the Metaverse 285

7.7   Conclusion..286

8   E-COMMERCE AND THE METAVERSE................288

8.1   Sales in the Metaverse...289

8.2   The Future of Sales in the Metaverse 290

8.3   Conclusion...293

9   LEGALITIES AND REAL WORLD ISSUES 295

9.1   Potential Snags in the Metaverse................................296

9.2   Legalities of the Digital Domains................................300

9.3   Lookouts for Future Iterations 302

9.4   Conclusion...304

10   Avatars of the Metaverse 305

10.1   What it means to Go Virtual......................................306

10.2   The Effect of the Avatar 308

10.3   The Monetization of the Virtual Avatar 310

10.4   Virtual Avatars, Virtual Economies and Games 316

10.5   The Assurance of Identities 318

10.6   The Importance of Identity in the Metaverse 326

10.7   Authentication and the Zero Knowledge Protocol 332

10.8   Conclusion...334

11   The Game Economy... 335

11.1   Attention Economy...336

11.2   Application of Games into the Metaverse 341

11.3   Virtual Items in the Virtual Economy of Games 342

11.4   Game Currencies 349

11.5   Conclusion...354

12   THE FUTURE IS NOW.. 355

12.1   Opportunities for Furthering the Metaverse 355

12.2   Evolution of the Metaverse..357

CONCLUSION 358

REFERENCES.. 359

Please remember to **leave a review of this book on Amazon**, even if you obtain the book on other platforms.

1 INTO THE METAVERSE

The Metaverse is a different kind of universe, defined not by a series of tangible concepts but a universe crafted entirely within the realm of technology, grafted onto our world through the use of myriad technological advances that serve as the bridge between our world and the Metaverse. If you are reading this book, the chances are that you would have encountered the term Meta in some form. But, again, the philosophical aspect is taken into account. Meta connotes transcendence and the ability of an object to surpass what has been expected of it. Gamers, for instance, would see this term in the context of the best character, skin or weapon there is in a game. Digital entrepreneurs, on the other hand, would view Meta as a domain that goes beyond what we have in our world. For the novice, the Metaverse is a world where virtual interactions enable one to transcend the boundaries of time and space and promote shared experiences with people worldwide.

1.1 What is the Metaverse?

The Metaverse was first coined in the 1992 cyberpunk dystopia in Neal Stephenson's Snow Crash. It would be more familiar to movie buffs in the universe depicted in Steven Spielberg's Ready Player One. Despite the futuristic connotations of the Metaverse, we have lived in one throughout all these years. How? The use of the chat room was one of the earliest iterations of the Metaverse. The dawn of the World Wide Web, where the fledgling online communities have found their origins, has led to the development of chat rooms in the 1980s. Multimedia Online Role Playing Games became a means to visualize the digital universe at the dawn of the new millennium. Lately, there are various platforms wherein one can easily engage with other people online.

From this, it can be gleaned that the Metaverse is a digital universe, shared by all those who can access it, wherein the Metaverse is accessible through cloud storage that enables one to combine aspects of the virtual world with that of the physical world through the use of the augmented reality technology. While it can be said that Metaverses could theoretically exist due to the presence of multiple platforms created by various developers, it is accepted that there is only a singular Metaverse, in that all the existent Metaverses are a summation of what the Metaverse is. While we may have gone into the metaphysical definitions of what the Metaverse could be, this means that each platform through which we access our version of the Metaverse exists in a singular linear model, where each forum lies along the same path. Although they are all connected through each other with the help of standard accounts such as our Facebook or Google Play accounts, we would eventually be able to interact more with other people and collaborate on other tasks within the scope of the Metaverse.

Specific characteristics distinguish a Metaverse from the closed world we often see in games. Because any iteration of the Metaverse is ultimately comprised of a code that exists on the Internet, the Metaverse has no defined end. It does not begin from somewhere, nor does it end at a particular point. As with the various combinations of the Metaverse codes, it is infinite in its possibilities.

Unlike closed worlds in the games that we encounter, where the worlds and events take place once the game starts, the events in the Metaverse occur in real-time. That is to say, everyone in the world who is in that particular domain at the moment is part of a collective of shared experiences, albeit with slight differences in time to accommodate the capacity of servers to hold all the individual IP addresses. While in the shared experience, the inhabitants of the Metaverse are differentiated from each other and can take part in the events that are slated in the said world, server accommodations aside, they would be able to fully immerse themselves virtually, as though they were in a digital facsimile of an actual event.

Like with other worlds and nations, as you could consider a Metaverse to be one in certain aspects, there would be some form of economy that would enable the world to flourish. Just as the world functions on businesses, the Metaverse is not only an immersive world for shared experiences- as this would severely limit its potentials, but a place of business where one can engage in practices that are valuable to the existence of the Metaverse. At the core of it all, the Metaverse is a world grafted to our own, where it does not exist only for entertainment purposes. To keep it afloat, it must also engage in business, where one can take part in the Metaverse development.

Earlier, we touched on the root word of the Metaverse, Meta, the Greek word for Beyond, and a transcendent experience. The Metaverse, as we reiterate constantly, is a fully immersive experience that links both physical and virtual experiences through specific servers, both public and private, and on platforms that may or may not be readily accessible to all people. Because of its transcendent nature, it becomes possible to link other platforms with the Metaverse you currently are in. Think of the transference of the aspects of one game, such as skins and items, through a medium, and you can use this in another game. On a relatable note, please think of how we link our games with our Facebook or Google Play accounts and how we can use the same data we have on another device. While the latter example is limited in that it is constrained within the devices, it becomes possible for the data to transfer to another app because of the existent link between the two disparate apps. This is how the Metaverse intends to function.

Lastly, the Metaverse differs from closed worlds. In the Metaverse, anyone can have a hand and contribute to the development and creation of worlds and features present in that platform, unlike closed worlds where the creation of the world-building features are primarily within the purview of the development team who created the game. In the Metaverse, however, the creation of content and other experiences are developed by anyone who has the technical knowledge on how to deliver the content on the said platform. If you are an avid gamer and a coder, you can think of it as a mod that you can share with other participants.

For a Metaverse to be defined, the characteristics mentioned above are central to its existence. However, a different approach can be seen with the Metaverse development. Some point out that it presages the result of a newer form of the Internet that transfers control from the digital conglomerates and allows other people to have a say in how the Metaverse is developed. This echoes the last characteristic that enables other independent developers or lesser-known tech groups to create shareable content that other participants in the Metaverse would access.

1.2 The History of the Metaverse

When it comes to the realization of the Metaverse as it exists in its current form, we have to delve into the history of the infrastructure that underlies the Metaverse. This refers to the Internet. While the technologically initiated will know that the Internet was developed to transfer files and data across a secure network, at its inception, the Internet was primarily used within the networks of the Department of Defense when it was known as the Arpanet. As we know it, the Internet was conceptualized for public use on August 6, 1991, when Sir Tim Berners-Lee enabled collaborators to work on what would be the Internet with the development of the World Wide Web. Earlier, we mentioned the 1992 Neil Stephenson novel Snow Crash, where Metaverse was first coined. In the novel, humans were able to interact in a three-dimensional dystopia in the form of avatars, wherein their digitized form, it became possible for humans to interact with data and software virtually.

One of the main mechanisms in the Metaverse would be the Proof of Work, wherein it functions as a safeguard used by Cryptocurrency transactions to ensure that each transaction in the network is validated. This mechanism came into being as early as 1993, where its original function was to prevent those pesky spam emails and prevent anyone from spamming anyone with emails. However, it was only in later years that the Proof of Work protocol became such an integral component in the Metaverse development, where it began to function as a means by which transactions that take place can be vetted and legitimized, especially with Cryptocurrencies that require mining. To link with the concept of Cryptocurrencies, the basis for Cryptocurrencies was first created in 1998 using B-money, which was the earliest form of Cryptocurrency. Conceptualized by computer engineer Wei Dei, it envisioned a decentralized currency that would be used in the Metaverse. However, this idea did not come to fruition but was later carried on when similar characteristics and concepts were embodied with the emergence of Bitcoin later on. Therefore, as a companion to the Proof of Work protocol, the Proof of Stake protocol was developed to mine data algorithms based on the developer's current holdings of Cryptocurrency, rather than the sheer volume of power that a person can wield with a particular program.

The conceptualization of the Metaverse was purely theoretical in its origins, but the components central to its infrastructure were laid out. As we would know, the Internet is central to the existence of the Metaverse and the Proofs of Work and Stake protocols that ensure that the transactions that take place within the Metaverse are safeguarded and would provide the continued safety of its patrons. The development of Cryptocurrency, though initially mothballed, was later used as a basis wherein one could establish a means to pay for transactions while within the Metaverse. Onwards into the new millennium, newer technological advances enabled software engineers and computer scientists to create a virtual world similar to our own. Digital Twins were first conceptualized in 2002 and were defined as a counterpart of a physical object in the digital world. This idea originated from Michael Grieves, who was, at the time, from the University of Michigan, while at a conference of a Society of Manufacturing Engineers. Grieves intended for the Digital Twin as a concept that would underlie product lifecycle management.

As the Metaverse can be envisioned as a digital world, the creation of Second Life in 2003 by Philip Rosedale and the development team of Linden Labs was an iteration of the Metaverse that featured an elaborately crafted digital universe. However, despite the innovation brought about by Second Life, it was hindered from further usage due to a low bandwidth capacity and a high-resolution time, which made it less than optimal for continued usage by Netizens. Despite its deficiencies, Second Life remains in use to the present day, where at least a million people continue to interact within its

proto-Metaverse environment. Three years later, we see the development of Roblox in 2006. Roblox, for the newbies, is an online platform that remains one of the more popularly used Metaverses nowadays, enabling a person to develop and play games that other users created. Roblox experienced an increase in the number of users amid the Pandemic. It provided a reasonably safe space wherein community members could interact with one another. Because of the uptick in the number of users in the pandemic-induced lockdown, Roblox ranked among the three highest-grossing games of 2020.

Aside from the gaming applications of the Metaverse, we head once more into the domain of Cryptocurrency, where Bitcoin came into being in the year 2009. Satoshi Nakamoto was the enigmatic creator of Bitcoin Cryptocurrency, who mined the first 50 Bitcoins when he mined Block Number 0. The same creator also conceptualized the idea of blockchains to servers as a means by which each transaction that involved Bitcoins may be recorded. Though Blockchains were initially believed to be invented earlier than Bitcoin, Nakamoto is credited with the development of the Blockchains as it became a usable protocol with the development of the Bitcoin.

A more familiar sight in the history of the Metaverse would be the development of Play-to-Earn Technology, Known in Japan as Gacha games, and this type of technology came into being in 2010. While the player plays the game, they would be able to earn currency that could be used to participate in a draw that would give them rare in-game items that would provide a considerable power boost to their character. This scenario would be highly familiar to gamers who frequently engage in RPGs where the microtransactions in each game enable the player to purchase weapons, skins and other characters that would boost their performance, or a chance to win the currency that would allow them to obtain these items. Think of it as a means to earn premium items such as gold, gems and crystals as a few examples. 2011 contributed Ready Player One, a novel we discussed earlier as one of the more comprehensive portrayals of the Metaverse.
The Spielberg film based on the book released in 2018 provided a more visual aspect of how the Metaverse and its myriad interactions are depicted.

2012 saw the development of the Non-Fungible Token, where the token represents a unique item rather than a fungible item. Fungible, in legal terms, is where an object may be exchanged for another thing that is equal in value. In this instance, this form of a token cannot be exchanged in any form. Coloured Coins were among the earlier form of NFTs, in their abbreviated aspect, where though similar to Bitcoins in function, because of the composition of their code, the coin cannot be exchanged as it is unique in itself. Vitalik Buterin conceptualized the NFT as he sought to improve the blockchain method of Bitcoins.

Vitalik Buterin is one of the many names that would be associated with the creation of the structures that underlie the Metaverse. The Thiel Fellowship would be central to the formation of the Metaverse Infrastructure. When Peter Thiel and Elon Musk formed a merger to form the service we know as Paypal, which eBay then bought for $1.5 billion, this resulted in a big payoff for both Musk and Thiel. Thiel, in 2010 created the Thiel Fellowship, which provided a hundred thousand dollars worth of grants for students who were under the age of 22 to leave school for other opportunities. Among the grantees was the then 20-year old Vitalik Buterin, the creator of the NFT and later co-creator of Ethereum. Ethereum was later launched in 2015 with the combined efforts of Buterin and Gavin Wood. At the same time, the Ethereum Blockchain was also released.

2015 saw the formation of a Metaverse called Decentraland, which provided land to users through the Proof of Work Algorithm now employed as a Metaverse Protocol. An increase in the worth of the NFT led to the sale of the "plots of land" in Decentraland, which fetched prices that reached up to $100,000.00. Also, in 2015 was the creation of Smart Contracts. However, these were initially conceived in the 1990s, where these contracts were defined as digitally made agreements, which obligate the parties to act upon the arrangements made within the contract. Despite the legalese explanation of the Smart Contract – which we can construe to bear similarity to contracts in a legal context, the Smart Contract now refers to a computation on a blockchain or a ledger.

In 2016, Pokemon Go, the viral hit game created by Niantic, became essential in the history of the Metaverse as it was the first game to integrate aspects of the Virtual World with the Real World. If you are familiar with the game itself, you may have seen the game's mechanics where players use their devices, with the help of GPS, to capture, train and battle other Pokemon within the scope of their environment. On a more serious note, 2016 also saw the inception of the Decentralized Autonomous Organization, which takes its name from a crowdfunded company of the same name established in 2016. The DAO, as it is abbreviated, set the record for the largest crowdfund and was initially founded to be an alternative venture fund based on the Blockchain of Ethereum that would be the initial model for a decentralized fund system. However, an exploited vulnerability in the security of the DAO allowed users to remove a third of the funds of the DAO into a subsidiary account which led to the demise of the DAO. Despite this, the groundwork for the establishment of a Decentralized Autonomous Organization was laid and allowed for the creation of more DAOs and other Metaverse companies governed by their respective participants in the Metaverse with their separate rules and transactions safely recorded on the Blockchain.

Fortnite was released in 2017, and it was a wildly successful game, as this introduced people to the idea of the Metaverse and Cryptocurrencies and how these would function in a virtual world. Fortnite became a place then to play games and for people from all over the world to interact in a shared world. In line with the use of Cryptocurrencies, the creation of the Dai Stablecoin in 2018 was introduced to compete with Bitcoin and Ethereum. Unlike other Cryptocurrencies, however, Stablecoin was valued based on the US Dollar, which lessened its volatility as a Cryptocurrency and enabled it to gain a foothold in the Cryptocurrency market as a more reliable form of currency for Decentralized Finance. Blockchain-based banking services gained a foothold due to a stabilized Cryptocurrency. They became available across multiple platforms to enable potential investors to borrow, lend and invest in Cryptocurrency and the Metaverse. Decentralized Exchanges, despite the negative press attained by Bancor with the loss of $13.5 million to hackers, became one of the primary means by which cyber currencies may be traded by the Smart Contracts that were executed, rather than with a centralized exchange. 2018 also saw the rise of Axie Infinity, a virtual reality game that revolves around the use of NFTs. As of 2021, the NFTs of Axie Infinity attained the highest value among play-to-earn platforms.

When the Pandemic struck in the first quarter of 2020, the lockdown imposed by national governments inhibited the ability of the people to assemble for their shared interests physically. The imposed quarantine saw the world population face a severely limited number of options on what they could do while confined in their homes. The Metaverse became the prime spot where the digital inhabitants could meet their friends in a pandemic-free zone. At the same time, the entrepreneurs would still be able to close deals within the protocols enforced in the Metaverse. The continuation of the Pandemic has propelled more interest in the expansion of the Metaverse. As such, it becomes possible now to be able to do more as more investors become interested in the idea of the Metaverse. 2020 was a good year for the growth of the Metaverse, as Decentralized Apps- open-sourced, transparent programs enabled one to take part in games and conduct financial transactions to potentially increase the value of their respective investments. This way, it was seen that the profit to be earned by investors would be significantly increased as the decentralization of apps eliminates the need for an intermediary to broker the transactions between two parties. On a lighter note, 2020 saw the first virtual concert in the Metaverse created by Fortnite. On the Cryptocurrency market, the Solana Blockchain Decentralized App was introduced, with the Sol as its currency. Another protocol to augment the Proof of Stake Algorithm employed by Solana called the Proof of History tool allowed for the insertion of timestamps into the blockchain transactions that are performed. Later in 2020, another Decentralized App called Alien Worlds came into fruition. With a name evocative of intergalactic adventures, the characters comprised the NFTs that could act in a Decentralized Autonomous Organization where their characters can mine tokens and perform other tasks. Though it can be initially perceived as such, this game began to teach its players the basics of Cryptocurrency and Crypto-Mining.

1.3 Other Metaverses

Metaverse finds its origins in the Greek word Meta – which means beyond and the universe. Despite the technological advancements made to conceptualize the Metaverse, the current iteration that we have as of 2021 is considered a primitive form of what the Metaverse can be. For potential investors, this may seem to dishearten prospective investments. However, the Metaverse is a universe in constant development. Developing a universe to its advanced stages takes time, and investments would help propel the Metaverse to reach its fullest potential. Subsequently, it becomes necessary to glimpse the other platforms developers have created to visualize all the Metaverse's potential. Earlier, we have touched on the gaming aspects of the Metaverse and the Metaverse as a place for businesses to trade in Cryptocurrencies, among other fungible items.

The version of the Metaverse developed by Microsoft is oriented towards business transactions, as well as for users who are engaged in the development of software. The Metaverse of Microsoft involves the development of accessible platforms where users can share and collaborate on the digital counterparts of actual physical items or collaborate on protocols that would enhance the functions of the Metaverse. Microsoft geared its Metaverse towards the development of environments with varying complexity to the development of products in general. The Microsoft Metaverse is oriented towards the logistical side of business wherein in their iteration of the Metaverse, it

13

becomes possible to locate items that have been purchased from its stores and its warehouses, and to identify the progress of apps, ideas and detect the value of stocks in the Metaverse market.

On the other hand, Nvidia has a more simplified Metaverse, which is referred to as the Omniverse. The applications, however focus on the enhancement of

Collaborative practices between engineers enable them to replicate physical items on a digital platform to ensure that engineers and other collaborators can work on the said idea. Facebook's latest rebrand into Meta is one that is unlikely to be forgotten, and its Metaverse revolves around the ability to meet people virtually. The Facebook Metaverse allows a person to create virtual rooms that enable people of like interests to share collective experiences regardless of location and time.

Aside from this, however, it can be seen that the Metaverse can still find its ubiquitous applications in games, like Minecraft, Roblox, and Fortnite remain prime examples of Metaverse with its gaming applications, though platforms such as Fortnite have evolved into a place where people could meet, more than the actual game itself. For example, Fortnite has been described as a game where numerous franchises could interact within the same platform. This has been advantageous for the game itself as it has begun to be considered a proto-Metaverse due to its added functions.

1.4 What to Do in a Digital Universe

As of December 2021, the current state of the Metaverse still revolves around the development and promotion of shared game experiences that are visible in the game as mentioned above platforms in the previous section. However, advances have been made to such a degree that one can add to these functions while immersed in the Metaverse environment. As with Pokemon Go, to cite an example, there are activities and features that, with the help of Augmented Reality Technology, enable the virtual and physical worlds to crossover through the use of an app. Aside from this, with Fortnite as an example, the focus is less on the need to complete the game and more on the use of the game and its servers as an alternative environment that focuses on promoting social interactions rather than the initial goal to complete the game. Furthermore, because the Metaverse was intended to enable other developers to contribute to the available features, one would support the environments and other items that the other users of the Metaverse created.

Like most nations, and if you have played world-building games like the Sims, for example, the importance of economy is present, more so when the Metaverse itself is designed to provide different opportunities for investments that would enable investors and entrepreneurs to link their physical investment portfolios with their Metaverse counterparts seamlessly. This would allow the trade and investments in various Cryptocurrencies, as well as the exchange of Non-Fungible Tokens as well as stocks.

As the Metaverse can be best described as an immersive experience, it can be seen that essential to its function would be the presence of the Virtual Reality and Augmented Reality Software, that allows the physical and Metaverse worlds to combine. Subsequently, the necessary hardware would also need the technical support available in the Metaverse itself.

However, these functions are just a mere representation of what is possible in the Metaverse, as it can be considered a Nexus of Possibilities, limited only by the creative prowess of the contributors who enable the Metaverse to expand. Earlier, we touched upon the role of the Metaverse in the transference and democratization of technology from the hands of technological giants into the hands of other developers. Thus, with many ideas that can exist within the same space, it can be reasoned out that the Metaverse applications would result in a multitude of possibilities. The uses now depend on the developer's ability to create a tool that would answer a need and the availability of the technology needed to execute the said tool as it is, the further expansion of the Metaverse sets of an impetus that would ensure that it continues to function for a prolonged time.

1.5 Conclusion

Creating a whole new universe out of code would involve the establishment of a strong foundation on which developers can lay out the groundwork. The Metaverse in its current form is imperfect in its manifestation as it has yet to permit the total immersion of the user into a virtual space, and with the constant need to innovate how one can assemble virtually over large distances, there remains the need to constantly reinvent and redevelop the foundations that enable the Metaverse to exist. While there have been advances made with regards to the development of a strong Metaverse economy, such as the rise of Bitcoin, Ethereum, and the Stablecoin, and a means to safeguard the transactions made with each currency such as the Proof of Work, Proof of Stake and Proof of History protocols, this creates limitations wherein the Metaverse is embedded into the game and Cryptocurrency niches. Though developments from major tech groups such as Microsoft and Facebook permit ease in the collaboration between like-minded engineers and developers, future results are to be made to ensure that the Metaverse can exist in a way that simulates the physical world. Thus, to answer that immersive need, it becomes essential to know what makes the Metaverse tick. In the second chapter, what is discussed are the fundamentals that comprise the Metaverse and how it enables a different universe to coexist alongside ours without the need to resort to science fiction.

Thanks for buying my book. Here is my **gift to you**, two free online **courses about NFTs** that you download for free from this link:

https://dl.bookfunnel.com/5265zz3f4i

Please remember to **leave a review of this book on Amazon**, even if you obtain the book on other platforms.

2 BASICS OF THE METAVERSE

In Chapter 1, we have touched upon the definition of the Metaverse as a universe that goes beyond and that enables the user to transcend the limitation of time and space to assemble with other users in a digital environment. In the same chapter, the characteristics that define the Metaverse are highlighted, with particularity given to the infiniteness of the Metaverse as it continues to develop.

2.1 The Data Needs of a Digital Universe

One of the more essential components of the Metaverse is the presence of mobile internet. In Chapter 1, we have dealt with the necessity for the internet and how it evolved from a means to simply transfer data across secured channels to being the digital behemoth that it is today. However, though the 90s saw the inception of the World Wide Web and increased usage of the internet, albeit, in its dial-up state, the internet at that time remained limited in that only a few households had internet access, and that the internet was solely accessible through a handful of servers, and only through a desktop computer. There was no Wi-Fi then, and laptops, though present, would need a physical connection to a modem that did not enable a person to take advantage of the afforded mobility. Though the content of the internet has grown throughout all these years, and even into the dawn of the new millennium, the internet became the information superhighway that we know, but navigable only through the use of desktops and modems. Thus, a true Metaverse cannot have been born yet, as most people were unable to access the internet in its current state, save for the use of the internet cafes that became a means where people could congregate. A proto-Metaverse took place with the rise of online games and chat rooms where people could meet, but these Metaverses at that time were limited in their function. Game-based Metaverses were limited to game functions and server caps, while

chat rooms were limited to only chat functions. While these enabled people to meet up, they could only do so using specific credentials and avatars and were not wholly immersive.

The basis for the foundations of the Metaverse were believed to be sown with the rise of the Mobile Internet. The mobile internet age was thought to be ushered in with the iPhones, as it enabled the use of multiple features that the internet had into a particular device. This allowed mobile data access to be more portable. The iPhone then utilized 3G data services, enabling the phones to link up with the signals transmitted by the data provider and allow the user to access the internet through their phone conveniently. The development of apps that augmented the phone's functions became an essential part of the foundations of the Metaverse. As these apps were coded upon Java, Unity and HTML for starters, they enabled collaborators to contribute to the development of the apps. The mobile internet also made it possible to initiate the microtransactions that allowed users to pay for premium features. It then followed that the data needs for the Metaverse would involve the need to ensure that data transmission is at its optimal capacity. When mobile internet officially took off, we started with 3G data, which allowed us to load a page or two at a slightly lower resolution per our data plan. Fast forward a few years later, along with several upgrades to the internal components that allowed for faster data processing, such as more microprocessors in the phone, and we have moved on to 5G internet, which enables us to access more services that are similar to the what the Metaverse intended to be.

In its current state, the Metaverse cannot fully function as a wholly immersive experience for a significant population due to several reasons. Foremost, the technology that would enable a large population to enjoy a synchronous event over cyberspace does not exist. The 2019 concert of the DJ Marshmello conducted over Fortnite can be taken as an example. Though the attendees' data registered at approximately 11 million users, they did not occupy the same network or the same server at the same time. The concert itself was divided into a hundred thousand instances, which played the concert at different times. This concept is essential as it emphasizes that one of the actual characteristics of the Metaverse is a complete shared experience. The fact that though there are 11 million attendees who have attended the concert, they did not as a whole share the same experience due to the lack of synchronicity with each of the 100,000 instances that were documented.

This highlights the current limitations for the Metaverse in that, rather than its ability to accommodate an infinite population within its domain. It remains capped at approximately a hundred thousand users on each server. Though Metaverse platforms could accommodate more than a hundred thousand, it remains in that specific denomination, as it cannot accommodate a million. The problem here lies with the capabilities of the internet at the moment, as at its core, the internet was only meant to share files, hence the development of the World Wide Web, in its current state, it was not designed to process large quantities of data that would encompass the population of a small country. The internet at this point can be reduced to two different servers that communicate information to one another. Social Media, popular it may be, and despite our apparent attempts to continually update our lives, our information does not get directly transmitted to other social media users. Instead, our information from our personal computers gets sent to a centralized server, which relays the information that we have given to the user who requested to access the said information. Even chat rooms maintain this functionality despite the simulation of real-time chat. The internet was never meant to process a continuous flow of information, nor can it accommodate the processing power needed to ensure that the data processed is synchronized across all servers worldwide.

What the Metaverse needs is internet with the capability to process data similar to that of video conferencing programs and video games as these two programs function due to a continued connection that allows for constant communication and that allows for updates to be implemented in the program without cessation in how the program works. If you are an avid gamer, you may have been able to play the game while the game updates. You would also see the patch notes that provide the updates for each program. However, despite the apparent synchronicity with the program, servers and its updates, the programs cease to function once a particular population has been accommodated in the server. For example, should you opt for a video conference, this would compel you to conduct a live stream to the other participants. Despite the life in its connection, the live stream is not live. However, because of the synchronicity in mobile games, their relative popularity has risen as players can compete in real-time. However, this feature is not relatively new, especially if you have played games developed by Blizzard Entertainment and other developers. The earlier iterations of game interactions were hindered by specific servers that cater to a particular location. Subsequently, the players can only interact with players who are within the same server. To join another server would result in disconnecting from the current server and loading your data into another. Should the game reach its capacity to accommodate a certain number of players, then the function of the game ceases to be optimal. As a result, for the Metaverse to evolve beyond its current status, developers must first seek to address the issues that relate to the infrastructure of the Metaverse that would allow for the continuous processing of vast amounts of data.

The second issue that must be addressed with the creation of the Metaverse would be the development of existing protocols. The current internet iteration utilizes protocols that allow the user to download web pages, view videos online and communicate with others. These protocols enable the swift identification of specific files that will allow the computer to execute the user-initiated action. Subsequently, it will allow our computers to communicate with other servers to perform the task that we had requested. While we have touched upon the Metaverse and some of the protocols that run it, precisely the Proof of Work, Proof of Stake and Proof of History protocols essential to Cryptocurrency transactions, these are just a few of the protocols needed to ensure that the experiences that are relayed in the Metaverse are executed smoothly, and its features can be utilized without any problems. The Metaverse, however, requires more than these three to function, as the protocols needed would have to be broad in their development, complex, and resilient in their execution. Because these protocols are unaccustomed to the need for continuous communication between servers, the Metaverse protocols would have to accommodate these. However, the applications and files would have to undergo a fundamental form of alteration in how they are transmitted. Attention must be drawn to the varied types of image files, accounts, and apps that exist on the internet. Some of these programs cannot make a smooth transition, as can be experienced why we can use our data in some apps, but not in another app. This, however, would be a matter best relegated to the technological corporations as this issue stems from their dislike to share the data of their programs to allow the cross-integration of their systems that would permit the smoother transition of data. Because of the current state of digital programs, it may cause the user just to cut the usage of the program altogether and migrate to another service provider or another app that affords them the same functionality with the features they need.

This issue surrounding the Metaverse development is among the most difficult to address. This involves concepts that pertain to the development of new protocols to accommodate all the data processing needs and the legalities involved with these protocols. There are legal issues that must be addressed, particularly in the sections of Internet Law that deal with the security of the data that are processed, stored and transmitted; the length of time it would take for the data to be stored, the compatibilities of the developed protocols for each platform, and the performance of certain transactions. Additional legal issues that the Metaverse would be embroiled in include censorship laws, the control of communications (to ensure that these do not infringe on any legal rights), regulatory enforcement (as assurance that the data processed and the functions performed are regulated and are not freely executed), tax reporting (as the Metaverse would be an abstract entity, there would be legalities that arise with the jurisdiction of cases whose cause of action originated in the environment of the Metaverse), a reduction of online radicalization (without infringement on the freedom of expression), and a multitude of other legal issues that a user may face in the real world.

To address these legal issues would take decades, especially when there is the need to unravel the legalese that enforces the restrictions on cross-sharing in the different Metaverse platforms. Despite the best efforts of all involved, the legal issues would always continue to come into play, as the key industrial players would encounter apprehensions that pertain to the operations and security of their data. It is heavily dependent on the human factor, wherein their opinions regarding certain aspects of the Metaverse are likely to change over time. It would be virtually impossible to address the immediate needs for a Metaverse to be fully realized. The development of the Metaverse cannot result in creating a fully developed world. As the computation and legal requirements are built upon, the most developers can do is create a microcosm in cyberspace wherein the developers gradually develop and expand according to the available technological advancements. The real issue lies in the politics that govern the Metaverse as the key industrial players would want to be the sole voices in how the Metaverse functions. As a result, the dissonant opinions of the developers will eventually conflict with their wants and needs, which could hinder the development of the various protocols needed to ensure that the data from one platform remains usable in another.

Another need related to the Metaverse is the protocols that populate the Metaverse. The developed protocols and data requirements would have to be of a sufficient quality that convinces other collaborators, investors, and developers to accept the Metaverse presented to them. A place of congregation does not automatically build itself up once the Metaverse has been realized. This can be compared with the logistics needed to develop an actual economy, where business areas that contain a few interactive sites gradually build up over time to become the town's economic hub. The same analogy can be carried over with the construction of the Metaverse. The hubs of the Metaverse are created over time, with the population that congregates in that particular area of the platform. For instance, the social media titan, Facebook, did not immediately spring into its current form as a means by which friends could communicate. If one has watched the movie The Social Network, it originally started off as a means to rate a person's attractiveness before it evolved into a cyberspace yearbook that gradually included messages as part of its features. Data then and the protocols that the Metaverse needs must ensure that the Metaverse created is capable of population and not just simply be populated. There must be a draw that entices people and developers to set up their accounts with a particular platform, and the data needs must be able to accommodate an influx of the population.

Popular game platforms should be considered more than games, as this severely limits their potential. We reiterate the appeal of Fortnite, as it became more than a game. It became a place where others could congregate to share their unique interests. This strikes a chord in what the Metaverse can be, especially as one can log into the game and converse with their friends without the compulsion to continue with the game's quests. The platform, as it should be called, had shown its versatility in the accommodation of other ideas when it allowed the integration of various franchises into its platform, and the establishment of different media within it, such as the broadcast of trailers, concerts and behind the scenes looks on our favourite series. About the hubs mentioned above, specific areas of the Fortnite Metaverse were accessible to certain users who have interacted in some form with a particular collaborator to enjoy premium events that were broadcasted through the platform.

Additionally, the same platform became a means where a digital economy had flourished. Users of the platform can purchase premium items to unlock additional advantages while immersed in that Metaverse. Subsequently, it can be said that among all of the existing proto-Metaverse platforms there are at the moment, Fortnite is the best example as the progenitor of the ideal Metaverse.

At the heart of the data needs of the fledgling, Metaverse would be the need for constant communication between all servers for the Metaverse to update itself as a simulacrum of the physical environment continually. As a result, the data that is needed to undertake such as herculean task entails the processing capabilities which are yet to be developed, and the data must be able to support a large population in asynchronous means to ensure that it is indeed a shared experience, accessed and experienced in real-time. Additionally, the protocols needed to support the data must ensure that the user can transition from one platform to another without any form of data loss or interruption that would negatively impact the user experience. Interoperability is an essential concept to the data needs of the Metaverse, and it is through here that perhaps, would be one of the major hindrances to the development of a true Metaverse. Other platforms, however, have made it possible to link game accounts across different platforms so you may continue your game progress from any device, regardless of the developer used.

2.2 The Tools to Create the Metaverse Domain

While the Metaverse in its most authentic essence has yet to be fully realized, in the previous section, we have touched upon the need for an improved internet speed to facilitate the sheer volume of data that must be concurrently processed and the need for protocols that would permit the increased interoperability of each platform. At the same time, these protocols would ensure that the finances and investments of contributors remain safeguarded. In addition, other tools are needed to ensure that the Metaverse becomes a wholly immersive and, more importantly, safe place for the future of the digital industry.

One of the essential tools needed for the Metaverse is repeatedly, faster internet. In this instance, our internet speeds are usually capped at 5G, ensuring a quicker browsing experience. However, despite the relative ease by which we now access our internet (remember the dial-ups way back when), our internet needs to move faster to accommodate the requirements of the Metaverse. This necessitates the need for the 6G internet speed. The sixth-generation internet promises a speedier internet connection with minimum lag as it communicates between servers- an essential aspect when you consider that true synchronicity remains an issue with the Metaverse regardless of the platform. With speeds purported to clock at one terabyte per second, this internet speed also ensures that the Metaverse can process a large amount of data at a constant rate. Current telecommunication companies are on the verge of ensuring that their mobile devices remain compatible with the afforded increased internet speed. While the current state of phones is that they can accommodate 5G internet, software and technology departments are searching to ensure that the phone can adapt to 6G internet when it becomes possible. It is mentioned that this form of the undertaking is quite monumental, and subsequently, this form of the internet would be viable towards the next decade. The Metaverse, if one would recall, is reliant on the use of Virtual Reality and Augmented reality. The 6G internet would ensure that the functions of these two systems operate at their optimal state. It would permit the ease at which users could interface with their devices and promote the faster creation of digital twins, which enhances the collaborative aspect needed to complete the infrastructure of the Metaverse.

Data Exchange Layers (DXL) involves the development of a centrally managed protocol that permits the user to access a specific number of applications and available digital services. Through the use of the data exchange layer, companies, public and private, can link with a user through identifiable credentials unique to the user. The user's data for the company they linked to is stored in a secure server that allows access only when they input their data and links the information across a secure channel between the company and the user involved. Data Exchange Layers are best appreciated in areas that have made advancements in the use of electronic data, as evidenced with the likes of Finland – whose economy has transitioned to the use of mobile devices that contain a unique identifier for each user that allows them to access various services permitted to them. The ease of transactions is made possible with the use of two keys. Authentication keys will enable the transmission of the user information through a secure channel.

In contrast, a signing key ensures that the user is indeed who they say they are and determines the ability to access the user data linked to the encoded credentials. Data Exchange Layers are a necessity in the Metaverse mainly as it is this protocol that allows mobility in a digital environment to ensure that each person with access to this Metaverse can sign in with a unique signature that will enable them to sign documents, obtain permits, and in turn have their actions regulated by a governing authority in the platform that they have signed in. The Data Exchange Layer is essential in the Metaverse as it addresses the specific issue of interoperability, mainly when the Metaverse involved is in Cryptocurrencies and the business operations of the Metaverse economy. The only problem is that some Cryptocurrencies operate under different protocols, and because of this, the data exchange layer is unable to facilitate the interoperability of the Metaverse business platforms. The advantage with the Data Exchange Layer in the Metaverse is the added security it provides, particularly with the use of various blockchains, the validity of the smart contracts, and the ability of the DXL to work with the Proof of Work, Stake and History protocols for the Cryptocurrencies, the DXL allows for increased transparency, accountability with each transaction, and the afforded ability to trace each transaction as it takes place. It empowers the user to have more control over who can access their data.

Edge Data Centers are a crucial part of the infrastructure of the Metaverse, as their strategic location on the fringes of most geographic server hubs allows for a closer relay of the data towards the users who are clustered towards that Edge Center. As a result, there is a faster data processing and a reduction in the lag experienced by users who have accessed the platform in these particular servers. Additionally, because these data centers, in essence, speed up the upload and download times of the various Metaverse platforms, this allows for a more immersive Metaverse experience.

Free Space Optical Communication enhances how data is transmitted across the internet. The use of lasers as the medium by which a user's information is transmitted enables this form of communication to be attachable to various satellites, drones, and even boxes that are installable on higher ground where the laser may transmit uninterrupted. The use of lasers as the medium of transmission becomes cost-effective for the data service provider as this requires no additional cables or towers, and such reduces the overall cost of data transmission. This form of communication is ideally used in areas with remote

communications. This entails that the most far-flung locales can join the internet mainframe through these connections. The one flaw with the use of the lasers as the means of transmission is that lasers can be interrupted in the event of inclement weather, which may significantly impact the quality of data transmission, and becomes the main hindrance to the full implementation of the concept. When applied to the Metaverse, the use of laser transmission of data implies that the internet infrastructure of the Metaverse exhibits a reduced incidence of increased latency. Therefore, there should be minimal lags when this form of transmission is present. Thus, if the hindrances are addressed, this would significantly enhance the quality of the shared experiences within the Metaverse. Regarding the economic implications, this allows collaborators from lesser developed countries to join in the Metaverse and invest in the digital economy.

With an increased internet speed comes an alteration in the processing capabilities of our devices; hence one of the tools needed by the gadget manufacturers includes the Photonic Integrated Circuit. Unlike the conventional processors that populate our computers and phones, the Photonic

Integrated Circuit integrates the use of light as a means to transmit and process data. In line with the use of light as a medium to share and process data, the use of Photonic particles increases the gadget's ability to process more significant amounts of data. While the use of a device entirely depends on light as the primary medium has yet to be developed, hybrid versions that incorporate this form of technology are under development, particularly with semiconductors that can accommodate this form of transmissions. The use of the Photonic Integrated Circuit would ensure that the data that is processed is vastly improved from its current speeds. The improved speed at which data is processed would potentially increase the power needs of the gadgets involved and the electrical requirements of the servers needed to run the Metaverse. The proposed solution to this would include the need for a Piezoelectric Generator.

Piezoelectricity is briefly defined as electricity generated from the electrical charges in certain non-organic materials (such as crystals-think quartz) or organic matter when it responds to certain stressful stimuli. The use of generators that could harness these types of energy would complement and augment the electrical capabilities of the servers and gadgets that run the Metaverse. Subsequently, the devices that integrate this form of electrical capacity can be self-sufficient in their operations and increase the portability of the devices that link the user to the Metaverse. This greatly enhances the immersive experience for the users in the Metaverse as the generator components could be seamlessly integrated into various devices. This allows for a more energy-efficient means to power systems that run on Virtual Reality and Augmented Reality Systems. It also helps that this form of energy is ecologically and environmentally friendly and ultimately the more sustainable option for developers.

One of the requirements for a feasible Metaverse includes populating the Metaverse. Another tool essential to the expansion of the Metaverse includes platform-agnostic Cloud Computing. This entails the developer's ability to create a computer network that exists in cloud storage that enables users to access the same network they usually would be unable to access because of the remoteness of the server that generally hosts a particular application or platform. The developer, in essence, uploads a facsimile of their network onto the cloud, wherein authorized users would be able to access certain features through the cloud storage and interact with other authorized users on the same cloud storage. This heightens the lack of synchronicity, one of the more prevalent issues in the Metaverse development, and seeks to partially address this as it allows increased accessibility to some platforms. However, because these developer-created platforms were created in line with specific technical requirements, proper accessibility depends on the capabilities of the accessing gadgets in the cloud to enable the platform to run in its optimal state. Despite this, the use of this form of cloud storage applies to all devices authorized to stream from the cloud storage. The use of this form of cloud storage is viable for limited use between gamers for co-op games. However, the use of this technology in the Metaverse increases the ability for developers to collaborate and contribute to the Metaverse and allows other devices in remote areas to access the Metaverse from their place. To augment the knowledge of the Metaverse and the servers that run it, the use of Exascale Computers would provide the necessary computation and processing power needed to ensure that data analysis in the Metaverse would take place at an enhanced speed. This computer system focuses less on the entertainment aspect of the Metaverse and more on its characteristics on the engineering, business, and collaborative elements. This allows for the rapid analysis of data and the development of simulated environments based on the data synthesized from the data analysis. Once applied to the other aspects of the Metaverse, this would address the issues that pertain to the synchronous experience essential to the functioning of the Metaverse.

With the need for the formation of the Digital Twins needed to enhance the collaborative aspect of the Metaverse, the use of the 3D scanner becomes essential in the development of the necessary hardware to interface with the Metaverse to improve the immersive experience significantly. The 3D Scanner is precisely what you would expect. It is a scanner that can take in the physical surface of the object; it scans and creates a visual replica of the object in the Metaverse environment it was linked to. Though the machines that have the full capabilities to do full 3D scans are complex and immense in their structure, our phones are reasonably close in integrating full 3D Scans, which enhances their portability. Since the Metaverse was meant to be a replica of the physical environment, the 3D Scanner would enhance the graphical aspect and create a realistic simulation of the climate rendered using the 3D Scanner. Augmented reality would benefit from using the 3D Scanner as this allows for the enhanced creation of virtual realities necessary for the Metaverse. On the economic applications of the scanner, it enables developers and independent creators to scan natural objects into a digital form and empower them for virtual ownership. With the use of the Digital Twins, it becomes possible to enhance the entirety of the locale of the Metaverse and form a true digital metropolis capable of population. Aside from creating the environment, an essential and familiar part of the Metaverse is creating an Avatar, the digital representation of a person in the Metaverse, and effectively, this would serve to populate the Metaverse. The development of an AI Avatar can range from simplistic designs to more realistic interpretations of humans rendered through motion-capture technology that would include the entire range of human actions and emotions. The avatars spoken of in this instance are created for the Artificial Intelligences within the Metaverse. This would allow the AI to increase its interactions with other users and the user's avatar, in turn, to perform fundamental interactions and maintain a digital presence within the Metaverse. The economic applications of the Avatars would enable the user to multitask, as the user can perform tasks in the physical world. In contrast, the digital avatar would perform its pre-programmed functions while in the Metaverse.

Augmented reality is a crucial concept to the existence of the Metaverse, as can be seen in interactive games such as Pokemon Go. When this is integrated into a piece of eyewear, Augmented Reality becomes more portable and more accurate in placing the image overlay in the physical world. This often takes the form of smart glasses that, though not commercially successful, have found their niche with more delicate operations such as Telehealth and research. Once it overcomes its limitations, the Augmented

Reality Eyewear would include microscopic versions of the equipment needed to scan, render, and transmit data from the environment and allow these to be controllable by the user. However, the applications of this form of eyewear are centred on its medical applications, though when applied to the Metaverse, it enables the user to experience a mash-up of virtual and physical worlds and allows the user to switch between both environments at will.

Artificial Neural Networks are an aspect of the Metaverse defined as a set of computational systems, similar to artificial intelligence, that mimic how the human brain generates and processes ideas and thoughts. Because this technology seeks to replicate human intelligence, it allows artificial intelligence to make informed decisions about the habits and preferences of the user it has been linked to. An innovative aspect of this would be the ability to predict outcomes through careful data analysis. It analyzes the data presented and formulates a decision based on the identified potential outcome. Once fully realized, the implications of this technology would be enormous in that it can locate probabilities and potentially address the pitfalls it foresees in these probabilities. Before our thoughts go into Skynet-type scenarios, its decisions are based on the user's habits, making the decision process critical and heavily dependent on the user it has found its analytical patterns on.

The technological ability of a Brain-Computer interface would allow users to link their brain with their computer and establish a linkage between the two without the need for physical communication. This option, however, requires medical intervention as to select the communication link, there must be the implantation of sensors of the brain whose consequences have yet to be fully explored. Because of the potential medical dangers of this technology, other forms of thought transmission are required, and safer, non-invasive means of interfacing are needed, such as using advanced machine learning sensitive to the neural impulses transmitted throughout the body. The use of an alternative means to control the environment of the Metaverse through the power of thought would lessen the need for additional hardware to interface with the Metaverse and ensure that the user feels the whole immersive experience. Additionally, the linkages between brain and machine would be an avenue of communication, especially for those users who are disabled and have no other means of communication available to them.

With the development of the Artificial Neural Networks, which to recall, are meant to simulate the thought process of the human brain through the use of predictive learning and specific algorithms to predict outcomes, comes the development of the Generative Adversarial Network, which features two of these neural networks in a competitive environment. To ensure that the decisions that these two machine learning algorithms remain rooted in reality, the data that is provided to these two artificial neural networks offer the algorithms that enable the machine learning program to establish realistic imagery and environments. One pair is encoded to specifically identify outcomes that would then be processed by the other neural network, which determines if the synthesized outcome is realistic. This allows both machines in tandem to create data that could be used to develop various training scenarios. Through this, it would be possible to develop hyper-realistic simulations synthesized from the data captured for the Metaverse. Through the Generative Adversarial Network, artificial intelligence can create different people to populate and interact with the Metaverse and provide opportunities for creators to develop new means to create images that could impact the communication process and augment education, media, medicine and other fields of study. Additionally, because of their added capabilities to simulate various realities and scenarios, the use of the GAN provides an additional layer of security to the servers that run the Metaverse as it would be able to simulate scenarios, identify potential adverse outcomes and assist the developers of the Metaverse platform in developing solutions that would counteract these flaws in the program and ensure the continued safety of the Metaverse and its populace. This way, it also provides that no part of the Metaverse would be rendered vulnerable to hackers.

To significantly improve the potential of the Metaverse to be truly immersive and as realistic to the physical world, the interactions within the Metaverse need to stimulate our senses. Through the use of Haptic technology, it becomes possible to replicate the sensations of touch in the Metaverse which allows the user to exert more control over the environment in the Metaverse as this reduces the need once more for additional hardware and can be used to develop simulations of real-life scenarios such as medical procedures, sports techniques, the rehabilitation of a patient, and even provide a more realistic environment for gamers. Through this technology, it would be possible for the user to feel the digital product they would buy while in the Metaverse and improve the quality of interactions with the other inhabitants of the Metaverse. To link with the improvement of the quality of interactions in the Metaverse, the use of the intelligent Virtual Agent (IVA) would be essential in the daily functions of the Metaverse. Artificial intelligence takes the form of these Virtual Agents to increase the rate of interactions and provide the needed assistance to these users who interact through these agents. The use of the Intelligent Virtual Agent would find widespread usage amongst the various government agencies, corporations, and those businesses that find themselves with the need to interact with other users constantly. Natural Language Processing is a crucial part as this enables the artificial intelligence to understand the user's query without the user having to resort to rather elaborately worded and stilted phrases to get the results they require. The same algorithm allows for identifying emotion and behaviour in the user that the AI may generate the most appropriate response. To improve upon the aesthetics of the avatar of the AI, it can also change its appearance to relate more with the user. Once applied in the Metaverse, the IVA would guide the newbie on navigating through the Metaverse, whether it is for exploration, games, or business. It would also provide customized assistance identified from the data it had gathered from the user. For the business aspect, the use of the IVA would significantly enhance the customer service experience, as the AI would be able to more accurately understand the needs of the customers who interact with it. The improved and streamlined interaction and presentation of solutions would make the IVA a valuable tool for businesses.

The enhancement of interoperability across platforms is a necessary tool in the Metaverse to ensure that all users can use their data regardless of the forum they initially linked their accounts with. Despite the legal tangles involved regarding data security, among other issues with the cross-integration of platforms, some protocols vary from platform to platform. This results in the need for machine translations, which enhance the interoperability of these platforms and improve the user's interaction with the Metaverse. The identification of the text and voice of the user allows the Metaverse to generate more accurate responses to correspond to the stimuli it had detected from the user. The use of machine translation would improve the overall game experiences and the quality of business transactions within the Metaverse economy and lessen the restrictions implemented with the help of different platforms to access the Metaverse. The removal of the developer-imposed limits would increase the capability of other developers to collaborate regardless of the platform used and provide additional work opportunities for the users in the Metaverse.

The safety of the Metaverse is among the more prevalent issues that developers must address and must be part of the initial infrastructure before the Metaverse could potentially expand. The use of a Trusted Execution Environment ensures that our linked electronic devices are protected as it locally stores the encryption keys needed within its hardware. The TEE takes the form of a miniature computer within our devices, independent from the various operating systems within our gadgets, incapable of duplication to another device, nor can it be linked to the internet. Through the device, itself may be compromised, and its contents are hacked into, the TEE would ensure that the encryption keys needed by the device are protected. This means though hackers would steal the data, the hackers would be unable to decipher the data as the lack of encryption keys would ensure that the data remains unintelligible. The use of the TEE is slowly incorporated into modern gadgetry as an additional layer of protection against hackers. Within the TEE, the user can store sensitive information such as biometrics that allows for the user's identification. As a result, not only does this protect the user and their data, but it also protects the data of other users from manipulation by a third party in the enforcement of copyright laws.

We have touched upon the necessity of Smart Contracts historically, but its application within the Metaverse is far removed from its legal relations. The use of the Smart Contract involves implementing a computer program that fulfills an obligation in the Blockchain once the obligor has met specific conditions. Through the Smart Contract, both parties can authenticate (validate the terms) of the contract and document that the obliged party has sufficiently met the obligation in the contract. Contracts, in this instance, are meant to ensure the validity of a transfer and facilitate the trade of virtual assets in a decentralized digital economy. At its heart, the Smart Contract remains a legal document, despite its digital applications, in that it enforces the fulfillment of obligations. Like a physical contract, the Smart Contract allows the transaction that became part of the obligation to be traced within the boundaries of the Metaverse. Because contracts can be taken as part of the evidence, they improve the relationship between both parties and show accountability if the contract comes under legal scrutiny. The contracts can also be used to digitally identify a user, as used by the Estonian government, and allow this person to operate a business strictly regulated by the laws of the governing country where the contract was issued.

Furthermore, the Smart contract enhances the interoperability of the Metaverse as, with a unified identity recognized in the agreement, it allows the user to link each account across different platforms with a single log-in credential. Furthermore, in decentralized finances, the intelligent contract streamlines the speed at which each party consummates transactions and economizes the paperwork for financial transactions. Lastly, the smart contract provides another layer of protection for creators as creators would mark their virtual assets as their personal property throughout all platforms. This amplifies the value of each asset and renders it unique across all Metaverse platforms.

We have touched upon Blockchains as the measure that ensures that each transaction in the Metaverse is duly recorded by the Proof of Work, Stake and History protocols integrated with each Cryptocurrency used as the basis for each transaction. A Sidechain forms part of the Blockchain, where it is a secondary yet independent portion of the chain with its benefits. The Sidechain allows the Blockchain to process additional data that the main Blockchain relegates to it. As a result, the main Blockchain would process the primary transaction faster. The presence of numerous side chains along the main Blockchain ensures that the transactions within the virtual economy are expedited and allows for the transfer and sale of assets at a larger scale, which would be ideal for investors who wish to invest in the Metaverse. The sidechains, however, allow the involvement of risk without potentially compromising the primary transaction—this aids in the facilitation of decentralized apps.

With the lockdowns induced by the pandemic, we have become familiar with the concept of Digital Wallets. However, when applied to the Metaverse, the wallet does not contain value computed immediately in dollars but instead includes Cryptocurrencies and other digital assets such as Non-Fungible Tokens. The wallet allows the user to store, purchase and collect more financial assets and provides a secured place accessible only through chosen identification methods. Once it becomes implemented as a standard throughout the Metaverse, digital wallets would have to accommodate the various Cryptocurrencies that exist in the market. The ability of the digital wallet to facilitate interoperability between the different platforms of the Metaverse would ensure that the digital wallet can link the user's data across these platforms and allow the user to easily transition from one platform to the other for ease in the completion of the transaction. The digital wallet, in its potential, could be the primary means by which financial transactions in the Metaverse are completed.

2.3 Ethical Considerations of the Digital Realms

The Metaverse at its heart permits expedited communications between people across time zones and distances. The existence of the Metaverse would then create an ethical dilemma wherein there is the question of privacy and security among all the users who have linked with the Metaverse platform. The various tools that were mentioned in the previous section have all provided opportunities, and at the same time, raised the possibilities on what could go wrong should these tools be wielded against the other users of the Metaverse. Case in point, we can go to the Artificial Neural Networks used in tandem with the Generative Adversarial Networks. Between the two, when used correctly, it can identify logical outcomes and identify solutions to counteract the adverse effects that the machine algorithm has predicted. Conversely, these could also be used to identify loopholes that can be exploited and overcome these counteractions. This scenario aside, the need arises to regulate and police what goes on in the Metaverse.

From this point, it can be understood that the Metaverse is a simulacrum of our actual physical world. Because it has an infrastructure that underlies the entirety of the digital universe and the protocols that allow for financial transactions and game microtransactions to be protected, there is also the need for the laws to regulate what can and cannot happen within the constraints of the Metaverse, just as we have our rules on how we can operate in society. Thus, there arises the question of security. Just how much freedom is there to act in the Metaverse? True, it was earlier said that the Metaverse was intended to democratize the use of the internet and move its control from the hands of a select few developers towards the capabilities of independent developers. In its ideal state, that would show that the internet and the world of the Metaverse is a democracy. Like a government, however, there has to be a system of checks and balances, and part of the balances lie in the ability of the developers to allow modifications within their platform and to prevent the independent developers from the implementation of too many concepts that may prove detrimental to the overall function of the Metaverse. The ethical question here is who would do the policing of the Metaverse and hopefully avoid any scenarios that speak of the dystopia in the book 1984. Is it possible to peacefully co-exist within the Metaverse, given that, though the Metaverse would be open for all people to modify, contribute and collaborate, the unique collaborations that are added would have to be regulated by the developers of the platform who may or may not nix the contribution in an arbitrary application of their ability to regulate? This is best answered using open source and free software movements that allow for the modification of programs. Though one can freely create these programs, it also becomes necessary for these developers to ensure that these contributions do not drastically alter the structure that underlies the Metaverse. One can develop as much as they want, but within reason, while the developer may regulate all they want but not arbitrarily negate each reason. While this issue is easier said than done, it is a question that will constantly arise the more the population becomes digitally literate and realizes their ideas on what they want to do in the Metaverse.

The next issue stems from the user's privacy, which can extend into the realms of copyright laws and laws on virtual ownership. At this point in our lives, and without any offence, we cannot deny that the world has become relatively shallow in that it panders to the vanity of those who seek to make their private lives public and those whose lives were public, to begin with, lose all semblance of privacy. It would be possible now, in an immersive environment, to have all of these laid bare for the world to see.

In the name of interactions, it becomes possible through social media to share videos, post photos, and share thoughts with a broader audience compared to the age of the Internet Freedom of expression is a right that is often bandied about when we post on social media. It is this freedom that empowers us to voice our opinions. However, opinions are just that, opinions, and the fact that social media panders to the bit of narcissism that is present in a person this serves as the impetus to blur the lines between privacy and publicity, which could lead to a lack of security that would protect the privacy of the user in the Metaverse. The issue of privacy within the confines of the Metaverse is an issue best answered with the use of regulatory powers enforced by the authorities that govern the Metaverse. The main catch is that there may be no anointed authority that could exert its regulatory powers over the contents posted by the users in the Metaverse. Hence, there would be no limit as to what can be posted, what cannot be posted, and until where the issues of privacy can be enforced when the posts themselves are up to the caprice of the user. This is just on the virtual aspect. Regarding the opinions of the sharer in the Metaverse, there remains the need to vet shared information, which would entail a particular invasion into the user's privacy, if only to verify the shared data.

Given that the pandemic still rages on around the world as of this writing, it becomes necessary to distinguish fact from fiction and ensure that the content within the

Metaverse is not deceptive in its information that the users may listen to without fear of deception from misinformation. This issue of privacy lies within the personal level. As more info begins to be uploaded into the internet, particularly those governed by intellectual property laws, we begin to blur the lines of privacy, security and copyright laws. In the previous sections and the chapter before this, we have spoken about the Metaverse as a platform that intends to be truly immersive, where we would be able to interact with other people. Among the tools necessary for this function are recording our movements and habits. If we go back once more to the Artificial Neural Network, our habits, behaviours, traits, and customs are all assimilated to simulate how our brains think.

Given that our every move, the way we think, and how we come to a decision can potentially be replicated within the Metaverse, we may give up our privacy while in the Metaverse as it records everything about us. What was recorded about our personal traits that can potentially be used against us, which is personal? The ramifications become more high-stakes and complex, mainly if the part of the Metaverse that is affected involves the higher echelons of the government. Personal information remains a valuable commodity, and despite the security measures intended to safeguard this information, the fact that it is within the data set of the Metaverse is no comfort as it already renders us vulnerable to a certain extent.

2.4 The Need for Protocol Requirements

A critical concept that must be explored with the Metaverse involves the protocols that go into the operation of the Metaverse. The Metaverse needs more than just the Proof of Work, Stake and History protocols which find their application within the realms of Cryptocurrencies. There is the part where information from all over the world tends to be uploaded exponentially. While there is the question of free and open-source software, the accessibility of this information needs to be regulated. Otherwise, this would upset the copyright laws that govern the data uploaded and affect the intellectual property rights of the writers of the information in the first place. Firstly, some protocols must be implemented to properly organize the data uploaded in the first place. Unlike the standard library classifications that are commonplace with public libraries, the classification and categorization of the Metaverse are more complex than that. The use of the Artificial Neural Networks takes into consideration the types of material we would often use and the method by which we select the material from which we gather the information that is needed. Aside from integrating a numerical system of classification for the uploaded data, there needs to be a thematic one as well. The protocols that enable this classification of information must be able to operate across all platforms.

We spoke about the potential for misinformation with the increased accessibility given to the users in the Metaverse to share their opinions and thoughts. Because this information requires verification, there needs to be a protocol that would fact-check and verify the information transmitted before the rest of the population can access it. This stems from the need to ensure that the information that is uploaded and accessed to the internet is verifiable and that the Metaverse would serve as a medium between the user and the database of information, that in line with the categorization protocols, would ensure that the user can appreciate and access the full scope of information that can be made available to them. This falls less in line with digital literacy and more on a protocol involving media literacy, as the protocols should differentiate facts from opinions. This imparts the need for regulatory protocols aside from the ones used in the enactment of blockchain transactions. In line with the imposition of control, there is the concept of Digital Twins, where because modern technological advances would enable the developers to create a replica of the item, environment or idea, it becomes difficult to distinguish the more valuable concept and blurs the lines of virtual ownership within the Metaverse.

2.5 Innovations of the Metaverse

In essence, the Metaverse contains various features that enable developers and users to gain the fully immersive experience of a whole new universe that simulates our physical world. In the second section of this chapter, we have touched upon the various tools that form an integral part of the functions of the Metaverse. We have touched upon some features such as that of the Artificial Neural Networks, which simulate how the human brain processes thoughts. When paired with the Generative Adversarial Network, we can identify potential outcomes in various scenarios that it had run through from the input data set. Other innovations that form part of the Metaverse include enhancing the immersive experience, which is done through the hardware that is interfaced with the Metaverse platform. Innovations such as Haptics, which enhance the user's sense of touch, allow the user to experience an approximate sensation of touch while logged into the Metaverse. Other more essential innovations involve using the Artificial Intelligence Avatar, which allows the user, developer or agency to maintain their presence inside the Metaverse. This differs from the avatars that we have due to the AI, which will enable them to interact on our behalf based on the habits and behavioural patterns that it has gleaned from us.

A more innovative and essential technological advancement to be had in the Metaverse would be the concept of Neurostimulation, where these procedures, invasive or non-invasive, attempt to control the impulses that are generated by the neural network of the brain through the addition of induced electrical impulses that would regulate brain activity. In the medical field, there are two different forms of Neurostimulation. Deep brain stimulation involves the delivery of electrical impulses through electrodes implanted in various areas around the brain (save for its underside). These electrodes are then linked to an electrical pulse generator. This would be the more invasive option. The non-invasive option involves the transmission of these nerve impulses through the skull via magnetic coils that were laid on the scalp. This allows the Metaverse to be an area where users can seek treatment for psychiatric conditions and seek relief from their pain. While the medical applications in the Metaverse can be groundbreaking in their application, the same inducement of stimulation can be used by advertisers and developers should they wish to evoke certain emotions among their audience. At its core, however, this innovation allows the Metaverse to be used as a platform for Telehealth options, useful in a world still ravaged by the pandemic.

To increase the accessibility of the Metaverse, the use of the Microelectromechanical Systems would be integral, as these devices, as one can get from the individual components of the word, contain both the electrical and mechanical aspects of handheld devices, on a smaller scale, that can improve the function of an object. The use of engineering on a microscopic scale would allow for the widespread manufactures of these immersive devices and make the Metaverse more accessible to the population. Aside from this, however, the devices through which users can access the Metaverse would have their power requirements reduced to a more manageable quantity which could make the Metaverse more economical to run in the long term and ensure that the platforms and devices through which one can access the Metaverse can become readily adaptable for public use.

Other components form part of the innovations of the Metaverse. These are, however, best discussed in the context of their role in the functions of the Metaverse, where some will be addressed in the subsequent chapters of this book.

2.6 Conclusion

It can be observed that the versions of the Metaverse that we think we have cannot be indeed considered the Metaverse in itself as these lack several components needed to make a future Metaverse a more viable prospect. The infrastructure required to support the functions of the Metaverse has yet to be fully realized in that the internet speed alone, as well as the supportive structures needed to run the internet, need a complete overhaul that the internet could support the perpetual, rather than the intermittent transmission and processing of data sets to ensure that the Metaverse remains a completely synchronous experience rather than fragments of several incidents that are never felt in real-time. Aside from these, a few more physical world issues render the subject of the Metaverse into a more grounded hindrance, such as the power requirements needed to run the Metaverse. Though sustainable energy is among those under development, its integration into the components of the devices that make the Metaverse a more accessible platform remains one of the necessary aspects of accessibility that need to be resolved. However, despite the hindrances, the devices that are under development to heighten new experiences verge on the miraculous and fantastical, to include the innovations that allow the disabled to experience functions as the average person would function in the physical world; allow patients to receive treatment, and allow for a more immersive and realistic simulation that would replicate real-world outcomes, through digitally-based executions. There are also the legal tangles that would have to be unravelled before true interoperability becomes a reality, as well as the ethical issues of regulation of content, the security of the stored data, and the assurance of privacy within the Metaverse itself. The Metaverse cannot be built immediately, barring the occurrence of a specific mechanical breakthrough. As a result, we have our proto-Metaverses that serve as a basis from which the Metaverse could be built upon. As one would develop a hub, we can grow our Metaverse slowly around these worlds until the Metaverse, in the minds of the developers, can be fully realized.

3 WHEN REALITY GOES VIRTUAL

When taken into the Metaverse concept, virtual reality is a relatively novel concept, which has led to the formation of a culture that revolves around the virtual world. Once thought of as only existent in the world of fiction, virtual reality has become an essential part of our vocabulary. When the world was brought to a standstill with the imposition of a worldwide lockdown, virtual reality became the space where we assembled for the sake of education, work, and to meet up with friends when restrictions forbid us to simply. The presence of virtual classrooms, virtual boardrooms and all sorts of applications to which this qualifier has been affixed is just a microcosm of what virtual reality can be. If you happen to be immersed in gamer culture, then by now, you have an inkling of what virtual reality can be. Because of the increased need for virtual interactions, developments in virtual reality have begun to advance faster to ensure that the virtual requirements needed by the public are met with technology sufficient to sustain the virtual reality created to address that specific need.

3.1 The Definition of Virtual Reality

Virtual Reality has a varied definition in accordance with the context it is applied in. Still, with regards to the Metaverse, it would be necessary to distinguish between the two since these two are often confused. The Metaverse can equate to virtual reality, but virtual reality does not necessarily equate to the Metaverse. The latter is simply part of the technology needed to make the reality within the Metaverse a more tangible concept. Virtual Reality has no fixed definition as it continues to evolve following the available technology. Virtual Reality is defined as a representation of reality from a digital perspective. Virtual reality can be interpreted, too, as a medium, where objects and interactions coexist in cyberspace, wherein their appearance would influence a person's behaviour as they interact in the Metaverse. This virtual reality is made possible through the use of Virtual Reality equipment, such as headsets, gloves and haptic technology that provide the immersive experience sought in the Metaverse.

For a reality to be considered virtual, it must-have features that in their amalgamation make virtual reality distinct from all other forms of perception available to the human mind. These features that are inclusive within the realm of Virtual Reality include the manipulation of time and space, the ability to participate and interact with the environment in real-time, and the ability of the user to control their setting to an extent where they can push through with their version of their narrative. Subsequently, it is meant to trap and enrapture the user's senses and render the user unable to distinguish between the virtual world and the physical world.

For Virtual Reality to be considered virtual reality, many developers of VR Technology have agreed that Virtual Reality must consist of 5 distinct characteristics. These include Intensive, where the technology should be able to amplify our sensory capabilities through the use of various technologies (such as haptic and auditory enhancements; Interactive in that the virtual reality is not merely there to showcase imagery, the user would be able to interact with the environment as well. In addition, virtual Reality must be immersive, in that the reality it generates must be able to fully capture and evoke all senses (as much as possible – taste sensations, however, are still under development); Illustrative, in that Virtual Reality must be able to differentiate between abstract and concrete concepts while in the Metaverse; and Intuitive, where the reality would be accessible to accommodate your perceived needs in the virtual world.

3.2 A Glossary of Common VR Terms

To grasp the terms underscored in Virtual Reality, this is a glossary to help you understand what these concepts are all about.

3.2.1 Virtuality

Virtuality does not refer to the actual physical existence of an object when applied in the context of technology. Still, it relates to the presumption that such an object exists in virtual reality. It also encompasses the sensation that a person believes that they are entirely part of the virtual reality and can exist within this realm and take part in its interactions.

3.2.2 Virtual Object/Image

Virtual images are generated using hardware and software to describe and render a concept in two-dimensional figures or three-dimensional renderings. The virtual image quintessentially is any object in the virtual world that can be perceived through an altered perspective. The thing rendered virtually forms the smallest part of the environment that comprises the entirety of the virtual world. This fundamental unit allows the user to visualize the Metaverse in a more concrete form when applied to the Metaverse.

3.2.3 Virtual World/Environment

Contrary to what the name depicts, the Virtual World does not necessarily include the representation of an entire universe or open world within Virtual Reality. It can be part of a world. However, this part must be rendered entirely within a virtual space. The virtual world is a mixture of two-dimensional and three-dimensional images and virtual objects to form the entirety of the virtual world. What makes a virtual world distinct is that while it functions, it also provides a synchronized and perpetual network of individuals that the user can interact with through avatars and other computer networks linked to interact with the virtual world. Virtual worlds must exist, even without the software that enables users to interact and immerse themselves within the virtual world and is distinct from the virtual environments depicted in movies and other films. As the current technologies have rendered, the Virtual World can fully immerse the individual in an environment where the user would be able to interact and explore. Additionally. The Virtual World would exhibit naturalism in the background and the full spectrum of human emotion, behaviour, and interactions through the avatars that populate.

3.2.4 Presence

Presence is often defined as an abstract concept related to the sensation that you are in a virtual environment as felt through Virtual Reality Technology. Presence is best indicated when the user can perceive the environment through their senses in the presence of a computer-generated environment. The sensory indicators do not include only sight. With the use of additional hardware and software forms, the user would sense and perceive tactile and auditory stimuli. As of this writing, these three senses are the limitations within the virtual world as there currently exists no form of technology that could replicate the sensations of smell and taste. These two senses aside, through sight, hearing and touch, the user would be able to interact with the Virtual World in real-time as though they were in the physical world, and these interactions would generate the illusory aspect that the user is in that specific area and is experiencing the scenario generated. More sophisticated forms of Virtual World designs allow users to share an upgrade in the quality of presence as they can relate their sensations from the physical world into the virtual world. Presence, to augment the definition initially provided, is best identified through the ability to stimulate cognitive processes in the user and evoke emotional responses from them. The best virtual worlds would be able to elicit presence through place illusions, which are necessary to the success of the virtual world.

Presence becomes a palpable concept with the aid of two types of illusions: Place Illusion and Plausibility Illusion. Place Illusions are developed with the use of Virtual Reality Software. They can generate the illusion that the user is in the virtual world through the use of hardware that influences the sensorimotor functions of the brain. Place illusion software is often supplied through sensors that track the movement of the user's head and eyes. Through this, it can manipulate the user's perception by altering the environment to adjust to the user's current perspective. Through place illusion, you would be able to see, for instance, a sidewalk or a field of grass rather than a series of pixels from an environment that was not fully rendered.

On the other hand, Plausibility illusions are responsible for the user's ability to interact with the objects while in the Virtual Reality environment. They are manifested when there are spontaneous responses to the user's actions. If you are a gamer, you would have experienced this numerous times, such as throwing an object into a body of water or interacting with other NPCs. Unlike the place illusion, the plausibility illusion allows the user to experience and interact in the virtual world, believing that the virtual world is similar to the real world.

3.2.5 Telepresence

Telepresence is defined as the ability of the user to manipulate and control natural objects remotely. It is further quantified as the ability to detect presence in the context of virtual reality within a specific environment. Presence in this instance differs from telepresence in that presence refers to the perception in accordance with our senses. In contrast, telepresence refers to mediated perception, which requires a computer-controlled display system to heighten our ability to interact with another object. One of the more common applications for this would include smart glasses to control aspects of our environment digitally.

3.3 Other Virtual Worlds

There are several variations on virtual worlds that exist with the use of VR Technology. Therefore, to make distinctions with each type of virtual world would create numerous variations centred on the kind of technology utilized to create the virtual world. Subsequently, it is agreed that the virtual worlds can be best categorized into those immersive worlds and those that are non-immersive.

Immersive Virtual Worlds include worlds that promote sensory immersion, immersions based on challenges, imaginative immersion, actual immersion, symbolic and narrative immersion, and social immersion. Non-Immersive Virtual Worlds include desktop-based, vehicle-based and internet-based immersions. A hybrid immersive virtual world is often semi-immersive, which provides for hybrid immersions and immersions through assistive devices.

To function as part of the Metaverse, the ideally created Virtual World should be a wholly immersive virtual reality that can provide the user with a higher level of presence obtained through any of the variations listed under the immersive virtual worlds in the previous paragraph. However, there are limitations to the types of virtual worlds that exist, and these include the expenses incurred to run the servers where the virtual world exists and where its data is stored; the usability of the software or platform through which the user can access the virtual world, or in this instance, the Metaverse; the lack of software that supports the functions of the virtual world, and the content that goes into the creation of the virtual world- as the development of new content for the Virtual World would prove to be difficult without the software and hardware needed to render the assets of the virtual world.

Immersive Virtual Worlds are focused on the concept of immersion, where it is defined as a digital experience that involves the ability to put the user in disbelief. An actual or total immersive environment is where the user experiences a complete and wholly immersive experience in the virtual world and cannot perceive stimuli from the physical world. To enhance the quality of the immersive environment for the users, physiologic components amplify the immersive climate experienced by the user. For a total immersion to be attained appropriately, the software and hardware must generate an illusion so comprehensive in its rendering that it renders the user's physical senses unable to distinguish between the virtual and physical worlds. Once the sensory capacities of the user have been fully immersed into the software, only then can the user be able to engage their mentality into the environment. This would, however, cause the necessity for hardware components in the use of immersive virtual reality, wherein the physical stimuli would be inutile if the mind were not fully immersed in the first place. To ensure that the user can generate a presence within the virtual world as defined by the terms in this chapter, it becomes necessary to ensure that the user's mind can respond to the trickery elicited by the illusions from VR Software. The actual immersive virtual reality environment provides all user sensations and perceptions to create a presence within the virtual world. The reality generated by the immersive environment must be of a quality that the feelings stimulate the mind and senses of a person within the virtual world.

For the generated virtual world to be prosperous in the eyes of the users and the context of the Metaverse, there needs to be the development of trust by the user in the virtual reality platform. Most users would trust VR platforms to be those that can provide a truly immersive experience in an environment that is, at the same time, responsive to their respective actions. Though it can be misconstrued that Virtual Reality is a field that relies mainly on the graphics needed, this is a gross oversimplification of what reality is. Just as our physical world is constituted of various microscopic components that impact at a macro level in the Metaverse, the environment rendered needs to showcase the ability of the user to interact with the servers that generated the place illusion of the VR World, and that there must be a way for the user to perceive the interaction between themselves and the virtual environment. Additionally, the user must exert their control over their virtual world area. Finally, the servers must respond to the commands initiated by the user through the interfaced software.

For a highly immersive virtual environment to exist, there must be several components needed aside from the hardware (which fosters the responsiveness of the user and their ability to interact with the virtual environment) and be able to work with the software, where both their capabilities have been amplified to create high fidelity, three-dimensional environments, objects and interactions. The fidelity of virtual reality is often evaluated by using several criteria, including interaction fidelity, display fidelity, and scenario fidelity. Interaction fidelity is defined as that which is related to the data obtained from the input of virtual reality software and the capability of the user to view how they can interact with objects in the environment through the use of a display system that records their interactions while immersed in the said reality. Display fidelity differs in that it concerns itself solely with identifying the user's presence while in the Virtual World. Lastly, scenario fidelity considers the combined actions of both the interaction and display fidelities, evaluates scenarios' development and generation, and provides realistic outputs derived from how the user interacts in the virtual world. Once these three are satisfied, only then can a virtual world be qualified as a highly immersive virtual world. In conjunction with the presence generated, this provides a better VR experience.

Sensory Immersive Virtual Realities are three-dimensional virtual worlds with an auditory capacity that find typical applications in games. The virtual world is made possible by using software that can be worn by the user or through a specialized area such as domes, where virtual reality can be manifested.

Because the environment generated results in a significantly augmented presence in the virtual world, the users can perceive and develop a company with the use of most of their sensory functions in that each nuance of movement exerted by the user would be amplified with the help of haptic and auditory technologies that allow the user to interact with the virtual objects within the generated environment. Furthermore, the responsiveness of the domain is imparted with the use of sensory feedback obtained from the user, where the use of challenge-based immersion is used in conjunction with sensory immersion to produce a heightened interactive experience.

On the other hand, challenge-based immersion is immersion based on the user's interactions and the environment. Therefore, it is best applied when used in simulations meant to develop individuals' motor skills and develop their cognitive ability.

Imaginative Immersions are virtual realities where the user can enact their fantasies, ideas or alternative experiences, similar to realistic situations in the physical world. The virtual world is deemed an imaginative immersion reality when it can allow other users to experience the world through another person's perspective through the manifestation of that person's thoughts. This concept is presented through the use of player avatars and stories. The imaginative immersion is best utilized to simulate real-life experiences that would otherwise be deemed high-risk in the physical world. This would allow the user the entire experience to reduce the danger they would typically face.

Actual immersions provide the user with opportunities to experience virtual actions in the real world, similar to how the Pokemon Go app allows the player to simulate the game using Augmented Reality. The catch with actual immersions is that users would experience the consequences of their actions when they enact certain decisions through real immersion. It differs from the imaginative immersion in that the scenarios presented are more realistic, and thus, the user would be keen to observe the consequences of their actions.

Narrative Immersion is also known as symbolic immersion. It is described as a type of immersive virtual reality that can manifest an environment that resonates with the psychological experiences of the user. The narrative, in this instance, is defined as a component of learning that significantly motivates the intellect of the user. The virtual world, in this instance, causes the user to be fully immersed in a scenario that stimulates their mind, emotions, and behaviour through the imposition of systems that trigger all three. In addition, however, the narrative immersion would allow the user to switch between the various stimuli by providing options to control what they see.

Social immersion, lastly, is a virtual reality immersion where the world can be modified for single or multiple users. The internet is required if the virtual world must accommodate numerous users simultaneously, that the users may experience the same events at the same time. However, true synchronicity here cannot be truly established. Though many users may share the same event, they are accommodated in various servers with the most minute of time differences that separate the relay of each information transmitted to each server. Because of this, social immersion, while it can be said that this would closely simulate the Metaverse, would require the implementation of more concrete forms of hardware needed to support its functions.

Through those mentioned above fully immersive realities, it becomes possible to create place illusions and generate plausible fantasies that would cater to the psychology of the user. It would depend on the existing software that would allow the virtual world to respond to the actions and choices generated by the user to permit increased responsiveness within the virtual world.

Non-Immersive Virtual Realities to be distinguished from Immersive Virtual Realities in that, where the Immersive Virtual Realities rely on the use of multiple pieces of hardware to create the virtual world, the non-immersive version relies solely on the desktop as well as the use of the monitor and a hand device that allows the creation of the two or three-dimensional virtual object. The typical computer monitor serves as the hardware where the user manifests the virtual world. In contrast, the handheld devices- such as the mouse, joysticks and other peripherals allow for limited interactions within the virtual world. At the most, this is the most common form of virtual reality, as this is most often observed in the games encountered, in that we travel through a virtual world but are constrained by the lack of options where we can interact with the environment. However, the non-immersive virtual reality can be modified to accommodate multiple users, and at the same time, find widespread usage for businesses that focus on the training of drivers and pilots, one of its more common applications.

Though the virtual environment generated by this virtual reality does not create a fully immersive experience for the user, they develop the needed presence and immersive experience at a significantly lower quality when contrasted with a fully immersive world. However, the immersive quality can be modified through adjustments with the quality of the graphics, the size, and the resolution of the images to improve upon what has been there. Computer games and experienced gamers have probably taken steps to modify their computers to simulate the immersive environment through the use of double monitors, surround sound and high-resolution video cards to make what would typically be a non-immersive game into one that is close enough to a fully immersive experience. However, the quality of the experience depends upon the user's expectations with the design of the game, how the user's actions are manifested in the virtual world, and how consistent these actions are when seen in the virtual world. Unlike the use of fully immersive virtual realities, which are heavily dependent on the hardware, the use of non-immersive virtual reality would be a more viable option in that it is easier to access for general use, and that it would be easier to add more content into the programming, as can be observed with the numerous mods that exist from the highly experienced gamers all over the world. Here at least, it becomes possible to contribute to the game more cost-effectively.

3.4 Equipment and Key Players in the VR World

While in Chapter 2, we have touched upon the use of Haptic Technology, as well as the use of 3D Scanners to simulate touch, and to facilitate the creation of digital twins within the virtual world of the Metaverse, there are other pieces of equipment necessary to the function of the virtual reality that is generated within the platform of the Metaverse. These can include items such as:

Head Mounted Display (Output Device)

This piece of equipment is deemed one of the essential components for the virtual world, as the power of sight is the most critical sense that is triggered with the environment of the virtual world is rendered. The head-mounted display can surround the user's perspective and transmit what the user perceives through the use of various display systems. As of this writing, there are three types of HMD's employed to benefit Virtual Reality, including a tethered HMD, a mobile phone integrated head-mounted display, and a stand-alone version of the head-mounted display. Within this device are various specifications that would determine the quality of the images that the virtual world has rendered. Alongside this, the shows can integrate either an LCD, an LED, a projection, or a tiny CRT. The use of the LCD, similar to our smartphones, is the most preferred method developers opt to display the virtual world. The Head Mounted Display, to some extent, can also be categorized as an input device, as with the trackers that detect movement from the user, whether it is the angle of the head or the direction of the eyes, the display uses the data and movement from the user to manipulate the environment to suit the user's perspective.

Latency remains an issue with virtual reality and the rest of the Metaverse, as a high latency would result in a lag of the rendered images. If you play games and experience the lag, you may know what is described here. Hence, it is necessary to lower the latency to prevent cybersickness, as this can affect the user experience in virtual reality. Frame Rates are how the visuals can refresh their frames and are often measured in frames per second. For example, a good HMD would have a frame rate of 90 frames per second for the images to be refreshed.

For the HMD to be fully immersive, It needs to be paired with motion tracking technology. Otherwise, the interactions between the user and the virtual world would be severely limited by the types of actions that may be performed. Several kinds of HMDs are available though most generally are used by developers who need these to see how the virtual Metaverse manifests. Makers such as Oculus Rift, Razer and Samsung Gear were made publicly available for users. They were made more cost-effective enough that the public may use these to begin their own immersive experience in the virtual world. However, despite the cost-effectiveness for some HMDs, some, like the tethered HMDs, prove to be too expensive to mass-produce and require the user to be well versed with the insertion of the hardware to ensure that the hardware and software are properly interfaced. However, the Oculus Rift was said to have developed a more compatible product that can be operated with any operating system, which makes it the more viable HMD as of this writing.

Stand-alone HMDs, on the other hand, allows the user to experience virtual reality without the need for a phone or a desktop computer, as developers have come up with a wireless product that has its processors, batteries and sensors that allow the user portability with the use of the Virtual Reality. This form of the HMD would require a wireless internet connection, and it is believed that this would be a solution to promote wireless charging to solve the power constraints of this device. The HMD is just one among several devices needed to fully immerse the user into the virtual world, as other peripherals include trackers for the head, eyes and hands; trackers for the positioning of the body as well as the gestures made with the hands; speech recognition for better interaction within the virtual world, as well as other platforms; and various controllers that would allow the user to influence the virtual world, to include more futuristic equipment such as vehicles, and surgical robots. While numerous, these equipment are necessary to generate the complete responsiveness of the virtual world. Through here, the virtual world becomes an authentic replica of our physical world. However, despite the need for controllers, the ideal immersive virtual world would have to forego the need for controllers and instead rely on sensors, which are more subtle in their construction. The use of sensors is less complicated when contrasted with integrating other devices. The sensors themselves can be integrated into a particular device, the HMD, and they would be easier to integrate with the software for the virtual world once in this form. Haptic feedback mechanisms are necessary for the proper functioning of the virtual world, particularly when that aspect of the virtual world can have potentially fatal complications – as with surgery and the manipulation of vehicles for one. Before haptic technology can be genuinely perfected, it must undergo several innovations, which include the ability of the user to detect other tactile sensations such as heat, texture, pressure and the density of an object, as most haptic technologies that currently exist contain features that are limited to the detection of the position of the hands and fingers – which are more physical aspects compared to the sensory elements needed to pull off the convincing illusions necessary to make the virtual world a more realistic place. Key players for the haptic technology include the likes of SensorYX VR Free, the Hi5 VR Glove, the Manus VR, and the Capto Glove, which all strive to answer the haptic needs needed for the VR Technology to work fully,

Aside from using the display devices, another piece of equipment needed is a panoramic camera, which entails that the user would have a 360 degree perspective of the rendered virtual world. The use of this dramatic option requires the camera and the ability to record and generate images and edit these images into a cohesive product. GoPro, Insta360 and iZugar are among the key equipment makers for the Panoramic 360 camera. The use of the camera, however, depends upon the user's purposes, whether it is simply to take photos or to record video. Cameras used to record videos may require higher quality imagery and more balanced software to ensure that the panorama does not become distorted.

The software needed to render the virtual world is a crucial aspect as for the Virtual World and the Metaverse to function optimally, the software that helps run it needs to sustain the functions programmed into it. While there is numerous software available to develop virtual worlds for newbies, their ability to shape a virtual world is rudimentary at best entirely. It would be ideal for those who wish to get their hands wet as they practice with their environments. More sophisticated forms of software would allow for several vital functions to occur in creating the virtual world. The development of three-dimensional virtual objects, the development of the three-dimensional virtual world where these objects are set, and the promotion of continued interactions between each model and the user. Additionally, to allow for the contribution of independent developers, the software must allow the developers, regardless of their experience, to create their contributions into the virtual world, such as the use of pre-existent virtual objects or simply the ability to create a new thing from scratch – which could later turn out to be a business venture for NFTs. The power of the user to interact with the environment results from the use of game engines, where users would be able to create an environment without the specialized knowledge needed to contribute to the Metaverse.

Game engines, in particular, are software that finds their use in the development of the virtual world. They also found it added functionalities to develop two and three-dimensional games (in the name, after all) for computers and other platforms. Through the game engine, the user can develop videos, animations, simulations, model objects, and create other functionalities within the game that the user wishes to make. Subsequently, this extends to the ability of the user to contribute to their area of the Metaverse and allow other users to join in the same shared experience. Of the software companies that are key players in the game industry, there are Unity and Unreal Engine.

Unity is a free game engine platform that has two variations available for the skill level of the game developers, with a professional feature for those with more skills. Unity gains its popularity from the ease in the use of its interface, the unrestricted use of its software, the simplistic primary structure and the presence of various assets, tutorials to help develop the game, and the quality of the visuals rendered within the game engine. In addition, the Unity game engine finds compatibility with most VR peripherals. It can function with several operating systems that allow for the platform's interoperability and allow for the extended reality to allow for the creation of another virtual platform.

Unreal engine is the main competitor of Unity. It shares similarities in that it does not cost anything to download the engine, and it has a wide selection of assets for the developer to choose from. The unreal engine also shares the same compatibilities with other operating systems, ensuring the virtual world's continued interoperability across different systems. What distinguishes it from Unity, however, are its extensive features which permit two-and three-dimensional modelling, the creation of blueprints, photorealistic rendering, panoramic video productions, the ability to animate and create cinematics for the game (think Blizzard), the capability to edit the Virtual World, simulate the virtual world, enhance the auditory experience, and browse for more content. The drawback is that this engine, with all its advanced features, is more suitable for the advanced user, although newbies can use some of the tools within this game engine. More importantly, the use of Unreal Engine allows the collaboration of several users in the development of the virtual world and enables these collaborators to work simultaneously to model objects and enhance their abilities with the C++ Code.

3D Modelling tools are necessary to the Virtual World, as this allows the user to develop more realistic virtual objects rather than to have the things generated from a shape. Those with an artistic bent and the necessary technological experience can compare this to sculpture within the digital world.

3Ds Max is one of the 3D Modelling tools commonly used by developers. It is an Autodesk software that allows the user to model objects, render them, and animate them. However, unlike the game engines, the software needs to be paid for. Still, this payment includes the use of various assets, textures, special effects, filters, light and shadow effects, and other tools necessary to craft a design for an object, which can then be integrated into the virtual world. Fusion 360 is another software from the same maker and is relatively easy for novice designers.

Blender is one of the modelling software that begins to gain prominence with 3d modelling as it permits interoperability across platforms and is free, open-source software. Blender carries the same features as other 3D modelling software but has the added functionalities of 3D pipelines, animations, simulation, rendering, and the ability to render and integrate motion tracking. While it has a game engine that augments its functions, it is best used as 3d modelling software.

Google enters the market using SketchUp, which is appropriate for rookie designers who wish to learn how to do 3d modelling. However, it is limited because users can only discover within a 30-day trial period.

Other software needed for the functions of the Virtual World include the following:

Adobe Premiere and After Effects to properly edit the videos for a panoramic setting allows for the ease of use and collaboration between users for the final product.

Vizor is a web-based video editor that allows the user to create interactive virtual reality experiences, and at the same time, provides for the use of audio within the video.

InstaVR requires payment before the user can use all features available within the tool. This allows the user to create 360-degree videos, panoramas, including creating three-dimensional objects and increased interactivity to allow for high-calibre virtual worlds. The use of this software does not require specialized knowledge in coding.

3.5 Conclusion

The use of virtual reality allows us to observe various situations from an alternative perspective and with safety in mind, particularly when we wish to simulate different real-world problems that would otherwise put us in mortal peril.

The Virtual Reality System promotes safety. It allows us to interact in environments in which we usually would not find ourselves and act with a lesser degree of caution than in a realistic environment. It becomes possible to test the limits of our imaginations and theories through the virtual world, which makes the most integral part of the Metaverse. It allows for the visualization of a world beyond what we can imagine.

Additionally, the use of Virtual Reality Technology, both hardware and software, allows for the collaboration of works between like-minded developers and promotes an educational environment where the user can learn, create and simulate situations where learnings can be put to the test. Lastly, the Virtual World affords the user a certain degree of flexibility when applying knowledge as it becomes possible to observe various realities when specific interactions are made. Ultimately, it becomes a cost-effective measure as it dramatically reduces the real-life risks that the user can experience. Though admittedly, it has its effects on the physical body attained with improper or prolonged usage, the benefits to be had from VR Technology are boundless. Because it allows for the creation of virtually any object, it becomes possible then to exercise our imagination without any limitations necessary for the expansion of the Metaverse.

4 AUGMENT REALITY

It would be wrong to make a finite distinction between virtual reality and augmented reality when the latter falls under the wide categorization of what virtual reality actually is. Where virtual reality has its sole focus on the virtual world crafted by collaborators throughout the world, Augmented Reality serves as the bridge that combines elements from the virtual world into the physical world. However, despite the lack of total immersion in the virtual aspect of the world, augmented reality utilizes more of virtual reality in that it is able to operate with a variety of mobile technologies. One of the best examples we have mentioned earlier was the use of Pokemon Go by Niantic, which overlaid aspects of the virtual world, with the physical environment to create the cities and environments commonly encountered within the Pokemon anime. The use of Augmented Reality is not solely limited to the use of mobile devices as it too, can be used on the HMDs, and other peripherals for the display of the virtual world. IN this instance, Augmented Reality is able to provide a depiction of the Virtual World, for other users to observe, from the perspective of the user, similar to how virtual reality would work.

Augmented Reality and Augmented Virtuality in this context are to be considered a pair, and both are often said to be the main components of what augmented reality actually is. Though these two components combined form what we perceive as augmented reality, there are a few distinctions that must be made. Augmented Reality integrates aspects from the virtual world into ours, and if you have played Pokemon Go, you may have had an inkling on how this goes, as you would be able to search the parks and other locations to capture the Pokemon you need. Other apps developed by Niantic allow you to partially immerse yourself in other fandoms such as the Harry Potter franchise, where you would be able to participate in tasks and explore Hogwarts. Here, Augmented Reality does not need to create a virtual world from scratch, it simply adds to what is already there through the use of various peripherals, and through your mobile device.

Between Virtual Reality and Augmented Reality, the more feasible option to integrate the use of the Metaverse into the lives of the public would be through the use of the Augmented Reality as this answers the questions that relate to necessity and affordability of the public with regards to the accessibility of the Metaverse. Augmented Reality changes the way we view our world, and allows us to interact with it in a limited capacity, where day to day functions would allow us to have added functionalities to our daily tasks. Just as the virtual world makes adjustments to our interactions within the virtual environment, Augmented Reality interacts with use through the provision of the necessary data that we need in accordance with our environment. Augmented Reality, as with its name, adds to the content of a particular object, and makes that particular object unique to the user when compared with the actual object – just as a museum or a park becomes a Pokemon center in Pokemon Go. Through Augmented Reality, with the use of the current example, it becomes possible for the user to unlock additional functions and manipulate the environment in a way that ordinary physical interactions would be unable to produce the same results. A counter for instance can be used to heal the Pokemon, when in reality it simply is the desk of a museum docent. Augmented Reality draws the user closer to the virtual world, while it allows the user to remain anchored without the use of full immersion in the physical world.

The biggest advantage afforded by the use of Augmented Reality is that it allows the user to actively participate in the virtual world, with direct reference to the current environment of the user, and in real time, which allows for full sensory stimulation, as is desired when we went into the necessity for plausible illusions in Chapter 3 to allow for a comprehensive virtual experience. The development of the content for Augmented Reality is deemed easier when contrasted with Virtual Reality as the AR developers do not need to create a whole new world from the pixel out; all they would have to do is allow for the enhancement of the environment that is already there. Through this, it becomes possible for the developer to create applications that simply allow virtual components to be made part of the physical world, and this would be all that is needed to make Augmented Reality accessible for the user.

4.1 What Augmented Reality is all about

We have touched upon the possibilities of what Augmented Reality can be, but we do have to take our cue from what Augment means, as it Is generally interpreted to mean to make something greater than it already is. While we know that the Metaverse and the digital world are great in themselves, this provides a lot of leeway for how developers choose to take up the gauntlet to augment something that has been considered one of the more revolutionary innovations to affect all of mankind. Augmented Reality at its heart simply adds digital components into the physical world, and adds to our perception of reality through the use of technology that heightens the functions of our senses – save that of taste. This easier theorized however, as for Augmented Reality to be successful, it needs to consider the physical location of the individual and the precise time at which the individual is able to perform that action and obtain the additional functions. Augmented Reality then integrates three key functions: It combines the physical and virtual worlds, where; it allows for interactions by the user in real time; and it seamlessly overlays the physical and virtual objects with each other. From this, Augmented Reality can be defined as a form of technology that incorporates components that are computer-generated into the physical world, that the user may perform the task that is needed without the need for tremendous effort. The environment generated within the Augmented Reality is existent and tangible, and it is merely expanded through the addition of the digital components. There are certain terms that the user must familiarize themselves with before we go into the world of Augmented Reality. These terms include:

- Inside-Out Tracking where sensors are integrated onto mobile targets that are capable of use regardless of the indoor or outdoor location of the target, or whether the target is immobile or sentient in their movement. This allows the AR software to place the aspects of the environment within its data processing.

- Outside-In Tracking utilizes fixed sensors within the environment to allow mobile targets to have their movements tracked. This form of tracking finds its use within AR systems that are fixed in terms of location.

- Marker-Based- this refers to Augmented Reality systems that need the use of fiduciary markers that allow cameras to recognize it so that the AR software would be able to respond with the necessary digital content.
- Markerless-Based Augmented Realities are those which integrate mechanical and optical sensors to include the use of GPS and image recognition software, as these forms of sensors do not require the use of artificial markers. These allow the Augmented Reality to function inside and in an outdoor setting.

4.2 Types of Augmented Reality

Unlike the classification of the Virtual Reality, the simplification of Augmented Reality is more complex in part due to the various technological components that are needed to make it function. There are various augmented realities that vary in accordance with the technology integrated into the functions, the types of interactions that would take place between the reality and the user, and the user recognitions that are integrated into the hardware. The basis for the classification of Augmented Realities starts from Marker Based and Markerless Augmented Realities. Marker Based Augmented Realities have two subcategories, which include Position Markers and QR Codes. Markerless Based Augmented Realities however, have a more diversified classification in that these are Geolocation Assisted, Inside Out, and Outside In trackers. Geolocation Assisted Augmented Realities include those that function with GPS and Electromagnetic Compasses that automatically orient the AR software with its location in the world. The Inside Out Augmented Reality utilizes Image Recognition Software, and Mapping Software to make the Augmented Reality possible. The same Image Recognition Software is also used as the subcategory for the Outside In Tracker Based Augmented Reality. These categorizations however, are not concrete, but are as general as possible to accommodate the broad distinctions that cause each AR System to differ.

Marker Based Augmented Realities are those that need a physical or sometimes virtual fiduciary marker that allows the software to release the digital content once it has been triggered, and allow the user to access the relevant content that has been integrated into the code of the marker. The rendered output can take several forms to include two-dimensional and three-dimensional images, videos, animations or even auditory triggers that have been coded into the marker once it has been scanned. You would find a similar functionality when you scan QR Codes to reveal menus or special content that has been embedded into certain products or events. A marker based AR would require a printed marker or visual information, an object that would trigger the marker (such as a camera), and the relevant digitized content that goes on display on the screen of your device.

For the marker based ARs, the cameras and visual markers are integral to the execution of the content that is present in the software, and through the use of a series of coordinates that determine the precise location of the triggered marker, the digitized content becomes available, and the user is able to visualize the content from various perspectives. The AR however, to be able to do this, has to have the capabilities to recognize the object over which it will overlay the aspects of the virtual world. Once the AR has recognized the object, the AR can then begin to integrate the aspects of the virtual world over the recognized object, and from there, the content is embedded in the virtual layer to complete the AR overlay. Once all of these processes are completed, all the user would have to do to activate the virtual reality is to scan the virtual object with the use of a camera to allow the embedded digitized content to be displayed onto the phones. This type of AR is more economical as this allows commercially available mobile phone cameras to be used, which increases its importance in the accessibility of the Metaverse. Because of its affordability, this type of AR is the most commonplace, and it allows for the easier development of content as this form of AR can recognize two-dimensional images and integrate it onto a three-dimensional object. As a result, this form of software is ideal for the novice developers and allows more individuals to collaborate and create their own content in the Metaverse. As a result, the developer would have no need for additional knowledge to code, as it would be quite easy to use. QR Codes have the same processes although it allows the user to access the digital content without the need to overlay this content onto a physical object.

Markerless-Based Augmented Reality Systems are more complex and broader compared to the Marker-Based AR as their systems and components tend to function independently of the other, and would require a variety of tracking systems to ensure that the user is able to access the data that is embedded into the physical object overlaid with the virtual object. The systems that form part of this type of AR must include the ability to detect location, motion, patterns, and objects that the system could take cognition of these objects and project their content for display in its monitors. The Markerless-Based AR finds similarities with the Virtual Reality Systems from the numerous components needed to generate the data from the physical object, as magnetometers and gyroscopes were among the sensors embedded into our phones and the HMDs just so the system would be able to detect movement from the user. As it is, because of the sheer number of components, this type of AR restricts the user from outdoor usage, and can only be used within a specified area. Inertial Sensors have provided some form of progress that this form of AR can be integrated within the smartphone, with the integration of GPS for a more accurate sense of the user's location to display the data needed. The use of the GPS however, is limited only to outdoor locations, and inclement weather can easily disrupt the transmission of the signals within the Markerless Based AR.

Current Markerless-Based AR Systems take several forms which include the use of the hybrid-tracking system – a portable version that is built-in into several devices, and the use of goggles and other mobile technologies to ensure that the user is able to experience the AR regardless of their position. Combined, the use of the portable hybrid tracking system allows the user to experience an enhanced version of the AR, as they would be able do visual searches, object recognition and be able to map the terrain. To improve the ability of the Markerless-Based AR to detect objects, the visual searches allow for model-based tracking or natural-feature tracking. Under Model-based tracking, this allows the AR to detect the edges of three-dimensional objects that its systems can begin to recognize the object that it detects that fit the identified parameters. Machine-Based Learning Algorithms help this form of tracking identify the specific object detected by the AR, which can include the use of image recognition software. The same image recognition software also functions in the detection of the natural features of an object, and when paired with the machine learning algorithm, it would be able to detect the same object and identify it in accordance with the data it has. The sole limitation however, is that the unconventional form of an object would prove difficult to identify, and here, there may be problems with the virtual overlay. The continued use of the Machine-Based Learning Algorithm however, may provide the means for the AR to recognize objects of a more unusual configuration. SLAM Algorithms are used by other types of AR systems which allow for the detection of familiar objects within an unfamiliar environment through the use of mapping technologies. As a result, this can aid in the detection of the natural features of an object that allows for the recognition of an object regardless of its position, location and distance from the camera of the device.

4.3 The Realization of Augmented Reality

For Augmented Reality to take place, it requires hardware and software to work in concert to ensure that the virtual overlay over a physical object is successfully executed that the user can simulate a fraction of the virtual experience seamlessly. The hardware that is necessary to the success of the AR includes the use of the Tracking Systems, specifically, the Hybrid tracking which itself is comprised of multiple components that allow the AR to accurately detect the position and location of a user in reference to a specific set of coordinates.

- The AR System firstly must be able to track and detect the physical environment of the user before it can begin to augment the reality it detects through the superimposition of the embedded data in the virtual overlay over the physical objects. As a result, the use of sensors in the AR technology are an integral part of the AR, and with the use of micro engineering, it becomes possible for the users to integrate the use of the software into mobile devices. Here, this form of AR carries similarities with the VR sensors, but includes more instruments to perform more accurate tracking. These can include:

- Hybrid Tracking
  - Active Tracking through the use of GPS, Gravity, Pressure, Thermal and Humidity Sensors around the user and their device
    - Mechanical Tracking;
    - Magnetic Tracking, and
    - Ultrasonic Tracking enables more accuracy in the detection of the position of the user relative to the software used.
  - Passive Tracking which simply uses optical and mechanical sensors.
    - Mechanical Tracking
      - Inertial Sensors
        - Accelerometers
        - Gyroscopes are needed to identify movement.

- o Magnetometer- which uses the magnetic field to identify location
- Optical Tracking, which allows the software to use the cameras of the device to track the position of the object relative to its location.
  - o Marker-based ARs
  - o Markerless-based ARs – which depend on the ambient environment to detect the user and the object.
    - Edge Tracking to help define the object
    - Natural Feature Tracking
- The tracking systems of the AR are just one of the numerous components, as the sensors needed for the tracking systems, the processors and the display systems all work in concert to produce the enhanced reality perceived by the user through the AR.
- The display systems of the AR are the secondary component as this allows the user to visualize the possible interactions with the virtual object, and also allows the user to access the data that has been embedded into the virtual overlay of the object. AR Display systems can take the form of head attached

displays, handheld displays and spatial displays. Under the head attached displays, the display devices include the use of retinal displays where the images are projected into the retina of the person (this being the anatomical point where light is transmitted to the brain through the optic nerve), the use of Head Mounted Displays such as those mentioned in Chapter 3, and the use of the HMP. Handheld Displays are perhaps the most familiar form of the AR as these can include our mobile gadgets. Spatial Displays on the other hand include the use of see-through videos that are projected onto a screen that other observers may perceive the augmented reality as well; spatial optical see through and the projection based spatial environment which can be likened to the rendering of a virtual world within the environment. Of these visual imageries, the retinal display and the Head Attached Displays provide the best options for the visualization of the augmented reality. Handheld Devices too are able to let the user visualize three dimensional objects from a two-dimensional perspective, and similarly, would be able to manifest the image through a hologram.

- Head Attached Displays are similar to the HMDs of Virtual Reality in that this requires the user to wear goggles that are mounted on the head to experience the augmented reality. Within the HAD are the sensors that permit the identification and detection of the objects in the environment and allow the user to interact with the virtual object. This is made possible through the use of a video see-through and the optical see-through technology. Video see-through technology is best represented as a mirror through which reality is reflected into the user's vision. This allows the immediate physical environment of the user to be recorded, where the data and virtual imagery can be overlaid before it is projected in front of the user to stream. For this instance however, the environment is digitized and modified before it is transmitted to the user to ensure that the imagery feels more realistic rather than unreal. For a more natural feel, the use of the optical see through technology is favored for its realistic visuals shown to the user.

- Retinal Displays involve the direct reflection of the physical and virtual components into the retinas of our eyes. Lasers that have been modified into a low-power setting generate the imagery to be projected to produce high-resolution images, with a minimal consumption of power. As a result, this is ideal for the use of ARs for outdoor usage due to their portability.
- HMDs are represented once more in the use of the hardware needed. They carry the same functionalities as their counterparts in the use of the Virtual Reality Systems. They do give several disadvantages when they are applied with AR software in that they are quite uncomfortable, are quite expensive and they have a low Field of View- they do

not allow the user to see much of the augmented reality. The HMD also creates latency issues when it has to render the physical environment and since the Metaverse cannot have latency issues, this would prove to be an error that must be rectified, and this can cause difficulties with the user. Other video see-through HMDs have display problems with the quality of the imagery provided to the user in the AR and severely constrain the use of this type of AR to indoor use.

o HPV (Holographic Particle Velocimetry) share the same characteristics as the retinal displays, with a modification in how the imagery is projected as this only uses half-silvered mirrors.

4.4 Key Players of Augmented Reality

With the various software and hardware needed to manifest the Augmented Reality, developers are able to modify the hardware needed for specific interests. Solo and Everysight Raptor for instance, have been developed for the use in sports and are suited for outdoor uses. These hardware consist of a variety of sensors used to detect the pulse rate, blood pressure and the body heat of the user in relation to the activity- which can also carry Telehealth implications should the user and physician choose to integrate this functionality. Through the use of Bluetooth Technology, it allows the user and other interested observers to monitor the vital signs in real-time, useful in the prevention and detection of medical anomalies within the body.

MS HoloLens 2 and Magic Leap are among the more popular forms of AR HMDs, which include the use of the SLAM Algorithm which allows for a more comprehensive mapping technology. The former can be used indoors and outdoors as it does not require the use of cables and is an untethered form of the HMD. It can be quite bulky to use however. The Magic Leap on the other hand was designed only to be used indoors, and this causes its functionality to be greatly affected by variables such as lighting quality and the shape of the environment. Magic Leap however, does not count as an untethered HMD as it is attached to a small computer mounted onto a belt. As it is, current applications for the MS HoloLens 2 and the Magic Leap center around the educational, professional and gaming industries. Third Eye and ODG HMDs are devices whose applications can span from personal to professional use. ODG particularly finds durability in its titanium structure and makes it a key player for devices intended for outdoor use. ThirdEye is favored by most professionals due to its AR Goggle Technology that enhances the quality of their professional learnings and simulations where the user is able to customize the settings that are available. Additionally, ThirdEye offers the use of the SLAM SDK for developers who wish to augment the content present in the display of the ThirdEye Goggle.

Handheld displays are perhaps the more common devices used to access Augmented Realities, as there are various types and sizes of these devices that afford the user the ability to choose in accordance with their frequency of usage, the length of time that they wish to use the device, the price, and the features that allow them to access the AR through each device. Handheld devices generally use see-through video technologies, though more complex versions that require the use of a projector for the display aspect of the device utilize the optical see-through technology in its place. These devices contain the sensors necessary to detect the user and the physical object before the AR software can begin the digitization process to link the virtual aspects of the software with the physical object to create the altered reality. From what can be safely gleaned, tablets, smartphones and personal digital assistants are popularly suited as handheld devices to ensure that the user can access the AR. This is important in the economic sense as this lessens the amount of equipment the user would need to access the Metaverse, and allow more people to populate the expanded environment. The cameras that form part of these devices allow the physical environment to be captured by the software that it may begin to integrate the digital overlay onto it. Developers of these devices are more concerned now with the need to ensure that the cameras of the latest models of smartphones and other handheld devices are compatible with the AR Software that could potentially use them, and ensure continued compatibility with other devices and programs needed to run the AR. This is essential in the expansion of the Metaverse as the use of mobile technology increased the number of users, and makes AR a more viable option compared to VR. However, the main disadvantage to be had is that full immersion in the virtual reality cannot take place as the size of the display severely limits the displays that are permitted by the device, and this limits the field of view that decreases the immersive experience of the user. Lastly, because our modern handheld devices require frequent use of our hands, the use of the handheld device in the AR limits our ability to interact – especially when we have to touch our phone screens every now and then to ensure that our phone does not get locked at the most inopportune time. Aside from the use of handheld devices, there are also handheld projectors, and despite their name, they are larger than the use of the HMDs, and are often disregarded for personal use. These projectors are primarily used by the Entertainment and Marketing Industries as these are more cost-effective solutions and are quite easy to use.

The software needed to run the AR has similarities to the Virtual Reality where the use of the game engines such as Unity and Unreal Engine remain key components. In the context of the AR, both developers have released applications to allow developers to create Augmented Realities regardless of the skill level of the developer. It stands to reason out that the creation of the environment of the Augmented Reality is more complex as this requires the software to interact with a variety of other hardware with other components. Where the creation of the Virtual Environment in a VR setting allows the developer to create an entire world from scratch, its distinct advantage over AR is that the VR Environment is easier to conceptualize. AR Environments are made more complex with the combination of virtual and physical environments, and thus before the design of the AR Environment is made, the ability to use the AR, its compatibility with the software, and the types of interactions available need to be outlined before one develops the AR environment.

Tangible AR Interfaces need physical objects to ensure that the software is able to manipulate the physical environment to create the virtual illusion that there is such an object in the physical world. Tangible AR Interfaces are dependent on the use of physical objects and this allows the possibility of collaboration for increased participation and the shared AR experience. In line with what the Metaverse is intended to be, the Tangible AR Interface allows users to share the same experiences across the same software regardless of the type of device, and that through the same software they would be able to visualize the same content. For this interface to work, the virtual environment needs to be stimulated through the use of several environmental triggers. It is possible however, through this software that 3D Visualization may take place on a two-dimensional object. The usual type of AR that uses this type of interface are the marker-based ARs as these require the presence of a physical marker that will trigger the development and digitization of the physical object into its virtual counterpart that the user may interact with it. The one downside to the use of this type of interface is the limitation in how the object is to be oriented, as the markers would have to be in their precise alignment to be able to recognize the object, which makes other orientations of the object impossible as the markers have to be continuously set in the same place for the virtual environment to be overlaid. Despite this, this type of interface is preferred for the use in aesthetics as decorators and designers take advantage of its relative ease of usage, and are best used for educational purposes due to the interaction between multiple users. More contemporary usages of the AR allow for an increased functionality as these allow interoperability between several devices.

Collaborative AR Interfaces enable localized or remote collaboration between developers, and are present in most AR displays, especially through handheld devices. This is not ordinary collaboration however, as we would compare it to Zoom or Google Meet meetings, this collaboration speaks of the ability of the users to meet in real time to interact with the same object and the ability of each user to manipulate the object that is their topic that the other users may be able to observe what is done in real time. This allows for the creation of digital content among users. Ideally, this is favored in the engineering profession as this allows collaboration over long distances, and the use of visualization-based Augmented Realities ensure that everyone is able to view the same object at the same time. Unlike the Tangible AR Based systems which require the use of markers to trigger the visual output through the environment, the Collaborative AR Interface allows the user to use the markerless-based ARs, visual search systems, SLAM Algorithms and various other display peripherals to display the object at the same time. Because of the nature of the equipment used, the use of the Collaborative Interface is only possible indoors as a connection with high speed internet is necessary to prevent latency in the delivery of the visuals, and to ensure that the image itself does not encounter any issues with its display in the collaborative environment. To overcome this however, most devices are constructed with the use of collaborative augmented realities in mind. It is hoped that the use of the Collaborative AR would allow for the improvement of the displays, to include physical avatars, Telehealth and the development of peripherals that are on the body to allow for a smoother interactive process within the AR environment.

Hybrid Augmented Reality Interfaces integrate the need for various software to communicate, between all the peripherals needed by the software to fully render the AR environment. These would include gloves, HMDs, sensors and the like. Unlike the Tangible AR Interface which is ideal for novice developers, this type of Augmented Reality Interface requires skilled technological capacity that the user may be able to properly render an augmented environment. Though complex in their construction, there are several Hybrid AR interfaces that are available, which integrate the use of an HMD and a wand among the peripherals needed to interact with the AR environment that was generated. Medical breakthroughs find common applications with the use of the Hybrid AR System as a paralyzed person would be able to move within the physical environment through a virtual body through the detection of impulses that allow another peripheral to manipulate the environment on their behalf. This allows for the implementation of a virtual presence as we have touched upon in Chapter 3, where the user would be able to manifest their actions within the virtual environment, necessary for the successful population of the Metaverse. Machine learning communications and a program that allows the software to understand the nuances of human language are under development, and this enhances the quality of the interaction between the user and software, and on a wider implication, the ability of the user to interact with machine-based artificial intelligences while immersed in the Metaverse.

Multimodal AR Interfaces allow the integration of human interactions with virtual objects, achieved through the use of specific physical hand movements (just as you would use a Wii), gestures, audio-based commands that recognize your speech patterns (as you would speak with Alexa or Siri), gaze tracking (as with games), and head movements. These are made possible through the use of microscopic sensors that are embedded within the devices used, but the interaction emanates from the combined aspects of the sensors with the software needed, the machine-learning capabilities, and the presence of a neural network system that improves the quality of the responsiveness of the virtual environment with the actions of the user. LeapMotion for instance, allows for the detection of movement of the hands and reciprocates the physical gestures made in the virtual setting that the user may interact with the virtual object. Gesture and speech sensors would allow however, for a more refined AR experience. Again, this type of AR interface finds a medical breakthrough in how disabled persons can take advantage of this type of technology to have experiences that they would normally not have.

The tools to develop an Augmented Reality are similar to those used by developers who go into a full scale virtual world. What differs, is that, because the Augmented Reality is dependent upon the existent physical environment of the user, the software has to make adjustments to that. The adjustments in this case would have to vary as well, in accordance with the intended use of the software. For instance, environments crafted within apps like Pokemon Go would be more light hearted and randomized to ensure that the player simulates the exploration of a real world. If it were a learning application for instance, such as flight or vehicle simulations, or even in a health care scenario, the information that would be presented would have to be strictly analyzed that the user would be able to accurately determine what would be the next course of interaction within the simulation. Thus, it can be said that this is arguably more complex than the development of a virtual reality due to the numerous applications that must be able to capably bridge the physical and virtual divide. Aside from the determination of the application's intended purposes, the developers of the AR would have to create the individual content that gets triggered when the camera of the device manages to scan the markers or identify the physical object that would trigger the type of content that is displayed onto the device of the user. There is also the question of the preparation of the virtual forms of the physical objects to ensure that the transition from the virtual to the physical worlds remains seamless. The components of an AR environment can be easily made through the use of the 3D modelling tools that were mentioned in Chapter 3, under Virtual Reality. The main issue is how to ensure that these digital twins are able to function within a physical world.

For developers to create an AR environment, it is necessary to identify first the type of interface that is needed for the application. Once the developer has identified the specific type of interface that must be applied to the AR software, there may be minimal coding knowledge necessary to execute all the intended functions, as this would be covered in the interface chosen. The development of an AR requires however, collaboration between the programmers who create the functionality of the code; the 3D modelers who create the digital objects that the AR Software allows the user to interact with, and the engineers to ensure that the peripherals and other components are able to work in harmony to create the AR sought by the developers. This ensures that the machine learning algorithms, the quality of interactions with the virtual world and the visual search based recognition needed by the AR to trigger the content are able to execute the tasks that they were programmed to do in the first place. As a result, there is no singular developer's tool that can be used to create the AR. We have touched upon Unity and Unreal Engine in the development of the VR, and these two game engines allow for the creation of an AR with the added functionalities within their software. The addition of a software developer kit into the game engine allows developers to use these two game engines to develop the AR environment and ensure that the kits are compatible with the type of software that must be used in the development process.

Each Software Developer Kit must be able to allow object recognition, as this is the foremost quality needed in the development of the AR. The recognition of two-dimensional and three-dimensional objects as well as the ability to recognize these objects from a certain distance or angle is necessary for the AR. Aside from this, the motion and location tracking are necessary, as well as the use of the SLAM Technology. The rendering technology of the software developer kits need to be considered, to include the use of the HMD Support, Hand-held support (the images that are on the display), and the display of the images in real time (necessary to the Metaverse for a true synchronic experience). Vuforia is one of the popular options as an SDK as this permits ease of use among novice developers due to the variety of functions and the presence of free and professional premium versions. Vuforia is able to operate within iOS, Android and Windows operating systems and is able to provide game support to the Unity Game Engine. With the use of Vuforia, it is entirely possible to detect two dimensional and three dimensional objects and the SDK would allow for the recognition of these objects, as well as word triggers from a lexicon of approximately a hundred thousand words. QR codes may also be automatically scanned with the use of this SDK, at a maximum distance of 4 meters through the use of the computer vision technology. The object scanner within this SDK allows for cloud storage of recognized objects regardless of their dimensionality, and once these objects have been stored and sufficiently identified, they may be downloaded from the storage to the Unity Game Engine that the developer may begin to create the AR and the virtual overlay. An added advantage when this SDK is used in conjunction with the Unity Game engine is that it can detect up to six objects at a time, which allows for more digital outputs, and it allows these objects to be viewed at different angles for a maximum perspective. The interface provided by Vuforia allows for a smoother interaction process and is ideal for handheld devices. It cannot however, be used in devices that rely on a GPS Tracking system.

Easy AR is another option compatible with Android, Windows and iOS Systems as well as the Unity Game Engine. This form of SDK is ideal for the development of the Smart Glasses, as well as Mobile Device based ARs. It cannot however, render two dimensional objects onto a three-dimensional environment, and this form of SDK, as with Vuforia, is incompatible with AR interfaces that require the use of GPS to track the location and position of the user. Easy AR is limited in that it can only detect three-dimensional objects at a maximum distance of 3 meters.

Wikitude is described as one of the more potent SDKs as it carries the same compatibilities as Vuforia and EasyAR, but is limited in its free use as more features require payment before they can be accessed by the developer. However, if you are willing to shell out the necessary payments, Wikitude provides linkages with the use of SLAM Technology – which to recap, allows the AR to scan for the objects within an environment at a farther distance to allow these objects to be virtually overlaid and mapped; and more importantly, allows for the use of GPS Tracking. Compared to Vuforia, it can only detect a maximum of five objects, but at a maximum distance of 5 meters. With the use of Wikitude, it is entirely possible for the developer to create ARs compatible for indoor and outdoor usage. Data can be safely stored in a cloud storage. This SDK is ideal for professional users, and supports several extensions including JavaScript API, Native API, Xamarin, Unity 3D, Cordova, and Titanium.

Kudan, is an SDK, best suited for developers of advanced iOS and Android ARs, as this form of SDK allow for the use of the SLAM Technology, the integration of AI, and the ability to interface with robotic technologies. It can be used with its own engine, the KudanCV, or as a plugin with the Unity Game Engine. It is ideal for mobile devices as the use of the SLAM Technology allows various environments to be mapped at the same time, regardless of its location indoors or outdoors; and its use of a markerless-based AR can be created to integrate the use of algorithms based on AIs. Through this SDK, it is possible for the developer to use all the various interfaces that were mentioned earlier in this chapter, and its ability to detect two dimensional and three dimensional objects remains limitless, and can also be applied for marker-based ARs.

ARTool Kit is the more popular option for AR Developers, due to its classification as a free and open-source software. Applications that use the Android, iOS, Windows, Linux and Mac OS as well as the applications that are compatible with smart glasses can be developed with the array of functions that are present with this SDK. Through this tool kit, it is possible for the developers to create apps that can identify the point of view of the user, through the use of intelligent computer vision algorithms that allows the digital content to be overlaid with the physical object in real time. This allows for a high quality image rendering of the digital output. The objects recognized by this toolkit allow for the recognition of up to six objects at a maximum distance of 3 meters, and allows the eye movement trackers to recalibrate in real time. SLAM Technology is also used in this SDK, as this allows the ARTool Kit to detect objects in 2d or 3D, and is compatible with other engines such as Unity, and OpenSceneGraph.

ARCore is an SDK developed by Google, that allows motion tracking, environment tracking and light estimation for the developers that opt for this SDK. This is limited however, to the development of ARs that are compatible with iOS and Android systems. This SDK however, can be used as a plug-in with Unity, Unreal Engine and Open GI, an advantage, where most SDKs are compatible with Unity, which allows the developer to opt for improved interoperability with the AR. This SDK is best used for the development of mobile applications, and it is possible to develop GPS-based and use Tangible AR-Based interfaces with this SDK, which allows the recognition of 2D or 3D objects and text, as well as the tracking and location of the mobile devices that carry the software developed. Environment tracking enables the developer to identify the size and location of the surfaces whose images are to be rendered in 3D. The use of the light estimation allows the AR to render the objects with the right lighting, to ensure it can be used outdoors. This SDK also allows the use of 3D modelling through Tiltbrush and Block VR Tools from Google.

4.5 Utility of Augmented Reality

There are numerous benefits to be had with Augmented Realities as these are able to heighten the types of interactions that take place between the user and the virtual world, in essence, the Metaverse manifested in our physical world. These allow the use of AR a form of versatility in the way that it lends itself to the application in several fields, and allows for a more stimulated environment as it makes great use of our sensory functions. You would be able to find Augmented Realities and their software used in the fields of Education, Engineering – where it becomes a great, cost-effective measure; Architecture, the Medical Field, Defense and of course, Entertainment. These applications however, barely scrape the potential of what Augmented Reality can truly be, as it is believed to contribute to the enhancement of the learning process as it boosts the confidence of the student, and stimulates their attention to a degree that has yet to be attained when compared to the more traditional methods of learning. Summarily, Augmented Reality provides the following benefits to the user, in that it allows the users to take part in the project, and provides opportunities for them to collaborate, and interact in real-time; the content presented is of an enhanced quality that responds immediately to each interaction that the user performs, and because of this, it allows the user to learn at a faster pace, with the reduction of strain on the brain, and fosters creativity, and stimulates their attention. Additionally, the AR becomes a cost-effective measure, and because it is portable, where it makes use of a variety of devices and cloud storages, it is more accessible.

It does however carry disadvantages in that not all AR software are meant for outdoor use, and the number of peripherals that may be needed to run more advanced versions limit the portability and usability of the application. The same peripherals cause a physical disadvantage in that these are quite heavy to use. Additionally, the full digitization of the physical environment may not be entirely possible with all AR applications as this is highly dependent on the type of interfaces and algorithms that the developer opted to integrate into the codes of the AR. Though we have touted the utility of AR in education, it finds resistance especially since most educators perceive this form of technology to be difficult to use, and this leads to a lack of customizable content.

4.6 Mixed Realities

Mixed Realities (MR) are defined as an amalgamation of Virtual Reality, Augmented Reality and Augmented Virtuality. It can be reasoned out that Mixed Reality results from the stimulation of our senses through the use of technology in such a way that the brain, while immersed in this form of reality, gains an altered perception of the reality presented to it due to the illusions generated by the peripherals that created the mixed reality. It can be seen that this is not a distinct type of reality on its own, but an umbrella term that integrates the entirety of both Virtual Reality and Augmented Reality. This form of reality is heavily dependent on the concept of Virtuality, where it allows for the duplication of our physical world, but also allows the user to envision the potential of what the virtual world can be, which links us back to the Metaverse, where it is believed that users would be able to create a personalized niche within the Metaverse should they have the skills to do so.

4.7 Extended Realities: Advantages and Disadvantages

Summarily, the main advantage of these extended realities are the enhanced methods wherein they are able to stimulate the sensory and cognitive functions of the user and allow the user to interact with objects in ways that are not ordinarily possible in the physical set-up. These allow for the application of these extended realities in a variety of fields which enhance the collaborative process which results in a cost-effective means to work, and learn.

Because of the sheer volume of peripherals that may be needed to run all the software and components, in both AR and VR, these may be quite costly from the onset, and this requires an optimal infrastructure, such as high-speed internet that ensures that the virtual experience, regardless of which form does not experience latency issues. There is the matter of the software and hardware, which can be both bulky, and difficult for the user to attach to the body. This aside, the benefits that the user attains from the use of the VR outweighs the disadvantages, as future developments may devise solutions that will counteract the disadvantages mentioned in this chapter and in Chapter 3, to make the VR and AR a more user-friendly experience.

4.8 Conclusion

Virtual and Augmented Reality are the key components of what would constitute the Metaverse, hence it would be necessary to go into detail as to how one goes about in the creation of a virtual world through these. Through a variety of software and hardware, it is entirely possible to create a world limited only by the imagination of the developers. Subsequently, this enhances our ability to interact with the virtual world, in a way that we would normally be unable to through the use of our computers. This reiterates the immersive quality that defines the Metaverse, and in the subsequent chapters, we delve into the interactions that help the Metaverse function similarly to our real world.

5 NON-FUNGIBLE TOKENS

In creating Bitcoin, the idea of trustless, digital scarcity has been established. The fact that digital copies were too costly before the inception of the technology was a barrier to widespread use.

Because of the introduction of blockchain technology, it is now feasible to create programmable digital scarcity. This technology is now being utilized for the aim of linking the digital world with the physical world. Non fungible tokens are the first type of digital assets that is playable (NFTs). This may serve as a catapult to enhance digital products scarcity.

ERC-721 tokens cannot be easily interchangeable, which means they may be used to represent unique assets and proposals. In other words, tangible assets like real estate, artwork, and antiques may be represented precisely using this model.

The collectibles market is now valued at $450 billion and has stayed mostly unaltered since the internet took off. Current authentication problems, fraud, and monetary restrictions are commonplace in the business. At this point in time, the market is ready for a shift since blockchain technology can provide trustless transactions to a whole new level.

Real-life assets may be tokenized using NFTs, which offer a trustworthy and trustless method to do so.

The majority of the NFT market was constructed around Ethereum. With all the extra activity on EOS, people have started to show more interest. In line with this, it's no surprise that NFTs (non-fungible tokens) are appearing on new blockchains thanks to investment fueling development.

Non-fungible tokens (NFTs) are digital assets having distinct characteristics. A particular asset may have any number of different NFTs (e.g., one piece of art or one piece of real estate).

With these distinct qualities, the object's digital representation may be created. Real-world physical assets may be represented using NFTs. In a trustless setting, a distributed, community-owned ledger may store a representation and exchange it with others without the requirement for a centralized authority.

NFTs are one of the primary pillars of the emerging digital asset class - assets that have been digitized and have their own cryptocurrency token associated with them. We will go through the many features of NFTs, and how they are linked to other asset types.

These subjects will be covered in this book:

NFTs are polyhedral tessellations. As previously mentioned, there are various kinds and characteristics of NFTs.

Tokens of different kinds (fungible vs non-fungible) (NFTs).

An introduction to NFTs and noteworthy projects that use NFTs.

Legal and ethical concerns that are associated with the development of NFTs. Where to find and keep them.

Additional issues relating to NFTs include: How NFTs connect to photography, music, and video makers.

Additionally, we will also address some of the most frequent questions surrounding NFTs and their solutions.

To find out how to make your first NFT utilizing the Ethereum platform and some other platforms, we shall examine how to do this in more detail later. We will then discuss the role of NFTs in the market.

This book will explain the following topics:

What are NFTs? The different types and features of NFTs. Difference between fungible and non-fungible tokens (NFTs).

The use cases for NFTs, and popular projects that use NFTs. Ethical and legal issues around the creation of NFTs. How to acquire and store them.

We'll also cover other important topics related to NFTs, such as:

The relationship between NFTs and Photography, NFTs and Video Maker, NFTs and Musicians and DJ.

We will also discuss some common questions on NFTs and their answers.

Later, we will go over how to create your first NFT using the Ethereum platform and some other platforms. We'll then talk about NFTs market's place.

5.1 NON-FUNGIBLE TOKEN - MEANING

NFTs are an abbreviation for Non-Fungible Tokens; they are Cryptocurrency assets that act as a rare and unique project, whether virtual or physical, such as digital art or real estate. NFTs are as unique as authentic pieces of art. Blockchain technology is used to recognize their authenticity to tell the difference between a replica and an original. This made it certified to be data carriers that act as the digital representation of a real-world asset. It represents physical assets, such as real estate, artwork, collectibles, and more. Digital assets like these have been touted as the next step for the global economy. They allow a real-world asset to be securely stored and transferred on the blockchain. Any item or artwork can be traced to the person who published it. This can be used to avoid fraud and manipulation prevalent in many markets today. Two of the most famous types of NFTs are Cryptototties and Cryptopunks.

NFTs are a unique digital asset. To be more specific, they are the first primary digital asset class tokenized on the blockchain. Since these assets do not conform to the fungible properties of traditional digital assets, we refer to them as non-fungible tokens. The term non-fungible is used because it implies that NFTs cannot be altered or duplicated without changing the value of the real-world asset being represented by them.

Through this feature, NFT offers buyers ownership certificates of digital items and protects the value of their upcoming transactions. A CoinDesk report claims that artists can digitally sell their artwork globally to generate higher profits at one-piece works and royalty plans. NFTs are a significant upgrade over previous types of tokens.

Gamers can also own in-game property or goods and sell them to earn money. Most NFT tokens are manufactured using the two Ethereum standards, ERC-1155 and ERC-721.

Cryptokitties, as a proof of concept, showed us that NFTs could represent digital collectibles. While this is a minor use case, it has proven that NFTs are something very new and unique. Furthermore, they have provided us with the foundations for bringing scarcity and digital ownership to a whole new level. However, the increased activity on EOS has caused interest to shift. With investment driving the growth of the blockchain, it is no surprise that NFTs are also starting to appear on new blockchains. NFTs are still very unique, and there have only been a few effective uses for them so far. However, there is a lot of potential for various applications of NFTs in the future. The rise of digital asset exchanges will bring a new type of liquidity that was not possible before. The current state of the NFT market is very similar to what the cryptocurrency industry was like in its early days.

There are still many issues with how NFTs are defined and classified. There is also no agreed-upon standard for their creation and storage. The NFT market is still experimental, but it has already proved its usefulness in niche markets. It will take some time before this technology can be implemented on different applications, but this does not mean that it will not eventually get there. All of these potential uses will require a solution to the problem of NFT interoperability.

No one owns real-world assets. The real-world assets that NFTs represent can only be owned by people who are registered as its owner on a blockchain. NFTs can only be properly owned and managed if their value is transferable on the blockchain. As with any other type of asset, a real-world asset's value can only be transferred if it has liquidity. Most people are already very familiar with the idea of owning digital items such as in-game assets, tickets, music albums, and others. The success that NFTs have had so far in these types of markets means that there will only be more adoption going forward.

As the public becomes more accustomed to using cryptocurrency exchange platforms, the demand for NFTs will also rise. It is often said that blockchain technology will disrupt a lot of industries. However, the industry where this could happen first would be online gaming. If NFTs can become useable on the blockchain, their opportunities for games will be enormous.

The use of NFTs in games has already started to happen. There are already several game developers that are using NFTs for in-game assets. They have made these NFTs available for gamers to use in their favourite games. The ownership of these assets is managed on the blockchain, which adds to their mainstream adoption. NFTs are not just limited to within games either. Some NFTs can be used for other purposes outside of the gaming industry. For example, NFTs can be used for in-app purchases or even as collectibles.

5.1.1   What is NFTs

Like physical money, cryptocurrency is just like material money, i.e., it is fungible. In other words, it can be used for buying or selling things or for exchange from one currency to another. For example, the value of one bitcoin will always be equal to another Bitcoin. The same is the case for the ether. Therefore, cryptocurrency is considered a secure transaction medium in the digital economy because of its fungibility.

NFTs change the crypto paradigm by making each token one-of-a-kind and irreplaceable, making them non-fungible, meaning that one token may be worth more than the others. Furthermore, due to distinct and non-transferable ID, digital asset representations are equated with digital passports to differentiate them from other tickets. In addition, there is the possibility of expansion. In other words, two NFT's can "breed" to form the third, unique NFFT.

NFTs, similar to Bitcoin, contain detailed ownership to make the verification and exchange of tokens between the holders a lot easier. In addition, the owners can add asset-related metadata or attributes in the NFT. For example, Coffee beans taken as the token can be included fair trade category. Alternatively, artists can use their metadata signature to sign their digital artwork.

ERC-721 standard was used to develop NFTs by the same person who manages the ERC-20 Intelligent Contract. The ERC-721 is used to define the minimum interface needed for trading game tokens. The interface includes property information, safety, and metadata. The ERC-1155 standard is described as decreasing the transaction and storage costs in a single contract as necessary for NFTs and batches in various non-fungible tokens. In November 2017, the most famous incident occurred in the history of NFT, i.e., the release of Cryptokitties. Cryptokitties are represented as a digital cat with an EthereumBlockchain unique ID. Each kitten is distinct, and its trade occurs in ether. They breed with each other and form new descendants with attributes and assessments that are different from their parents.

Cryptokitties, after its launch, in no time, accumulated a fan base that actively purchased, exchanged and distributed ether and spent $ 20 million. Some fans go far in their efforts to the point that they even went from $ 100,000.

Although the Cryptokitties' is considered unimportant, it has significant commercial applications. For example, NFTs have been used at the real estate level and for personal transactions. The benefit of allowing different types of tokens in a contract increases trust in these tokens, whether they are used for real estate or single transactions.

5.1.2 Fungibility in NFTs

The capacity of an asset to be exchanged for a similar item without losing its value is referred to as fungibility. The properties of an asset, such as divisibility and value, are also defined by fungibility.

For example, when compared, the value of two $ 10 bills remains the same. So, for example, when you lend a $ 10 bill, you can return it in the form of another type with the same value as this $10 bill instead of replacing the same note.

In the digital currency world, the value of one BTC is similar to that of the other one. But same is not the case for non-fungible tokens. In this case, the value of the NFT token will be different from the similar token. This is because each token has its own unique characteristics and the assets of the real world, such as the rare stones, artworks and luxury products of the collector.

5.1.3 Fungible and non-fungible

Fungible tokens are tokens whose value remains the same on exchange. As discussed previously, the value of Bitcoin is not dependent on its owner or history and remains the same. That's why it is known as a fungible token.

However, non-fungible tokens are distinct from one another, and trade cannot occur in another form. As discussed about bitcoin earlier, on the other hand, a non-fungible token is a unique trading card. Therefore, you can get something else if you exchange it with a completely different card.

5.1.4 Characteristics of NFTs

Rarity: Rarity defines the value of the NFT. Thus, the desired amount of tokens can be developed by NFT developers to increase its value. However, they sometimes restrict the development of these tokens.

Insaperable: NFTs are inseparable. They cannot be broken down into smaller units. You can either purchase the entire piece of digital art or not buy any art.

Unique: it is the most important characteristic of all. They register themselves as unique in a permanent information tab. They consider these features as originality certificates.

Whether a GIF or an image, creating your own NFT artwork is easy and requires less or no knowledge about cryptocurrency. NFT can be utilized in developing collectibles and also stacks of digital cards. Since the art is generated from the blockchain, it's possible to use an image created on one chain and transfer it to another.

NFTs can be created with any digital art creation software, such as Photoshop or The Gimp. You'll also need to convert your image into an ASCII art file for it to be readable by Etheremon or similar games. Some digital art creation software such as Gimp provides the option to encode the file into base64 or an image format that Etheremon can read.

Creating an NFT usually entails taking your piece of digital art and encoding it in a compatible image format. If you're not familiar with this, you may want to use Gimp to encode your digital art into a compatible file type. The final step is to transfer the file to the blockchain and register it with an address. What is the cost of making an NFT? Thankfully, there are currently a number of tools that allow you to create NFTs for free! Some of the tools include Etheremon, CryptoKitties, and CryptoPunks. You can also use digital art creation software such as Gimp.
One of the biggest hurdles is creating an account for your NFT. Since it's a digital asset, you'll need to register with a blockchain wallet service provider, such as MyEtherWallet or MetaMask.

Developers can use open-source tools such as the ERC-721 to create and manage the NFTs on the Ethereum blockchain. There are also several third-party applications developers can use to create and manage NFTs. Some of these include Ethers.JS.

NFTs are not limited to being in games; however, they can also be used for other purposes outside of gaming. Some of the uses of NFTs outside of gaming include:

- Art Industry: This allows artists to sell their digital work.

- Real Estate: Digital real estate and 3D assets like furniture can be easily transact using NFT.

- Musicians: Selling the rights and originals of their work and short video clips of their music.

There are so many ways that NFTs can be used in games, making them so exciting for game developers. Some of the limitations that developers face with NFTs include the size and complexity that they can have on games.

However, as more developers discover these possibilities, NFTs look like a viable option.

An NFT is a new technology in the gaming world that can create very powerful and flexible virtual items and experiences. They can do this by applying an Ethereum smart contract to a virtual item, allowing the item to be distributed ("leased") between two parties without ever having to touch it or interact with it. These types of contracts are useful in games and other industries as well.

In the real estate industry, a seller may not want to spend time and money finding a buyer for a property, but instead, the seller can "lease" it's listing to another real estate agent for a fixed fee. A contract can be drawn up that describes how the virtual property will be used and what will happen if the cause of action arises. The contract can also contain guidelines that describe how items in this virtual world must behave according to the specified design specifications.

Non-fungible tokens are more like digital assets than digital currencies. In order to transfer an asset from one party to another, the asset must be unique. These types of tokens are not interchangeable or divisible, as this would cause their value to change due to changes in supply and demand. The NFTs can be utilized for a wide array of reasons. Some of these include: NFTs are very rare and unique. If you combine NFTs with digital identities, you can create operable real-world assets on the blockchain. Traditional digital items we know today lack ownership and scarcity, so they cannot be considered real-world assets. Since NFTs are implemented with smart contracts, they can have fungible digital identities, which can also act as real-world assets.

NFTs can be used to facilitate smart contracts. In addition, they can be used to manage the digital assets on the blockchain. This means that they can also manage things like escrows, in-game assets, and more. Not only are they able to perform these tasks, but they can also offer a new level of complexity. The increase in complexity has many positive outcomes for all stakeholders involved:

Another use case relates to exchanging digital assets for real-world ones using NFTs as the medium of exchange. This scenario is more prevalent in the gaming industry than in other industries, but the idea of exchanging digital items for real-world ones is not limited to that.

In the gaming industry, a user can buy digital items within the game using NFTs. This gives them increased flexibility and control over their assets as they can access their NFTs from anywhere. Since these virtual assets are stored on the blockchain, they are much safer and more notable than traditional digital items. This means less risk of fraud and scams when dealing with NFTs. If players want to trade their digital items, they can easily do so outside of the game using NFTs as the medium of exchange. A user's profile is not only their in-game credentials and scores but also includes a collection of their digital assets. This allows them to maintain complete control over these assets while still using them in the most convenient way possible.

An example of this can be seen in the game, CryptoKitties. CryptoKitties is an online game that specializes in collecting digital collectibles. It allows users to purchase and collect kitties, which can be traded and sold – just like traditional digital items.

The player who purchases any CryptoKitties collects virtual assets that are stored on the blockchain. These virtual assets are unique and are controlled by the player only. This means that there is no risk of being scammed or losing access to them.

5.1.5 The Future of Art Market in the Blockchain industry

NFTs, blockchain, and others will stand out if the visionaries have their way in the future art market. But, on the other hand, if the skeptics have what they want, then the future hype will make art too expensive compared to awful work.

Mike Winkelmann, pseudonym Beeple, from the United States, has been releasing a piece every day for almost 13 years without skipping a single day. On Instagram, he has 1.8 million followers but no gallery. Justin Bieber wore his artwork during shows, and Louis Vuitton reproduced it on clothing. He is also a father and a graphic designer. And it's clear that art has been something he's done in the past because he's done it. And art has been something for him that he has done in the past because he has chosen this for himself. He states on his website, "He's dabbling in a wide range of artistic endeavours. Some of it is good, but a lot of it is awful. Every day, he's striving to make it less crap, so bear with him).".

In December of the last year, On Nifty Gateway was considered a digital art marketplace. There, he established an auction, when he earned almost $ 3.5 million for 20 of his paintings. Now at Christie's, it's a collage of about 5,000 pieces daily, it's been heard by experts that it sells for a minimum of $ 50 million, and it's still underrated.

5.1.6 Hype for art

'Beeple Mania': How Mike Winkelmann Makes Millions sold Pixels" was a few days ago, the headline of "Esquire." Furthermore, cat madness surrounds along with Beeple-Mania. "Why an Animation Flying Cat with a Pop-Tart Body selling for Almost $ 600,000, " on Monday, becomes the headline of the New York Times. The art market has everything. Each piece of art is very high, and media are turning over. Only now, things don't seem to be similar as they've always been, since digital art is now being sold for which there was previously no market. Although, in addition to the fact that almost anybody in the art world has noticed, it's already disappearing like hotcakes on the market. There is famous various art marketplace that includes Nifty Gateway, Foundation, Rarible, SuperRare, MakersPlace, Zora, and KnownOrigin.

All of this necessitates a great deal of debate. What's the big deal about this? Why do people purchase digital art in the first place? What are your plans for it? What role do NFTs play in all of this? And what exactly are NFTs? Clubhouse, an audio-based social network, is presently satiating the demand for information and interaction. The application is trying to explain the importance of NFTs in future for several weeks.

While sitting in the room, I often heard the statement "NFTs and the Future of the Art," and I hear it from time to time. People constantly talk about the destruction and democratization of cryptocurrency, crypto wallet, drops, and tokens, including Ethereum, BTC, Nifty, and super rare.

Those who know their way are sometimes getting new information and new ideas. You'll be embarrassed and angry and leave the room immediately. Suppose you don't know anything about NFT. Suppose an artist sells digital art for $ 1.4 million in five minutes. You cannot understand certain quantities if you are unaware of marketplace drop culture.

5.1.7 Key function

NFTs are sophisticated forms of basic encryption. The contemporary financial system comprises sophisticated trading and lending systems for many kinds of assets, from immovable to loans and artworks. NFTs are in the process of redesigning this infrastructure by allowing digital, physical asset representation. To make sure the idea of digital-physical asset distinction is nothing new and does not require separate identification. However, these ideas coupled with the benefits of size-resistant intelligent contract blockchain may become a strong force for change.

Maybe the efficiency of the market helps NFT directly. Converting tangible advantages into digital works may remove middlemen and simplify the procedure. For example, NFTs in block diagrams that depict accurate or digital drawings remove the need for agencies and enable artists to connect directly with the audience. They may also enhance their processes for businesses. For instance, the NFT of a bottle of wine will facilitate the connection and control of each participant's source, manufacture, and sales in the supply chain. Ernst & Young has created a customer solution. Non-fermentable tokens are also perfect for the maintenance of identities. For example, consider submitting a physical passport at all entrance and departure points. Each passport has unique identifying features by transforming individual passports into NFTs, which may ease entering and leaving countries. In order to extend this use case, NFT may also be utilized in the digital world for identity management.

NFT may offer a new investment concept by dividing them into various amounts of tangible assets, such as property. A digital real estate asset is simpler to divide into numerous owners than real life. This tokenization ethic does not have to be confined to property. It may easily be extended to other materials like images. So an artwork doesn't require a single owner. Many owners may have a digital equivalent, and each owner is accountable for a portion of the diagram. These contracts may enhance their value and earnings.

New kinds of investing and markets are the exciting potential of NFTs.

5.1.8 Benefit of NFT

Non-fungible tokens open a new dimension to the digital world.

Significant advantages of NFTs are:

- **Transferable**, unlike the exchangeable tokens on commercial markets. It is bought or sold on the NFT unique market. But its value depends on itself.
- **Real**, thanks to the technological power of blockchain is an NFT token. Therefore, you know that your NFT is real because it is almost impossible to use a decentralized and immutable master book to create forgeries. They hold

property rights. This also refers to using a decentralized NFT platform. The owner cannot change the data once committed.

5.2 ASSET FOR COLLECTIBLES

5.2.1 Main characteristics

The fungibility feature has been introduced in the previous chapter, but let's dive more into understanding what fungible assets mean. Fungible assets can be exchanged for other units of such assets. For example, one Bitcoin is the same as any other Bitcoin in circulation, similar to the Ether, Dollar and Euro. These are also divisible. In other words, they can be split into smaller pieces of units of the same asset. These assets are indistinguishable. This property is essential to enable all assets to be run by payment method.

In contrast, non-fungible tokens are cryptographic tokens that are uniquely indivisible. NFTs are based on contracts like ETH and DAI, but the contract also contains vital data that makes each NFT unique to the next NFT. As such, one NFT cannot be exchanged for another. Furthermore, it is impossible to break down one NFT into smaller units and use it. These properties indicate irreplaceability.

The idea of NFTs has been around since 2014, but it wasn't until 2017 that the first ERC-721 token was created. Since then, many games have created their own NFTs as in-game items. The most popular example is CryptoKitties, which went viral in late 2017 primarily due to each kitty's unique nature and the ability to breed them and create new variations. Although that game is popular, NFTs aren't limited to just the games industry; other industries are starting to see the possibilities that NFTs provide.

The most popular use case for NFTs is in the gaming industry. Game developers have been using open-source tools such as ERC-721 to create NFTs on the Ethereum blockchain since 2016. However, 2018 has marked a rise in mainstream interest in these types of tokens.

As one of the first developer communities with many active users, the gaming community was a driving force for NFTs in 2018. In addition, the idea of playing virtual items such as digital collectibles that can be traded and sold has already proven to be popular because of CryptoKitties.

However, NFTs are more than just a new form of in-game items. Multiple industries have found that NFTs can provide tremendous benefits to their business models.

These virtual items are registered on the blockchain and can be managed and transferred securely. The primary use case for NFTs outside the gaming industry is to create digital assets that will be used as a medium of exchange in other industries. The immediate use for NFTs in these industries lies in the possibility of creating real-world assets using smart contracts. NFTs can provide digital ownerships to real-world items through smart contracts. This means that one can trade their digital assets for physical assets outside the virtual world without relying on a third party or middleman.

The gaming industry is also interested in moving physical items out of blockchain and its network. This is because it would allow them to reduce costs and increase efficiency. For example, a high-quality game may have an inventory of tens of thousands of items. These items can be distributed using NFTs and "leasing" them to users through smart contracts. The users can then associate their progress with those virtual items and purchase them in the future.

The most common concern surrounding NFTs is that they could be imbalanced in the future. This is because they can potentially provide any player with the same level of value and status. This means that a newbie player and a veteran player may have the same value to the game. There are some ways to avoid this issue, though complementary features.

5.2.2 Complementary features

NFTs have proven to be a rare asset. Every token contains a code that indicates that it is the only asset with a unique digital ID. It helps generate your digital assets and can also represent rare assets (physical assets) whose tree of ownership can be traced. The possibilities for rare and exclusive items to trade, including game pieces and digital art collectibles, are endless. Platforms such as Nifty Gateway, Open Sea, and Rarible provide NFTs with an increasing consumer base. The use cases of NFT are as follows:

- Create digital or crypto collectibles.
- Proving authenticity of digital art, and at the same time allowing artists to retain their copyright and IP
- Management of digital items ownership within blockchain-integrated games
- Allows ownership of parts of expensive items such as real estate.
- Devised a digital ID system that enables users to control information by staying at one place.

A famous application for NFTs to date is CryptoKitties, an Ethereum- based game that allows for buying and selling digital cats, including their breeding. CryptoKitties was released on November 28, 2017, and recorded $ 15 million in transactions with more than 150,000 users for the first time in two weeks. One of the CryptoKitties, sold for $ 170,000, has created a viral sensation that has drawn the platform to Etherium and worldwide interest.

The success of CryptoKitties has caused severe transaction congestion on the Ethereum network. The result encourages the adoption of CryptoKitties in the press with a lot of money that is scrambled to counter the network's negotiability and exchanged for digital cats. This has resulted in great recognition for blockchain as an innovative tech that offers more than just a cryptocurrency.

5.3 HISTORY OF NON-FUNGIBLE TOKENS

Let's delve into the history of non-fungible tokens, where we understand their functions and uses and deepen our understanding of how they are being used in trade. Non-fungible tokens have been around since the beginning of blockchain technology. The first cryptocurrency ever launched, Bitcoin, created a digital asset that its developers completely controlled. These assets were referred to as "bitcoins," giving their owners a certain level of value. The coins could be owned by a user and used to purchase or sell real-world assets (mainly BTC) through the Bitcoin network. This meant that these assets could be used to create fiat money on the blockchain, which was unprecedented at the time. This gave Bitcoin early adopters an edge over others who were looking to purchase cryptocurrencies because there was a clear way of using them to buy real-world goods. Some of the first NFT games were created with Bitcoin in mind. For instance, Spells of Genesis (SoG) and CryptoKitties make it possible for users to spend their cryptocurrencies in a game.

The popularity of NFTs began to grow significantly in 2017 and 2018. This was mainly because of the increased attention and usage of cryptocurrencies on the blockchain. Up until this point, games using blockchain technology were primarily focused on creating a digital asset that could be exchanged for real-world assets (fiat). However, more and more users were becoming interested in using NFTs and other blockchain tools to create advanced game experiences. This resulted in the creation of CryptoKitties, which became an instant success. By the end of 2017, it received more than $12 million in funds from investors. This was huge at the time, especially for a blockchain-based game. The price of a CryptoKitty was reportedly so high that a digital cat went for $110,000. This means that it was on par with the price of a work of art! This shows just how valuable NFTs can be. They can be used to create assets that have real-world value, not just game value. It was after the success of CryptoKitties that the ERC-721 standard was developed. One of the main reasons this standard came about is because of CryptoKitties and the fact that it introduced NFTs to an even larger audience. This meant that people who had never heard about blockchain technology previously now understood what they were, how they worked, and how they could be used in a game. Around this time, blockchain technology started to become more mainstream, which also helped increase the number of developers who saw value in NFTs and other blockchain tools. Today, any game can use non-fungible tokens because they are easy to build and integrate. In addition, the popularity of NFTs has led to many other possibilities for games that were previously thought impossible. It's also worth noting that many games are now designed to increase the value of NFTs. As discussed earlier, NFTs are more valuable and have more functions than standard digital assets. For example, CryptoKitties tracks the total number of cats that have been created and even allows users to collect and trade them.

Soon, we will start to see a lot of games that use non-fungible tokens as their core currency. This will allow players to use NFTs to purchase items, services, and other assets within the game. These assets can be of any kind, including weapons and vehicles.

5.3.1 Non-Fungible Tokens Myths

Several myths surround NFTs and non-fungible tokens. This is understandable, considering that most of these myths have existed for years.
Here's a list of some of the more common myths::

1) Myth: "Ethereum has thousands of pending transactions" is one of the most common misconceptions about Ethereum. It reveals a misunderstanding about how blockchains work and how they process data. The number of pending transactions has nothing to do with the number of people using the network or its popularity. It simply means that there are many pending transactions in this block, which is good because many developers and users are using Ethereum. The more people who use Ethereum, the more valuable it becomes.

2) Myth: "NFTs are a scam" is another common misconception about NFTs. This is true in some markets, but it is not the case in most cases. A few years ago, this was true because people were unfamiliar with the concept of non-fungible tokens. However, as time went on and more people understood what they were, this myth died out. Today, many professional traders who understand NFTs and blockchain technology's benefits are starting to view them as an investment rather than a scam. This was shown by the fact that nine percent of all NFTs were traded on the Ethereum network during 2018.

3)   Myth: "NFTs are too volatile" is another common misconception about non-fungible tokens. The price of an NFT will go up and down, just like any other coin or token. This is because it is not linked to a specific item and can be used in any number of games. That is why it can be traded for games and real-world assets.

4) Myth: "NFTs are too expensive" – This is not true at all. The price of NFTs varies, but the average cost is equivalent to that of other cryptocurrencies, which are already cheap compared to traditional currencies. This means you can get as many NFTs as you want for a fraction of the cost of conventional money.

5) Myth: "NFTs are too complicated and hard to create" – This is not true, either. It all depends on the game developer and which blockchain platform they are using. Since there are so many different blockchain platforms, developers will use whichever one they prefer. However, if they use Ethereum, they can use NFT-Crowdfund to create their own NFT token. This means they can rely on a protocol to create their NFT without learning a new programming language or building their smart contracts. They will only need some knowledge about Ethereum and how it works.

6) "NFTs don't bring value to the gaming industry" – This is another common misconception about non-fungible tokens. However, there are a lot of games that allow you to collect NFTs. This means that these features can increase the value of an NFT. After all, NFTs can be used in many different forms, including virtual items in games such as CryptoKitties and Spells of Genesis.

5.3.2 Problems or Controversies

When you tear off the first layer of NFTs, some overlapping issues arise:

environmental, logistical, ethical, etc.

Many have pointed out the impact (extreme ecological impact) of NFT formation and trade explosions on planets already destroyed by climate change (climate change-related disasters, environment, racism, inequality). What is the relationship between NFTs and climate change? Simply put, a lot of energy is used along with the process of issuing NFTs, adding tokens to the blockchain and the wave of transactions (bidding, resale, etc.). Multiplying that by a vast market driven by greed, we are initiating new forms of environmental destruction. Ethereum is a platform that hosts a fixed blockchain with many of these NFTs. This promised to transform the system into a carbon-depleting form to keep it working safely, but this hasn't happened yet. The timing of this switch is still unknown.

From a fairness and an ethical standpoint, the choice to sell a particular art as an NFT may not have the right opportunity it has. Digital artist RJ Palmer recently warned that accounts extract art by minting tweets from fellow artists and artists and selling them as NFTs. The work of a budding artist can be severely abused if not properly enforced or investigated whether the person writing the NFT is the real artist, the actual creator, or the copyright holder. Furthermore, it has created an environment where the relative anonymity of cryptocurrency transactions can be exploited, stolen and harmed.

5.3.3 Make enlightened business decisions

Transitioning the practice of art into cryptographic art requires careful planning as a business decision and the selection of art dealers and galleries. The crypto art industry is now valued at $445 million, with Nifty Gateway leading the way in sales volume. Because the competition is intense, it's critical to grasp the terminology, choose the right platform, and seek out well-informed professionals for guidance. Do not focus on stable or fast profit yet. It is advisable not to allocate funds from the sale of cryptographic arts to pay the rent. Thus, it won't be different from the "old" art market. Studies show that, given the environmental impact of Ether mining, the footprint a computer needs to create a single board NFT is the same as the total electricity usage of EU residents in a month. In comparison, for 2020, Louvre Museum consumed the same amount of electricity as 677,224 households in Paris. Therefore, it would be good to invest some of the income earned from the art of cryptography to fund Jason Bailey's Green NFT grants and other attempts to decrease NFT consumption of energy. Just as you would experiment with a new medium, experiment with one piece at a time. It's a good idea to complete, embed, or create activated encrypted art by playing it back in media, such as playing it as an animation in .mp4

or .gif format, adding sound, or converting a picture into interactive digital art. You can also create an NFTonly series to see which works are the most popular. We experiment and research what's best for your target collector and you while staying true to your values and the brand community.

Therefore, as long as the legal consequences are understood, NFT can provide an attractive alternative to the usual art market. The choice of the market and the authentic artwork to be sold result from special consideration of commercial, practical and legal aspects.

5.4 CASES OF USE OF NON-FUNGIBLE TOKEN

Gaming

NFT is famous and well-known in the gaming world as it solves one of its inherent problems. Such as popular games like Fortnite do not allow anyone to sell rare skins, weapons, accessories and features.

With NFT, these features can be transferred and easily used in various games. Thus, non-fungible tokens help promote the economy of the game.

Digital Assets

Participants in Decentraland can purchase virtual land. ENS is another example close to home, using NFTs in the ETH domain for ease of sale and purchase.

Identity

NFTs are optimal to combat identity theft and can represent personal information by digitizing appearance, medical records and educational background. Digital artists can also convert their work to NFT for copyright. Testing IDs using NFTs can convert actual game tickets into non-fungible tokens and eliminate fakes.

Collectibles

NFT brings a new revolution to the world of collectibles. As a result, traditional collectors are now becoming digital assets. To understand the usage of non-fungible tokens, it is worth examining their standards and origins, which leads us back to ERC721.

Now I have listed some popular NFT use cases. The best question is that the NFT between finance, technology, sports, arts and music has not been sold. Soon all the popular names will enter this game. For example, Twitter co-founder Jack Dorsey sold his first tweet for $ 2.9 million on March 22. The tweet was, "I just setting up my Twitter." The money was donated to charity. A group of NFTs and art lovers bought a piece of Bansky's art, burned it down, and sold it as an NFT work for an estimated US$380,000. Lindsay Lohan sold her "Lindsay `Lightning` Lohan" as her first NFT for approximately $50,000 on rarible.com (she also promised to donate the proceeds to a charity that accepts Bitcoin to empower the young generation"). Rob Gronkowski sold a limited edition NFT tournament trading card for more than a million dollars. Elon Musk changed their mind about selling a techno song about NFTs as an NFT. Steve Aoki (Dream Catcher) limited art collection sold for a total of $4.25 million, and there are still many works for sale.

Let's not forget to mention that there is a cost of $100 for adding/listing "each" your NFT art to the Ethereum network. So unless you are famous already, you may end up with only one or two dollars as an offer for a listing that costs you $100.

5.4.1   What are ERC-721 tokens?

The ERC-721 token is another form of token created for the Ethereum network according to its smart contracts standards. At the end of 2017, a developer, Dieter Shirley, proposed the creation of this new standard, and it has been getting attention in the crypto world.

As discussed earlier, this standard was designed to create interchangeable tokens with unique and non-expendable characteristics, which will make each token unique in its entire existence and can neither be deteriorated nor destroyed.

The word ERC-721, when broken down, refers to the creation of NFTs on the Ethereum Blockchain as a means of establishing guide standards. Because of this, NTF is a sort of token built according to the Ethereum ERC-721 specification.

NFTs can be found in various decentralized networks, including Neo and EOS, in addition to the Ethereum blockchain. On the other hand, Intelligent contractability and a comprehensive set of NFT tools are required for these systems. For example, intelligent contracts enable the addition of specific descriptions, like metadata, in the contract.

5.4.2   Important information

Art of NFT

Digital artists have exploited non-fungible tokens (NFTs) to create NFT art. However, one factor contributing to the increased popularity of this specialized NFT market is the amount of money that artists can recuperate in NFT markets.

Crypto art data

According to a crypto art data and analysis platform that concentrates on cryptocurrency's art, the entire volume of NFT-based artwork will hit $ 8.2 million by the end of 2020. This was a considerable rise compared to the previous volume of 2.6 million dollars every month.

The market's total value is currently over $ 130 billion in value. The surge in market value reflects a shift in the perception of collectors from a simple recreational activity to a significant financial movement.

According to Richard Chen, the founder of Crypto art, a rise in awareness of what non-fungible tokens may accomplish to retain authenticity has increased the volume of bargaining.

Artists are working with digital media. In particular, we're able to sell their work at some of their best prices in the last months of 2020. For example, if the price of Bitcoin fluctuates in September 2020, a digital artwork created using NFT technology will be worth 262 ETHEREUM.

Earlier this year, another NFT designer negotiated the sale of the item for $131.250, which, at the time, was NFT's tallest product and hadn't been sold until a couple of months later. But, surprisingly, the best days for NFT artists were yet to come, as a collection of NFT artworks was sold for $ 777,777.78 just two months after the auction sale.

This dramatic change in value demonstrates that the value of each token is derived from the rarity and uniqueness. Thus, non-fungible token apps such as Decentraland, CryptoKitties, CryptoPunks and many others are in great demand.

5.4.3 What are the Cryptokitties?

In the decentralized protocol of ETH-Powered, a popular game known as Cryptokitties allows players to gather virtual cats and sell them to other players and reproduce them. As a bastion of Nft since its release at the height of that year's bull race, Blockchain of the 1990s Cult Classic Tamagotchi (in the same spirit, check out Defi'sAavegotchi!) has continued to serve as a source of inspiration for new players.

In particular, this game was the first universal use case in the largest b.lock of blocks that was devoted to leisure activities. Furthermore, the game opened the door to the possibility of DAPPs being used for recreational reasons. After its inception, Cryptokitties generated a lot of excitement across the Ethereum platform, which quickly turned into a negative thing as its popularity slowed down the network, pushing the prices up and causing transaction confirmations to take longer than expected.

Owners of Kitties and breeders of virtual cats can advertise their virtual cats through clever contracts. As a result, they attract the attention of investors and serious money to non-fungible token (NFT) markets like OpenSea.

If you are a cat lover and wonder how to purchase Cryptokitties, the process is straightforward. To begin, you'll need a Chrome or Firefox web browser, a MetaMask wallet, and some Ethereum (ETH) tokens to put in it. After that, go to the Kitties market and choose your cat. Then, pay for it, and you're done. Dapper Labs, the company that created Cryptokitties, has just followed up on its success with NBA Topshot, a market for digital memorabilia geared toward NBA fans.

5.4.4   What Are CryptoPunks?

In January 2021, a dark Cryptopunks "Alien" NFT WENT FAMOUS when it was sold for an incredible $ 760,000, equal to 605 Ethereum at the time. Cryptopunks is famous as the first NFT series, and its breakthrough idea predates both the Cryptokitties and ERC-721 blockchains, which were created in the same year. The outcome has been an increase in scarcity, with an average selling price of more than $ 6,000 in 2020. However, as explained by a spokeswoman for the investment organization, which includes many prominent members of the DEFI sector, digital art would draw a new market of younger collectors who would appreciate it over time and eventually evolve into "iconic" digital pieces. The question "punk," number 2890, is one of the nine existing "alien" collectibles carried out by Larva Labs and was released for the last time in July 2017 for only 8 ETH (around $ 1,500 at that time).

5.4.5   CoinMarketcap X the Sandbox: CMC Heroes

CoinMartcap and the Sandbox cooperated to create their own CoinMarketcap Hero NFTS line, released in January 2021. There are currently six CMC heroes available: CoinMarketcaptain, Protector, Hothead, Sage, Liquefier and Brawler. However, because of the shortage of resources, CoinMarketcaptain can only be obtained by those who have five other heroes.

5.4.6 What else can be converted into an NFT?

Compliance with Yeld Farming in Defi

NFTs are beginning to intersect with decentralized finance (DEFI), specifically agricultural techniques that create goods and services. Until 2020, the fruits of this new collaboration began to be seen in the marketplace. For example, the Yearn Finance protocol, which is a DEFI protocol, has developed an insurance product called Y. With the help of NFT approaches, Y. Insure depicts the distinctive properties of insurance contracts (ERC-721). However, for the most part, typical ERC-20 Tokens "didn't make sense" when used to express the specific aspects of an insurance policy.

Enjin, Bancor and Meme are examples of Defi's other ventures that have an NFT aspect.

Individual skills

Non-fungible tokens may be used to indicate the timing or ability of a person to monetize them. An NFT can be used for various purposes, such as movies, podcasts and bulletins.

5.5 POPULAR PROJECTS

NFTs are being utilized as collectable and tradable components in many applications. A selection of some of the most popular will be presented.

DecentralLand.
Decentraland is a decentralized virtual reality environment in which users can trade and own virtual land and various other items. Cryptovoxels is a players' game for the trade, development and creation of virtual assets.

Gods Unchained
This is a collecting game in which the cards are provided on the blockchain as NFT. Players may own and trade digital cards at the same property level as physical cards since each digital card is unique.

My Crypto Heroes
It is a multiplayer role-playing game in which users may elevate historical figures by completing objectives and fighting other players. The items and heroes in the game are represented by tokens stored on the Blockchain Ethereum.

Binance Collectibles
They are non-fungible tokens (NFTs) created in collaboration with ENJIN and BINANCE on a specific instance. Keep an eye out for our future raffles, and follow Binance on Twitter if you want to get your hands on one.

Crypto stamps
The Austrian Post Office distributed these to bridge the physical and the digital world. Like any other stamp, these

stamps transport letters and packages. But on the other hand, their automated images are saved on the Ethereum Blockchain, making them a marketable digital collection.

5.5.1 Top NFT Projects

Because the NFT subspace is growing exponentially, the number of NFT-related activities and objects has also increased. They range from gaming organizations to commercial facilities affiliated with the NTF. These are five of the most significant NFT initiatives underway presently.

OpenSea: This is where most of the NFT collectibles and art are sold the business. The objects that have been recorded range from ENS to virtual pets and plots of land. Surprisingly, the commercial area allows purchases to be made using a few virtual monetary forms such as DAI and ETH.

Async.Art: It is NFT's marketplace featuring programmable art. This platform's peculiarity is that the artist can create a dynamic art where the master art can be composed of different layers, and every layer can be customized. The master is the overall work, and the layers are the layers or elements that make it up. The customers can purchase the master or single "layers."
The artist can allow specific work parameters to be changed by editing individual layers. The different versions of the layers are called states. In every state, you can change colour, scale, rotation, transparency, and other parameters according to the limits allowed by the artist. Only the state owner can modify this state, and his modification will be immediately reflected in the master.

It is also possible to set specific parameters such as time, stock market trends, and weather. The work will therefore be "living" and will continually change.

CryptoKitties: Even though we have already discussed this assignment, it deserves to be included on the list of the most excellent NFT projects because it has brought the entire NFT game into the limelight.

Ethereum Name Service (ENS): This is a project for managing area names that began in the middle of 2017. The ETH domain names are non-fungible tokens (NFTs) that follow the Ethereum ERC-721 specifications and are available on NFT commercial exchanges.

Decentraland: Decentraland is a top-tier NFT project that creates a distributed virtual world. Members can purchase virtual land in this section. Furthermore, every "occupant" is equipped with an advanced identification system. An NFT (non-fungible token) is a unique cryptographically produced token that uses blockchain innovation to connect with a unique computerized resource that cannot be replicated. An NFT is a token that is not widely used and is made infrequently.

These non-fungible tokens stand in contrast to conventional digital currencies such as Monero (XMR), Bitcoin (BTC), and Ether (ETH), which are fungible; for example, you may trade one Bitcoin for another Bitcoin. Non-fungible tokens are those that cannot be traded for other tokens.

Although NFTs have spread to various endeavours, they are most frequently associated with the gaming and advanced collectibles industries, and they are most commonly encountered as a specific Ethereum token based on the ERC-721 standard. Although their use is beginning to extend to other blockchains in 2021, such as the BEP-721 standard of the Binance Smart Chain, it will take several years before it becomes widespread.

5.5.2 Latest Sells of NFTs

5.5.2.1 NFT sold a column from 'The New York Times' for 475,000 euros.

Kevin Roose, a New York Times journalist, has sold a column in the newspaper for $ 560,000 at auction. (about 475,000 euros) after turning it into an NFT (non-fungible token), a certification system of digital authenticity based on blockchain technology that has starred in some spectacular auctions recently, such as the sale of the first tweet for almost 2.5 million euros or a digital artistic composition for about 58 million euros.

The sale of Roose's column is non-profit making. In the same column that has been auctioned, which consists of describing the column's online auction project itself, it is specified that the result of the sale will be donated to Neediest Cases Fund, a charitable foundation of The New York Times itself.

After observing the phenomenon of the NFTs brought to art or the sale of NBA plays on video, Roose wondered if it could be applied to journalism. To experiment, he

146

consulted the newspaper and started it. The author relates that he decided to take the test after seeing how these digital certificates were spread in various fields, especially in the art world:

The column describes the process of launching the sale, which began for 24 hours and a minimum price of 0.5 Ether (a cryptocurrency like bitcoin), equivalent to about $ 850. The final result came to 350 Ether.

Even if they have paid almost half a million euros, the buyer of that first column will not have the article's copyright or any right of reproduction or retransmission. Instead, it will simply have the property title of the column in PNG image format. As a bonus, Roose promised to have the buyer's name published and to have The Daily host Michael Barbaro send him a personalized voice memo congratulating him on his purchase.

Roose's column warns that "the world of cryptocurrencies is full of scammers whose projects often fail." Additionally, critics point out that crypto-related projects and NFTs consume enormous energy and computer power, posing a threat to the environment as they grow exponentially. "The journalist considers it legitimate to wonder "what exactly NFT buyers get for their money and if those tokens will become broken links if the markets and hosting services that store the underlying files disappear."

Rose notes in her column that "it's easy to be skeptical of NFTs." "But I'm cautiously optimistic about them," he concludes, "for the simple reason that they represent a new way for creative people to earn a living online.

5.5.3 Expensive NFTs

NFT fans see great potential in the NFT Ethereum (ETH) space. On the other hand, criticism believes that the NFT market is excessive and that the hype on non-fungible tokens is nothing more than hot air. Nonetheless, NFTs are already being traded for enormous sums. So let's discuss some of the most expensive non-fungible tokens available today.

5.5.3.1 Beeple's Digital Art Collection - $ 3.5 million

Mike Winkelmann, a CGI artist, known as Beeple in the group, had the most important sales for NFT in its history. It all began with Beeple's announcement of selling 21 of his works on Twitter. Since his art was focused on NFTs, things moved quickly. All was also backed up by records and an accurate sample of Beeple hair.

The NFT Nifty Gateway Marketplace operated by the 'Winklevoss Brothers Gemini Exchange' received a share of sales revenue. The first ten auctions totalled almost $900,000. After that, ten further works of art were purchased for a total of $1.2 million by bidders. The last painting's auction was revealed just before it began. Tim Kang auctioned it off for $ 777,777. For $ 3.5 million, 21 works of art were sold. A video was shared on Twitter by the artist following the agreement, in which his pals greeted Beeple's performance with a shower of Champagne in celebration of their victory.

5.5.3.2 Rick and Morty ($ 2.3 million)

Justin Roiland, the renowned cartoon comedy "Rick and Morty" creator, was among the artists who sold NFT paintings at excessive rates. His collection of 16 pieces was auctioned for ETH 1,300 (approximately $2.3 million). In his statement, Roiland explained that the auction was a means for him to push the frontiers of cryptographic art while also contributing a portion of the revenues to help poor people without homes currently living in the streets of Los Angeles.

It's worth noting that some of Roiland's artwork has been reproduced as well. The works "It's Tree Guy Basically" and "Eligible Bachelor's" cost $10 and $100. Due to their rarity and originality, works of art produced in a single copy sold for a greater price—the play "The Simpsons" sold for $ 290,100. Initially, the auction's opening bid was $ 14,999, and its counterpart was sold at an equal price.

5.5.3.3 Axie Infinity Lands- $ 1.5 million

Axie Infinity allows users to create their empire, complete with fantastic characters. Lucia is the world's name where you can purchase virtual property, and there are only a few spots available. The entire plot is split into 90,601 smaller parcels, with players owning 19% of them.

Falcon said that the land he purchased is in an excellent position. Furthermore, as shown by the rising number of active users on Axie Infinity, the trend is gradually increasing. It would also be possible to plan activities on "your territory," like concerts or festivals, in the future, and thus earn profit.

5.5.3.4 The Crypto Punks

A game known as "CryptoPunks" was auctioned off on the NFT for 605 ETH at the end of January. Featuring over 10,000 unique digital characters, CryptoPunks is a digital universe inspired by the crypto art movement. They can be traded on a CyberPunks market. It should be noted that the characters in the game were initially available for free, with the only requirement being that you had an Ethereum wallet. It is NFT # 2890, taken in 2017 and then sold for an astronomically high amount a few months later in 2018. It's a scarce type of 'punk' to find.

5.5.3.5 One F1 Delta Time track

The area of F1 Delta Time was sold for almost nine million REVV tokens. As of writing this book, the REVV has climbed by 500 percent, and it would cost $ 1.2 million to produce the same amount of REVV at the current exchange rate. It comprises 330 tokens of this kind, divided into four tiers ranging from "Rare" to "Apex." The virtual circuit for the Circuit de Monaco is constructed using these tokens. Each token comes with a virtual track share and other benefits. This specific NFT had reached the "apex" of its development. Its purchaser will earn 5% of all in-game sales and 4.2 percent of elite staking income produced by player deposits. REVV utility tokens can be used to pay for both.

5.5.3.6 Finance Insurance for NFT

Thanks to a dedicated digital policy, you will get up to 5,000 ETH protection against Curve's smart contract errors. NFT costs 350 ETH, which is currently worth over $ 560,000.

The cover is another name for Yinsure. In a nutshell, it's a combination of Nexus Mutual-guaranteed insurance and a different form of tokenized insurance. Insurance plans are defined by the letter NFT. Each one is a one-of-a-kind NFT, also known as ayNFT, that can be sold, exchanged or purchased.

5.5.3.7 Virtual lands in Decentraland

On the Decentralandblockchain game, someone purchased 12,600 m2 for 514 ETH. The game is a decentralized virtual reality platform based on Ethereum. Users can develop, play with, and monetize their content and applications on the platform. LAND is a minimal 3D virtual space in Decentraland. Ethereum smart contracts manage this non-fungible digital asset, and the virtual landowner has complete power over it.

5.5.3.8 Land at 22.2 in Decentraland is available for purchase for 345 ETH.

Decentraland has made a resurgence in the world of technology. As a result, another tract of land at 22.2 acres in a "great location" is up for grabs.

The size of the land in Decentraland is predetermined. Decentraland sells and leases the majority of its space, with around 80% private. No one owns the remainder of the land, such as roads and squares.

Players can only walk their characters on their land or public land, so choosing the right location is critical. Lots in more popular areas will likely be more expensive than those in less popular ones.

The increase of non-fungible tokens and the sold may be another significant trend shortly after Defi. One of the features of NFTs is that they each have their distinct features. While NFTs continue to be a tiny business, they provide a wide variety of applications.

5.5.3.9 CryptoSpaceCommanders Battlecruiser - 250 ETH

It is a space MMORPG developed by Lucid Sight. The company received a total of $ 11 million to fund the development of its "scarcity engine," a tool that would allow it to bring its Blockchain-powered games to mobile devices, Personal Computers and Consoles in the near future. Video games are critical to the mass adoption of cryptocurrencies Ethereum is utilized for safeguarding game properties, executing all in-game contracts, and powering the game's free-market economy, which operates without the need for a developer.

Users can explore the world or engage in combat with other players searching for materials. In addition, players can trade, keep or sell the retained resources to profit at any point in their journey.
Each ship in the game is unique and has its own set of qualities, which you may learn about through playing the game. For example, the more valuable a ship is in generating wealth in the game, the more expensive it is to purchase it in the first place.
The Battlecruiser was purchased for 250 ETH when it first appeared on the market in September of 2020.

The Battlecruiser was the world's first combat ship of its kind to be built. It can be transferred instantly anywhere on the CSC globe within 20 light-years, making it ideal for creeping up on hostile ships and launching a lethal ambush.

5.5.3.10 Gods Unchained (Atlas) -210 ETH

It is a competitive card game built on the Ethereum Blockchain similar to the hugely popular game Hearthstone in terms of gameplay and mechanics. Gods Unchained's proprietary mechanics, made possible by the game's Blockchain-based nature, are the most significant difference between the two. Players may resell the cards on the secondary market if they so choose. Gods Unchained has been considered the world's first Blockchain-based e-sport, and it is now in its beta phase. An annual Gods Unchained World Championship will be held, with a prize pool of USD 100,000 and 10 percent of all card pack purchases going toward the winner. The estimated prize pool for the first Gods Unchained event is around $540,865.

Since the game includes an e-sport component, players want to be as competitive as possible and develop strong decks when competing in tournaments, increasing the value of the cards.

A maximum of four "Mythic" cards with powerful abilities in the game will be released by its team each year by the Gods Unchained team. Atlas is one of the Mythic cards, and he represents the god of the sky. It was discovered by chance in a deck of cards by a lucky player who had no idea how valuable it was. However, it wasn't until the Gods Unchained team confirmed the value of the digital treasure to the card's owner that the asset was able to capture their interest. It took five days for the auction to conclude, with the winning bidder receiving 210 ETH. Only time will say if this is a good investment, but the early indicators are positive.

5.5.3.11 Gods Unchained (Prometheus) -235 ETH

As a result of great anticipation, Gods Unchained's marketplace was introduced, which resulted in a flurry of activity as players started exchanging cards.

An additional mythological card, known as the Prometheus, had a one in a million chance of being discovered and was concealed in a random package. Given the card's one-of-a-kind characteristics, as well as its overall strength in the game, it was the ideal card for those who were serious about competing for a portion of the $ 500,000 prize pool.

Consequently, when Prometheus was placed up for sale by the player who found it, the card was in high demand, reaching a top bid of 235 Ethereum at an auction.

5.6 SECURITY AND NON-FUNGIBLE TOKEN

5.6.1 Standards for Non-Fungible Token

Because of their requirements, non-fungible tokens are powerful. In addition to providing developers with the assurance that assets will behave in a given manner, they also explain precisely how to interact with the assets' basic functionality.

This means that developers can create complex logic that can be applied to assets and offer them to users who may not understand how to interact. Standards also allow for interoperability between multiple NFT games, which opens up the possibility of trading assets (cross-game).

Four primary standards make NFTs work, and currently, only one organization is involved in designing standards for NFTs: the ERC-721 (Non-Fungible Token Standard). AGAME, a blockchain-based game platform, created this standard in 2018. This standard aims to create common rules and functionality that can be applied across every game that uses NFTs.

This allows for interoperability between all games and incentivizes developers to use this as the main NFT standard. Although some other organizations have started working on standards, none of them has been formally released yet. This means that ERC-721 is one of the only standards supporting NFTs and making them work seamlessly.

Some developers make design choices based on cultural norms and values. NFTs can also be a part of these norms and values if they look like real-world assets. For instance, certain societies in Japan have a unique way of thinking about non-fungible items (the same is true for many others worldwide). In Japan, things as simple as chopsticks and paper are considered unique and valuable because of the effort put into creating them.

If game creators opt to utilize NFTs to include this cultural element into their games, they will be able to generate game assets that are more valuable than what players can create on their own. This is one of the ways that NFTs may outperform conventional digital products.

The real potential of NFTs lies in blockchain technology. The blockchains they run on and the tools provided by developers can either work together or be completely incompatible. In the last year, there has been a significant effort to make NFTs and other blockchain technologies work together so that game creators can get more advantages and gamers can earn more value. This includes the need for numerous characters to have particular functions, such as avatars, that may be transferred to other game players.

NFTs are straightforward to create. The only requirement is to define a series of properties for it, such as name and image. These properties can then be used in the NFT's smart contract, which can handle all other details and make them work seamlessly with all other NFTs. NFTs are made on smart contracts that implement ERC-721.

NFTs are officially recognized by the Ethereum network and are therefore considered an Asset on the blockchain. This means that they have a unique address and ID to be managed just like any other asset. The only difference is that the NFT in question will always be a unique item. This gives them a certain level of value and status – just like fiat money. So, for example, if a user has created an NFT for their character in a game, that player can use it as a form of game currency.

This gives them an incentive to treat the NFT like cash and exchange it for real-world objects or services within the game (fiat). The most popular way to access non-fungible tokens is through the Ethereum blockchain. Even though several other projects support NFTs, the ERC-721 standard makes NFTs work seamlessly on Ethereum. The main benefit of this is that all the tools and specifications for creating an NFT exist on the blockchain. This means that developers are highly motivated to develop their smart contracts with ERC-721 to make it easy for players to use them.

There are three main parts of the smart contract for an NFT contract: primary functionality, describing its properties, and the token interface.

The first part is the primary function of an NFT. This refers to what a token can do when created and exists within a specific game. For example, this could describe how a particular item can progress in the game or what special abilities it might have.

5.6.1.1 Non-Fungible Tokens Metadata

As discussed earlier, the smart contract has three main parts, and describing its properties is the second main part of the smart contract.

In the non-fungible token smart contract, a list of attributes defines the NFT properties. These include its name and ID. For example, the following attribute is called "metadata." This information describes the NFT but isn't part of its properties. Attributes that can be used with this kind of metadata include "owner," "location," and "avatar."

The owner field refers to storing and keeping track of the NFT in question. This could be the game developer or a user. This is useful because it makes the owner of an NFT responsible for any actions taken in relation to it, such as transferring it to another player or destroying it, for example. Finally, the following field is the location. Since some game mechanics may depend on having this information available, the location could have many different meanings and interpretations depending on what kind of game is being developed. For example, "location" could indicate the position of an item in a scene. However, it might also refer to the part of an item relative to other items in a game.

An item might have a special "location" that determines when it is safe to interact with it. It could also be used to indicate the current condition of an item.

The metadata field is used to describe any unique details about an NFT that are not stored in the properties or defined through other attributes, such as its name and image. For example, these details can include creation time, creator, and image ID.

The final part of the NFT smart contract is called the token interface. This refers to how different smart contracts can interact with an NFT. It is useful for game developers because it makes it possible for them to create new NFTs without making any changes to their initial code. They can create a new "monster" (for example) and give it a specific combat power using the token interface. They can then include these details in the NFT's metadata. This means that new items can be created without creating specific points or levels. This creates more possibilities for in-game mechanics and design, making smart contracts more powerful and valuable.

5.6.2 Be smart about copyright

Any artist should know how and when to utilize copyright because it is a bedrock of intellectual property, especially for NFTs.

It is not necessary to register with the copyright office in the USA to exist. However, to apply against others, it is needed. The Copyright Act of 1976 provides exclusive replication, distribution and production of works by authors of pictures, sculptures or graphics. Therefore, platforms have to establish methods to deal with violating materials. However, it is easy to record a visual arts work within a couple of minutes, ideally before publication.

While it is tempting to convert pre-existing images into an NFT, doing so without significant alteration and a clear additional message is like walking on a tightrope.

Converting a digital artwork without the author's express permission may result in litigation, with the offender arguing that the use is "fair" under copyright law. Courts will evaluate the resemblance between the original and defendant's works, the market in which the parties operate, and the purpose and transformative character of the defendant's work when making fair-use judgments. A licensing agreement can avert complications and provide a fantastic opportunity to communicate with other creators. Furthermore, artists should be informed that unless a written agreement between the customer and the artist is signed, the NFT purchaser does not have the right to replicate the underlying work purchased from them. However, any NFT platform may grant itself a non-exclusive, global, and royalty-free licence to distribute and reproduce copies of the art offered for sale by using the Terms & Conditions of the platform. Unfortunately, the unfortunate reality is that these terms are rarely, if ever, negotiable.

5.6.3   Keeping your information safe

For artists, linking an NFT to a platform that accepts Ether is essential. Digital currencies can be stored in software wallets (like MetaMask or Coinbase) or hardware wallets (like a hard drive). Because of increased protection against hacking (internet fraud), hardware wallets are a better long-term investment that is more reliable.

When selecting a cryptocurrency wallet, it is recommended to look for two-factor verification, a secure way to store your seed phrase (same as password), and the ability to send and receive payments (same as a debit card number). It is also advisable to get into the habit of using a virtual private network (VPN) while trading cryptocurrencies. It is also recommended that artists examine which wallets are accepted by the NFT platform before creating their own (for example, Foundation uses MetaMask).

5.6.4   NFT FOR PHOTOGRAPHY

5.6.5   Photography And Digital World

Chemically developed light-sensitive emulsions have been the age of photography in the early 1900s, limiting the skills and usage of photography. The recent technology in photography can only be imagined by a maniac then. However, the 21st century digital age has brought a lot to the photography world. The shift to digital storage and capture technology from the early 1900s was started in the late '80s when the first consumer digital cameras were introduced, and Photoshop was first released in 1990. The program (Photoshop) extended the conventional darkroom by extensively using the classic instruments of two-colour pictorial photography (black and white) and also allowed photographers to go deeper into their creative explorations. The long-standing beliefs about photographic documentary or veracity "truth value" were nearly dispelled when technology-enabled photographers to alter an image's structure and even the substance readily. To some people, the medium's very nature has been changed, but the best is yet to happen.

The first decade of this century was when photographers and the world felt the full impact of digital photography – its usage, how it creates fantastic memories, and some business usage like marketing. It was still common practice in 2001 to use old film cameras to shoot breaking news events. However, the fast transmission and simple digital pictures led to the shift of journals and magazines into a digital method of operating and putting digital cameras in its photographers' hands geared to pros. The widespread use of digital photography has prompted various responses from photographers such as Jerry Spagnoli, Deborah Luster, Chuck Close Sally, and Mann. Some have reverted to traditional photographic processes such as daguerreotyping or working with wet-collodion plates, which is a photographic process that dates back to the nineteenth century.

Some other photographers, such as Alison Rossiter and Chris McCaw, have resorted to using antiquated enlarging paper from the mid-20th century for their work and printing it themselves. This was on the verge of reviving popularity in the art world, but it was projected to be rendered obsolete by widely available web photographs.

Others used this time to think critically about their new picture environment. Pictures of light trails made by satellites such as Trevor Paglen were taken as you travelled across the night sky. The convergence of pictures and videos still-digital and web design tools allowing audio editing, animation, and movement control also led to an arena in which photography was an instrument and a tool for creating multimedia experiences. In the 21st century, photography became online digital communication into the contemporary art world, transcending its previously distinct character and significantly boosting its importance as a means of visual communication. With widely accessible internet pictures, photo books can now be simply produced. Digital printing, moreover, reduced the publishing costs while enabling photographers to choose how their ideas were presented, both in story and context. The digital presence of photography can not be neglected, and its usage in the digital world is fascinating, but people need more. People need to feel that their digital image is not just out there on the Internet; they want value for their work. Hence, the creation of NFTs.

You must be wondering what an NFT was; don't be surprised because it is just an acronym.

5.6.6 Meaning Of NFT For Photographer

Non-Fungible Tokens (also known as digital tokens or certificates) are digital tokens or certificates saved on a secure distributed database and cannot be forged (blockchain). As a result, NFTs are one-of-a-kind digital assets that can be purchased and sold on a trustless platform, with each transaction being permanently stored on the blockchain.

Another way to think of NFT is as a certificate of authenticity that is permanently included in a database, including any future transactions in which ownership is swapped or transferred. You will be able to see who founded the NFT, who purchased it, and so on for the rest of the time. NFT is a unique technology that holds a great deal of promise but has yet to be fully explored.

The NFT can be thought of as a certificate of authenticity that is permanently stored in a database, then used to record any subsequent transactions in which ownership is exchanged or transferred. From now on, you can see who started the NFT, who bought it, and so forth. NFT is a one-of-a-kind technology that offers a tremendous deal of potential but has not yet been thoroughly investigated. When we talk about blockchain, we refer to the underlying technology that powers decentralized cryptocurrencies such as Ethereum and Bitcoin. Currently, NFTs are not entirely supported on all blockchain technologies because blockchain technology is still in its early stages, and each blockchain has a unique structure. Ethereum appears to be the most extensively utilized blockchain service for NFTs at the moment, but this is susceptible to change as the technology matures. Even though NFTs can represent both tangible and intangible objects, the recent focus has been on how they have been utilized for trading entirely digital items like animated GIFs, digital pictures, and other digital artwork. Non-fungibility refers to the absence of interchangeability of tokens, which indicates that an NFT cannot be traded for another; instead, each is entirely distinct from the others. Unlike fungible assets, which can be exchanged for other assets of equal value, nonfungible assets cannot be exchanged for other nonfungible assets.

NFTs became the most talked-about acronym in the news and on social media in an instant, like a nightmare come true. A single JPG file made by Winkelmann Mike – known as Beeple – was recently sold in an online auction for a whopping 69.3 million dollars. It was the world's first digital-only art auction, which means there was no tangible copy of the artwork up for grabs. Despite their sudden rise in popularity, NFTs have been around for a long time and are not a novel concept. However, the current surge is introducing more small and large creators to a marketplace where their work may be monetized within the bitcoin community, which is a positive development.

5.6.7 Buying An NFT – What Do You Receive?

Essentially, this means that you purchase the right to use a digital good rather than buying it. This could be one of many editions, a single edition, or a part of a collection, among other things. In most circumstances, you will not be able to claim ownership of the image, and this means that the NFT author will be able to edit or otherwise manipulate their digital asset as they see fit. It is also important to note that it does not confer exclusive rights to a digital asset, which means that there may be many copies of the same picture or gif available on the Internet for the general public to view. Still, only one unique NFT will be used to demonstrate ownership of the digital asset. This feature of NFTs may be difficult to fathom when seen from traditional asset ownership, but it presents a positive trend in value for digital customers overall. Sports trading cards, for example, are an excellent illustration of this. There is a chance that 1,000 copies of a player's rookie card will be discovered, but only one of them will have the player's signature on it; that card will be valued significantly more than the rest because it is the only one with the player's signature on it.

5.6.8 Digital Art And Physical Art Worlds – The Difference

Starting with the physical world and how selling printed copies of your photography works in artwork with excellent cameras.

You have to select one or a collection of your photographs to print as a physical copy. After the selection process is printed, and at this stage, you have to decide their edition. In simple words, you have to determine their availability in the market; hence, the value will be appreciated. Next, you determine if you are printing only one version – and edition of one – or an edition of 10, 50, or more. You can also choose to have an open edition, which means you have no limit concerning the number of times you can print and distribute your photograph.

The next thing is to give every print a signature, more like an edition number and an authenticity certificate. This certificate is your proof of ownership and your authorization for its distribution. Simply put, it shows that the print is authentic. This will also allow collectors to prove their ownership of the editioned print.

Imagine a scenario that someone walks into your gallery and snaps a high-resolution image of your collections, then the person decides to print it out and starts posting it to be real. Your proof of ownership can only be established with your certificate. This is precisely what NFTs do as well. Now let's apply our scenario to the digital world. Take NFTs as your signature or your authenticity certificate – deed of ownership. In the case of the digital world, you can also decide how much scarcity you want, and blockchain technology will ensure that the counterfeit can never be produced.

So, when you "mint" and "convert your art into NFT," you are establishing your right of possession of the art and how many editions of the image you want to be available. Then, blockchain technology will control and record how the digital art exchanges hands – who buys and owns your art.

5.6.9 Photographers And Other Digital Artists – How Can They Benefit From NFT Technology?

The conventional market for photography and other digital art has been limited to printmaking, stock photography licensing, and other avenues of selling physical copies or non-physical rights to a work of art. With huge market congestion in the last decade, most artists are increasingly challenging to make money from their work. Still, NFTs present an entirely new market and mindset for artists and photographers. Interested buyers in art and technology are now looking to support their favourite artists and acquire scarce digital assets that can increase value. NFTs are like aid to photographers/artists and buyers alike due to the unique structure of trustless blockchain technology. Each transaction is recorded for everyone to see and cannot be erased, misplaced, or undone. Artists can also benefit from the secondary market by including a particular percentage or commission in their NFTs that will be paid to them on any subsequent sales of their NFT. Most importantly, artists can hold on to their full copyright, unlike many licensing agreements.

5.6.10 How Can Photographers Use/Create NFTs?

Converting or tokenizing digital art (an image or anything) is a simple process that entails uploading and placing it for sale. NFTs marketplaces are managed within the blockchain, which requires cryptocurrencies like Ethereum or Bitcoin.

For photographers, after your image has been uploaded as an NFT, several verification steps will be required, like if you are selling multiple editions or original. You can even place a royalty – a commission for the photographer upon subsequent sales – on your NFTs, like 10-15% of all future sales, just as discussed earlier.

As said by Dinch, "With respect to photography, you can convert a photograph as a token, and this photograph is owned by whoever owns this token. People can download or look at it, but there is only one owner."

A landscape photographer based in Michigan, Bryan Minear, has always kept a close eye on the crypto space. So he did an NFT drop featuring five photographs ranging from 200 to 2,500 dollars. Within a few minutes, he almost sold out everything.

He commented that he was crying by the end of the day. And furtherly said that it's not like transformational money, but when you create for the love of photographs, and then that moment of validation finally arrived, which is, someone, somewhere loves your work so much that they're willing to spend some money to acquire it, it's another level of satisfaction.

Minear furtherly gave why he chose to hold on to NFTs; he said that he realized crypto was here to stay despite different speculation that the NFT market is a bubble.

However, he doesn't see NFTs as a medium to eradicate the potential of copyright, nor does he sees the blockchain as a way to control the distribution of his work online; instead, he sees a new opportunity to reach a passionate audience about digital art and willing put value on it.

5.6.11 How Do Photographers Determine The Cost Of Their NFT?

This was one of the biggest obstacles for most photographers before listing their NFTs on the marketplace. Artists decide the value of their NFT as they wish. Minear initially had to list his photos at a lower price to make them accessible, but he realized he didn't have enough data to create a more informed judgment because his art quickly sold out.

Then comes the big question, what is the difference between selling limited edition physical prints and selling multiple versions of an NFT?

The most significant difference between selling multiple versions of the photograph as an NFT and selling a limited edition hard copy of a picture is tangibility.

For Minear, it also comes down to his audience values. Do they want digital ownership or a physical poster on a wall? He then noted how he sold more value as a digital print than physical prints.

5.6.12 Copyright And Licensing

As previously stated, copyright in photography is the same as it is in other fields; the original work's owner will always be the original work's owner, regardless of whether an NFT of that work has been sold. This is because NFTs are digital reproductions of original works – not physical prints – and the original author retains complete control over the licensing of their work.

5.6.13 Can NFT Offer More Than Photography?

Photography is quite similar to Video making. Videos are images in fast motion, or a series of images played in a particular order or sequence at a specified time frame or rate, usually from software playing video (digital) or device (analog).

Can NFT offer more to Video making than photography? This is a bigger question that needs to be unravelled.

5.7 NFT FOR VIDEO MAKER

Joseph Niepce was the first person to take a black-and-white picture in 1826. Joseph Plateau, a few years after (1832), became the first to simulate motion images in his invention named phenakistoscope ("spindle viewer"). Video production has continuously evolved from the earliest days of "motion pictures" more than a century ago in reaction to new technology. As long as new tools, formats and platforms are widely recognized, every creative who works with video has to adapt.

While the way we see videos has changed continuously with technological innovation, distribution techniques and the creation of videos also need to continue to stay pace with this quickly changing environment. Over time, new video technology, job roles and the basic manner in which businesses integrate video into their broader strategy for commercial success have affected production processes. However, the digital video did not stop the change of television broadcasting, the video did not kill the radio star, and TV did not cease the creation of films.

On the contrary, the more than one century of film and video creation that before it laid the way for today's video environment is feasible. It has always been essential to adjust to new technologies, whether the future of video, to watch a video with a growing number of technology and media and many new tools and platforms to produce and distribute it.

5.7.1 How Can A Video Creator Use/Create NFTs?

The world feels like it's rapidly changing during the pandemic period, and Non Fungible tokens have come on the radar recently, with Digital Artists such as Beeple making as much as $69 million for an image file. Now seems to be the best period to learn some essential information about creating an NFT as a Video Maker. As a Video Maker, there are potentially many benefits if you can mint and offer your artwork for sale. Cryptocurrency technology will certify you as the original owner on the blockchain and continue to pay you some royalties (Just as discussed in the case of photography). Anything in the support file formats under a 100MB JPG, SVG, PNG, GLTF, GIF, MP4, WAV, WEBM, GLB, MP3, OGG can be created. As a Video Maker, you are likely to develop a good video below 100MB. In addition, you have the option to give unlockable content when someone purchases the NFT through an external link to another platform. Creating your video content can be done using any video-creating software. The final step is to mint the video with a platform available and put it up for sale.

5.7.2 What Can You Sell?

You can sell anything digital from tweets, contracts, images, video skits, an album, any audio, 3d model, e.t.c. Some platforms accept the following file formats: JPG, SVG, PNG, GLTF, GIF, MP4, WAV, WEBM, GLB, MP3, OGG. With a maximum file size of 100 MB.

5.7.3 Platforms To Sell Your NFT

Presently, there are many platforms on the Internet, and they all have their advantages and disadvantages, depending on what you are selling. For example, some platforms are SuperRare, Foundation, VIV3, OpenSea, Axie Marketplace, Rarible, BakerySwap, Nifty Gateway, and NFT ShowRoom. OpenSea seems to be better in terms of file size because they accept files up to 100MB, unlike Rarible, where the maximum file size to be uploaded is 30MB. Another advantage is that they seem to be more significant NFT marketplaces that don't require an invite, unlike other platforms like Niftygateway and Super rare. They also offer some great free information on using their platform.

5.7.4   Related NFT Video Sales

NFT has been very popular that everyone wants to mint their artwork (Image, Music, or Video) on supported platforms to get some returns. However, NFT created from an image seems to be the most popular, and other digital arts are getting some attention from creators.

One of the most popular NFT video clips is a 10-second video that sold for a whopping $6.6 million at the NFT auction. Pablo Rodriguez-Fraile, a Miami-based art collector, spent over USD 67,000 on a 10-second video in October 2020. The video could have been watched online without cost because we live in a technologically sophisticated age where everything is now available on the Internet. Still, he chose to spend $67,000 to obtain the video for his collection rather than do so. In February 2021, he sold the property for a total of 6.6 million dollars.

As discussed in NFT by photographer, the blockchain was used to authenticate the video created by a digital artist known as Beeple, whose real name is Mike Winkelmann, "the blockchain is a trustless platform that serves as a digital signature to verify and certify who owns it and that it is the original work."

Another popular NFT video that got people's attention is the LeBron James slam dunk sold for $208,000.

The launch of the U.S. NBA's Top Shot website has been the start of the rush for NFTs. It is possible to trade, sell or buy NFTs in video highlights from games on the website, which is open to anybody interested.

The platform says it has hit over 10,000 users buying NFT with nearly $250 million of sales. The NBA is also said to receive royalties on every sale on the marketplace. And February 2021 is said to be the highest sales on the platform so far, with a total sales of over $198 million, which multiplies January's sales of $44 million.

The most significant transaction on February 22 on the platform was when a user paid $208,000 for LeBron James slam dunk video.

During an interview with one prominent NFT investor, known as "Pranksy," he stated that he had put USD 600 in an early NFT project in 2017. His portfolio of NFTs and cryptocurrencies is now worth a total of seven figures to him.

Pranksy claims to have spent more than a million dollars on Top Shot and made approximately 4.7 million dollars from the resale of his various game collections.

You must be wondering this is it; NFT has nothing to offer another industry except an industry that involves graphics like image or video, but NFT has not stopped there; it is available for anything digital technology, even music. So how can music be displayed as an NFT? Well, it is like owning an album of music as one of your collections.

5.8 NFT FOR MUSICIANS AND DJ

The music industry started approximately a century ago when technological advances made it possible to record, store, and playback sound. Since its inception, the business has responded to several technical improvements in sound technologies, progressing from mono to high-fidelity stereo. Meanwhile, storage media technologies in the music industry moved from vinyl to cassettes and then onto compact discs and mini-discs. Then there was the evolution of gadgets used to replay sound, culminating in what we have today: portable audio players. While these transformations occur, industry players have either had to adjust to the new changes brought about by modern technologies in the industry or have simply disappeared quickly. The music industry in the twenty-first century is currently undergoing significant transformations, fueled by the rapid expansion of the integration of audio and computing technologies and the Internet.

After integrating computing technology and audio technologies, the industry was transformed into one that produces information products. As a result, the way music and songs are purchased and used in today's culture has been transformed by technological advancements. In addition, they gave ways to compose music at a low cost that can be easily made at home, mix and dub music, and the use of balancing and digital noise filters to improve the sound's quality. All of these things were did not exist just a few years ago.

Digital technologies such as mp3 have established themselves as a standard format. Many music software developers are satisfied with the MP3 format. These files can be tiny, making it easier to send music over the Internet. With the advent of compression technology, music files may now be compressed to a small size, making it easier to distribute music over the Internet. The introduction of the mp3 format resulted in portable audio devices that allow downloading music directly from hard disks and the Internet. Music listeners can easily distribute and download music over the Internet because mp3 does not have an anti-piracy feature (pirated and legal copy).

We were told that the Internet would save the music industry by allowing musicians to control their songs and make an honest career without being tied to any industrial music complex. Unfortunately, this hasn't benefited the artist at all.

Musicians get an estimated 12% of profits from sales or streams. The rest goes to intermediaries.

The Covid-19 pandemic forced all musicians to abandon their tour plans in early 2020. In addition, several artists were not earning anything because of the pandemic. In the end, they began to ask why they were working in a business where a significant portion of all streaming income went to a few top musicians, and the rest went to someone else.

All of these disappointments prompted a rapid adoption of the new technology circulating in the digital world; it may seem to outside observers that the music business has grown obsessed with "NFT," but it is essential to preserve their sweat and labour.

Many transactions have happened in the NFT-Music transaction, and millions of dollars have been made a profit. In February, Grimes, an EDM concept artist, sold USD 5.8 million in NFTs. 3LAU, another hot EDM/DJ remixer, sold USD 11.6 million in NFTs. Even more impressive: Kings of Leon released an entire album as an NFT. The DJ/Dance sensation Steve Aoki also made $4.25 million in NFTs.

3Lau	$11 Million
Grimes	$6 Million
Kings of Leon	$2 Million
Steve Aoki	$4.2 Million
Odeza	$2.1 Million
VÉRITÉ	$12,000
Lil Miquela	$82,000
Pussy Riot	$200,000
Young and Sick	$865,000
Zack Fox	$15,000
Ozuna	$11,000+
Intro to Music Theory	$12,000+

You must now be wondering what they are selling for them to make this massive amount of money. They have been selling primarily short music videos, fan experiences (either during the artistic process itself or looks backstage), and digital "collectible" versions of a record, all of which the collectors could display, sell or withhold to show the value of the artist to them.

Example of what has been sold are:

Kings of Leon - front-row tickets for life
RAC - NFT to a cassette tape tied to the NFT
3Lau- Physical waveform sculpture tied to the NFT

Intro to Music Theory - NFT-linked t-shirts scannable to their music streaming

Snoop Dogg - Digital Joint Art

Various - Unreleased tracks, exclusive music videos, digital art inspired by their music.

5.8.1 General Pricing Guide For Digital Artists

After reading every part of the book up to this section, I believe you must ask how I can start? When will I be able to sell my NFT at a high cost? Do I need to start competing with top established artists in terms of price or better under-price my NFT? The solution to these questions is highlighted below.

1. When starting as a new artist in the NFT industry, it is best, to begin with, humility, then steadily raise your floor consistently. The daily exchange in blockchain technology is enough to mislead any newbie, but as you continue to sell more frequently and steadily, you can raise your price. Sales are like your review; it shows your artwork is worth having as a collection.

2. Don't be too hastily to hit the 7 – 9 figures. Slow and steady is essential because the value of your artistry, especially long-term, isn't about a sale in the immediate, but how strong you have built your network. So when you observe that your work isn't hitting many sales, it doesn't mean you have to burn your tokens; hold tight, trust the process, keep the vision clear, and keep working.

3. As mentioned earlier, the marketplace is extensive, and there are many platforms where you can sell your artwork, make use of all of these platforms, but be consistent with your pricing. Don't forget that you can sell your artwork on any platform regardless of where it is minted. Collectors are spread across these platforms, so it is best to reach as many collectors as possible.

4. Don't be afraid to play with the pricing. Sometimes you need that bold side to come out big; it is a win-win case if it receives enormous sales. Don't be afraid of making mistakes; we only learn through mistakes.

5. ETH is not a fiat system of exchange. The value of one ETH is multiple to any currency in the fiat system. So, beware of undervaluing yourself because you're thinking in terms of fiat currency – government-issued currency.

5.8.2 What Are Charged Particles?

Before discussing anything further, let's see what charged Particles are. First, it allows users to give ERC-20 tokens into an NFT.

A scarce NFT (e.g. Collectible, Art, In-Game Item, Virtual Real Estate, etc.) can be transformed into a holding for other tokens.

It is now possible to deposit any ERC-20 token into ANY NFT. Still, it is noted in their forum, "for yield — Aave's tokens will be the fundamental interest-bearing asset available in the Charged Particles Protocol when we go live." Benefit for NFTs.

Yield-bearing tokens with programmable charges are among many assets that NFTs can hold. If you have several LP Tokens, speculative tokens or social tokens, you can deposit any/all of them inside a scarce NFT, and it is all possible.

In addition, it will be easy to deposit tokens/assets into other users' NFTs. So it is more like having your NFT wallet.

Customization of the NFTs configurations of their NFTs is now straightforward — Required Mechanics for Charged Particles include: Time-Locks: NFT assets can only be withdrawn after a specified duration. Charge: Aave token-supported asset will be swapped instantly, and you can then decide how you would like to treat the interest. E.g., a particular charge can be discharged to any different address depending on your choice — the NFT creator, a charity, or a friend.

Discharge: This is when you want to remove accrued interest – configurations.

Mass (Principle) Removal Configurations: Do you have to burn the NFT to remove the principle from the NFT?

However, by using charged Particles to construct NFTs, you enable them to have a programmable interest and readily hold other ERC-20 tokens.

5.8.3 Related Concerns To Nft Technology

It is worth noting that all new technology presents concerns while growing, and one of the concerns to NFTs is that anyone can mint them. This is problematic for digital artists and photographers because there is no legal precedent to guide sellers and buyers currently. For example, if someone downloads an image that is not theirs – they do not own the copyright, they can still mint an NFT with that image. The copyright owner would rightfully have an issue with another person profiting off their work without proper permission, but the recourse they would have is still unclear at this time. In addition, the large volume of sales on marketplaces every day could pose a severe issue for the marketplaces and artists. Who gets to pay in the event of copyright infringement? Who is liable? What constitutes copyright infringement? These are all legal questions that are yet to be answered. Another threat to NFTs is the inherent carbon footprint of blockchain and crypto technology, which is damaging the atmosphere. This is a severe concern for the eco-conscience because the blockchain and its related technologies require enormous computing power, which means considerable power consumption.

Each marketplace has been said to have its vulnerabilities to cap it all. For example, there have been reports of NFT vanishing from marketplaces without any notice. This could be a significant problem if it occurs after paying minting fees or buying NFTs.

The market is still gaining audience day by day, which means there may be some potential concerns out there waiting around the corner to be noticed.

5.9 PLATFORM TO SELL NFT AND ITS REQUIREMENT

After discussing the popular projects that use NFTs and the relationship between NFTs and other art (Photography, Video Maker, and Musicians and Dj), it is pertinent to discuss the platforms that support the trading of NFTs. Some of these platforms have been discussed in the previous chapter, but their requirements and how to trade NFTs on these platforms will be discussed further in this chapter.

Here is a list of platforms that allows easy trading of your Non-Fungible Tokens (NFTs).Here is a list of platforms that allows easy trading of your Non-Fungible Tokens (NTFs).

1. OpenSea: www.opensea.io
2. Rarible: www.rarible.com
3. SuperRare: www.superrare.co
4. Foundation: www.foundation.app
5. Atomic Market: www.wax.atomicmarket.io
6. Myth Market: www.myth.market
7. BakerySwap: www.bakeryswap.org
8. KnownOrigin: www.knownorigin.io
9. Enjin Marketplace: www.enjin.io/software/marketplace
10. Portion: www.portion.io
11. Async Art: www.async.art/

5.9.1 OpenSea

OpenSea boasts of being the world's biggest NFT marketplace. Collectibles, sports, virtual worlds, trading cards, domain names that are censorship-resistant and art are among the non-fungible tokens available. ERC721 and ERC1155 properties are included. In addition, unique digital assets such as Axies, ENS titles, CryptoKitties, Decentraland, and more are available to purchase, sell, and discover. They have over 700 projects, ranging from collectible games and trading card games to name systems and interactive art projects like ENS (Ethereum Name Service).

Using OpenSea's item minting tool, creators can build their objects on the blockchain. It helps you create a set and NFTs without writing a single line of code. For example, you can link to OpenSea by creating a smart contract for an online game or a digital item on the blockchain.

You can sell something on OpenSea for a set price, a falling auction listing or a price listing.

5.9.2   Rarible

It is an NFT (non-fungible token) marketplace owned by the community using ERC-20 RARI token as an ownership token. Variable rewards active users who purchase or sell on the NFT marketplace with the RARI token. Per week, it distributes 75,000 RARI.

The website prioritizes art assets. Rarible allows developers to "mine" fresh NFTs to sell movies, art, CDs, music and books. Those who visit Rarible can see a preview of the product, but only the customer can access the entire project. You can buy and sell NFTs in several categories like domains, music, sports, metaverses, memes, photography, art, and many others.

5.9.3 SuperRare

Super rare is primarily a marketplace for limited-edition and unique digital artworks. Tokenized works of art created by network artists can own and trade. They describe themselves as a hybrid of Christie and Instagram's, offering a new way to engage with collecting, culture and art on the web. Every art available on SuperRare is a digital collectible, encrypted and tracked on the blockchain. On top of the marketplace, SuperRare has created a social network. Digital collectibles are suitable for a social atmosphere because they have a clear record of ownership.

The Ethereum network's native Cryptocurrency, ether, is used in all transactions.

A form can be used to submit your artist profile and be evaluated for SuperRare's future full launch.

5.9.4 Foundation

It is a niche forum that brings digital developers, crypto natives, and enthusiasts to advance the culture. It is dubbed the "new creative economy." It is mainly concerned with digital art.

In their initial blog post in August 2020, they invited developers to experiment with value and Crypto and value. "Hack, subvert, and abuse the value of art," they advised.

In other words, when a collector resells their work to another person for a better price, the artist receives 10% of the sales value.

5.9.5 AtomicMarket

It is an NFT market smart contract with mutual liquidity used by several websites. Anything available in one place appears in every other place, known as shared liquidity.

It's a platform for Atomic Assets, a non-fungible token standard based on the EOSIO blockchain. As a result, a standard for tokenizing and building digital assets that may be used on the Atomic Assets marketplace can be employed. You can both search and list NFTs for sale on AtomicMarket. Genuine and well-known NFTs collections are recognized with a verification checkmark. Malicious collections are blacklisted.

5.9.6   Myth Market

It is a collection of user-friendly online marketplaces for various digital trading card firms. Shatner, KOGS.Market, Pepe.Market and Heroes. Market are all places where you can buy digital Garbage Pail Kids cards.
This is the featured market at the moment (for memorabilia relating to William Shatner).

5.9.7   BakerySwap

BakerySwap is a decentralized exchange (DEX) and Binance Smart Chain automated market maker (AMM) that operates on the Binance Smart Chain (BSC). It uses the platform's native BakerySwap token (BAKE). It is a multi-functional crypto centre including a range of Defi services, an NFT supermarket and a crypto launchpad.
With BAKE tokens, it offers NFT, meme contests and digital art. When you combine NFTs, you gain BAKE tokens. Moreover, it is simple to mint and sell.

5.9.8   KnownOrigin

KnownOrigin is an online marketplace for exclusive digital artwork. Each digital art on KnownOrigin is unique.

Creators can use the forum to display their piece of art and sell it to collectors. Ethereum blockchain protects them.
Users can upload jpeg or GIF files to the KnownOrigin gallery, which is kept on IPFS.

5.9.9 Enjin Marketplace

An exploration and trade platform for blockchain properties. An NFT marketplace powered by Enjin. Enjin Coin has been used to purchase 2.1 billion NFTs valued at USD 43.8 million. In addition, 832.7K deals have been made. The Enjin Wallet makes it easy to sell and buy gaming items.
For example, the Age of Rust and The Six Dragons multiverse have gamified reward systems, including NFT's (such as Binance and Swissborg), Microsoft Azure Heroes and community-created items.

5.9.10 Portion

It is an online Blockchain-based trading place that enables collectors and artists to own, sell and invest in collectibles and art quickly and transparently. This initiative is supported by Artist Collective, a decentralized global network of content creators and artists.Portion makes it easy to collect. Cryptocurrency can be exchanged for collectibles and art at one spot.
These ERC-20 tokens are used to vote and rule on the blockchain's future. Potential and existing team members receive new tokens. In addition, artists who generate new NFTs receive new Portion Tokens worth 500 PRT.

5.9.11 Async Art

Async Art is a blockchain-based creative movement. Programmable art can be created, collected, and exchanged. Both "Masters" and "Layers" are available for purchase. Layers are the different components that create the Master image. The artist decides what special abilities each layer should have. Whoever owns the Master picture will see any changes made to a Layer. Artists determine the parameters of their work and offer collectors complete control over every element. Users might, for example, change the context, a character's location, or the sky's colour.

5.10 HOW TO CREATE NFTS

You must be wondering that NFTs are excellent investments and would like to own some. The previous chapters gave us insight into how NFTs work and some popular projects used for. It's time to create a Non-Fungible Token. But before we create NFTs, let's discuss some problems that are associated with them.

5.10.1 Problems with the NFT

Non-fungible tokens are not without flaws, despite their impact on various businesses. Unfortunately, your issues stem from the its source - blockchain.

Decentralized networks aren't perfect, but developers are attempting to fix them. For example, verifying validity, selling, buying, and storing an NFT all require some knowledge of Blockchain technology.

The problem arises because most people are only interested in the product and not the technology behind it.

When it comes to NFTS adoption, Beeple, an NFT creator who sold some of his works for USD$66,666 cooler (and a record-breaking purchase of more than USD$777,777,777), observes that "the required infrastructure is in place," which would provide a great experience for customers.

The same goes for "Internet" and "smartphones." Most individuals have idea how these two work, but billions use them everyday. As with blockchain, we need the same experience in this case too.

Generating your own NFT artwork, as a photograph or a GIF, is a simple process that doesn't require much crypto knowledge. NFT can be used to create collectibles and other digital card sets.

You must first decide which blockchain you wish to utilize to create your NFTs. The most widely used blockchain platform for publishing NFTs is Ethereum.

However, other blockchains are gaining popularity, such as:

- Binance Smart Chain

- WAX.

- Flow by Dapper Labs

- Cosmos

- Polkadot

- Tezos

- EOS

- Tron

Each blockchain is compatible with its own standard NFT token as well as its wallet services and its markets. You can only sell NFTs on sites that take up Binance Smart Chain characteristics if you are using a Binance Smart Chain. That implies that you cannot sell it on an Ethereumblockchain-based platform like the VIV3 developed on the Flow blockchain or OpenSea.

Use one of various NFT-centric platforms to link your wallet and upload the file or image you want to convert. Ethereum NFT marketplaces are:

- Rarible

- Mintable

- OpenSea

Making NFTs on Makersplace is also possible, but you must first register as an artist.

Mintable, Rarible, and OpenSea all have a 'Create' button. This is how it works on OpenSea, the world's biggest NFT market in Ethereum.

To add your Ethereum wallet, click the blue "Create" button.

With your wallet password, the app connects your wallet to the marketplace. A digitally signed message in your Ethereum wallet will be required to transmit funds, but you can simply click to confirm your wallet address. The marketplace will immediately associate your wallet with your wallet password as soon as you input it when asked. To make sure your Ethereum wallet address is correct, simply click to check. There is no fee for the digital signature of a message. To prove that you are managing the wallet, this is just a demonstration.

The next move on OpenSea is to pick "My Collection" by hovering over "Create" in the top right corner. Then, as shown below, press the blue "Create" button.

When you arrive at the window, you will be guided to it, where you may name your artwork, provide a description, and submit it.

To complete this step, you will just need to create a folder for your freshly produced NFTs.

It will appear as shown below once you've assigned a picture to your set (blue). Click the pencil icon in the top right corner to add a banner image (red).

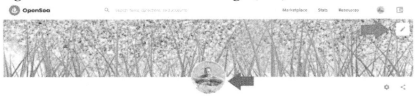

The finished result should have the same appearance as the sample to the right.

You will now be the first to create a new kind of NFT. Clicking the "Connect New Thing" button will cause your wallet to be used to sign a new message (blue).

Your NFT artwork will display in a new window.

The rarity and originality of your NFT on OpenSea and other markets should be increased. Creators may also have unlockable content that the purchaser can only access. Passwords to such utilities, coupon codes, and contact details are all examples of this.

On the Ethereum-based OpenSea platform, NFT traits are available.

When you're done, go to the bottom of the page and click "create" to confirm the NFT's presence by signing another message in your wallet.

5.10.2 Creation cost of an NFT

Some platforms demand a fee for creating NFTs on OpenSea. In Ethereum-based systems, this charge is called "gas.". Ether gas is the quantity of ether required to complete a certain blockchain function. That will be the launch of a new NFT to the market. Gas prices vary according to network congestion. The cost of gas prices rises as more people transfer value over the network,
Here's a helpful hint: Over the weekend, when transaction volume decreases, the cost of using Ethereum decreases somewhat. This can help you save money if you're selling multiple NFTs.

5.10.3 How to create and sell NFT of digital art

The configuration process varies per NFT type. If you want to configure Digital NFTs Art, you can use Opensea, a popular online seizure.
Create a digital wallet to hold Crypto and NFT. OpenSea suggests a meta mask wallet addon for Chrome.
Next, go to OpenSEA and click on my profile in the upper right corner.
Enter then follow the screen prompts to finish configuring your account.
After that, go to your account at the top right and click my collections.

Then create a new collection, click create, and enter the details.

Now, click Add new item, and you will be prompted to name your NFT and update the information.

Finally, click Create to finish.

Before listing anything on OpenSEA, sellers must first pay a gas price, which is the Ethereum Blockchain transaction cost.

OpenSea is one of the most popular NTF markets today, although Rarable and SuperRare are also fantastic choices. Artists can use them to make money on the crypto market while also reaching new audiences.

5.10.4 How are NFTs used?

NFTs can be used to show the value and scarcity of digital assets or other commodities. They can represent and receive everything from virtual games to artwork.

Non-fungible tokens are bought and sold in a digital market, not on regular exchanges.

5.10.5 What can NFTs do?

NFTS can be used with DAPPs to create Crypto collections and unique digital products. Investment product or a billable item.

The economic game is not new. Besides that, considering that many online games are already economical, blockchain adoption to tokenize game assets adds marvel. In reality, NFTs can reduce or eliminate the general inflation issue of many games. The tokenization of real-world assets is another fascinating use of NFT. As a blockchain token, this NFT can represent a real-world asset fraction. This can help many markets that lack liquidity, such as rare collection items, real estate, art and many others

Digital specification can also be of relevance to NFTs. Saving identifying and ownership data on blockchain will improve data integrity and privacy for many people. Parallel, quick and consistent transfers from these assets can eliminate global friction.

5.10.6 The story of Ethereum and CryptoKitties

CryptoKitties has been previously discussed, but its emergence is marvelous; hence, it is worth mentioning its relation with Ethereum.

Cryptokitties is an Ethereum-built game that enables players to collect, nurture and sell virtual cats, one of the first NFT initiatives to acquire popularity.

Each CryptoKitty has a unique combination of colour, breed and age. Also, they are not interchangeable. Cryptokitties tokens are indivisible, hence they cannot be split up (like the Ether for Gwei).

Cryptokitties gained prominence when clogged the block of blocks Ethereum due to heavy network activity. The all-time high (ATH) for daily transactions of Ethereum Blockchain remains about the popularity of the crypto cats. Like the first feather currency offering, other events also affected the Ethereum network (ICO).

Non-currency use cases for blocks date back to CryptoKitties. They generated millions in sales, with some rare artefacts commanding hundreds of thousands.

5.10.7 Detailed steps on how to create NFT art

Step 1: Create an artwork
The principal thing you should do to sell NFT craftsmanship is to make your specialty. This can be

practically any type of media GIFs, representations, recordings, 3D models and so forth. A quick walk around Rarible or Foundation will give you a general idea of the crypto art inclinations.

At the moment, it seems to be a preference for either very avant-garde, experimental abstract art or meme-rich internet cultural references. Not that this should necessarily determine your work - we won't get into a debate about "making for the market" here. Once you've decided what art you'd like to upload, you can move on to the next step.

Step 2: Create an Ethereum wallet

There are numerous wallets to browse to serve your public location and store your private key, however it is by and large prescribed to depend on an equipment wallet.

If you're new to cryptocurrencies, here's a quick crash course on how cryptocurrency wallets work: Basically, they're software or hardware that help you manage the public address on your cryptocurrency blockchain.

This public address stores the cryptocurrency and can be seen by anyone, although its ownership is completely anonymous (unless you make it otherwise). Each public address has a private key which is used to deposit, withdraw or send funds to and from that address. Think of it as a mailbox: everyone sees it, knows where it is, and can send mail to it. However, only the people with the mailbox key can open it and collect the letters it contains.

There are two types of wallets: online wallets, which provide more convenience for the user at the expense of less security, and cold wallets, which store information offline and are less convenient for frequent use but provide a much higher level of security for the user.

A famous example of a hot wallet is the widely used MyEtherWallet, while the best examples of cold wallets are the hardware wallets from Trezor or Ledger that we mentioned above, as well as pen and paper. Yes, good old pen and paper can also work as a cold wallet, although you will need to create your own public addresses, which can be unpleasant.

Step 3: Buy ether

In the whirlwind of news and growing interest in the NFT, it may be news to you that selling the NFT will actually cost you some money. Unlike Bitcoin, where miners are rewarded with Bitcoin for contributing the computing power needed to verify transactions and add records to the blockchain, Ethereum miners are paid in another blockchain currency called gas.

Each time a transaction is requested to be confirmed and added to the blockchain, a transaction fee is paid (presumably to cover the gas and platform fee) - Ethereum miners can choose which contracts they would like to allocate computing power to, so the more gas you pay for your transaction, the quicker your contract will be executed and added to the blockchain. This includes uploading your NFT.

Step 4: Select a marketplace

Once you have your piece, your wallet and some ether burning a hole in your pocket, you are ready to put your NFT on the market. What you want to do is go to ethereum.org and take a look at their selection of "Apps" - short for decentralized apps. Rarible, Nifty Gateway and Foundation are amazing good opening points to get started to get familiar with the Ethereum market and see your NFT. Each one caters to slightly different tastes, so be sure to check out all three, as well as many other marketplaces before settling on one.

Foundation seems to be best suited to digital painting, Nifty Gateway caters most to 3D models, and Rarible looks like a chaotic fusion of the aforementioned avant-garde and internet meme culture.

Step 5: Upload your artwork

While each principles will differ in where you press the actual button, they all start with connecting your cryptocurrency wallet. Each of the main sites will automatically create an account linked to your wallet and guide you through a fairly simple upload process, during which you will need to choose how many "copies" of the NFT you want to mint and what percentage of royalties you would like to receive once the product is resold.

The latter feature is an innovative step forward for digital artists who, unlike their traditional counterparts, have never been able to truly restrict the supply of any one work once it has been distributed and create a true "original".

The NFT essentially has a certificate of authenticity printed on the blockchain that proves that it is an original work, so that the original artist can get a cut of every subsequent trade/sale - a feature that even traditional artists cannot take advantage of. Once you have chosen your work, made your copies and set your royalties, you can move on to the final step.

Step 6: Pay the transaction fee

Once your NFT artwork has been locked and uploaded, all you have to do is pull the trigger and you can sit back and relax until your artwork is transferred to the blockchain and turns into an extraordinary substance on the organization, unchanging and impenetrable to any worker crash. The exchange expense will guarantee that your NFT is mined by any Ethereum digger who acknowledges the agreement and recuperates your charge for their work.

After that, your newly mined NFT should only be a matter of a couple of minutes before it hits the market, just waiting to delight the keen-eyed patron who sees it first.

5.11 NON-FUNGIBLE TOKEN MARKET

So far, NFTs have proven to be stable, and with all its use cases, it has gained more market place. Some of these market places have been discussed in the earlier chapters; it is time to discuss the step by step procedure on how to transact in some of these market places.

The crypto space has been fostering a new groundswell of institutional interest in the crypto industry for some time now. The newest company to invest in bitcoin is Tesla, the electric vehicle manufacturer. It also explains how to take an asset as payment in the future. This was a new development since it was owing to a discussion between Elon Musk and Michael Saylor, a wealthy tech entrepreneur, who bought bitcoin in 2020.

Tesla's announcement created a wave of enthusiasm among the crypto community.

While there is certainly a strong likelihood that loaded hedge funds would imitate the investing strategies of Tesla, Mass Mutual, Microstrategy, top digital funds, and inquisitive digital investors are seeking to identify the next big cryptocurrency investment opportunity (alts).

Divided Opinion on NFTs

New Financing Techniques are growing the digital resource market; meanwhile, the future of collectibles (in which digital tokens reflect ownership of either real or virtual items) is the means for users to verify their ownership by creating unique digital tokens stored on the blockchain. However, unlike crypto assets, the community has noted doubts about the real-world volume NFTs would drive. On the other hand, over 500 billion dollars' worth of weekly BTC futures trading volume took place in January of this year, and as of the time of this writing, NFT market trading volume has reached $8.2 million.

To far, NFTs such as digital paintings have failed to attract a strong trading market. However, with the sector maturing, it's possible that larger and more stable markets may develop. Of course, bringing in investors such as Paul Tudor Jones, Saylor and Musk is no different from previously having considered them mythical in cryptocurrencies.

With other items, you should be able to deposit your money on a blockchain and own collateralized fiat-pegged stable coins or borderless digital assets.

It's unclear if NFTs will be able to stay in the same slipstream as other cryptocurrencies like bitcoin and altcoins, and yet yield a profit. This is very important because is it able to make ordinary investors who spend small amounts of money in high-end auction houses and the preserve of high-net-worth collectors accessible to them?

Celebrities and NFTs

Already, Lindsay Lohan has started luring Bitcoin followers to her Twitter account, and billionaire Mark Cuban recently sold NFTs for about $1,000 to investors interested in selling his tweets as an NFT. Soon, other celebrities will jump on the bandwagon, and it will only be a matter of time before more elites join the movement.

In other words, Ethernity is trying to get famous individuals on board by selling digital artwork (including the aforementioned personalities) with every NFT. Paolo Maldini, Michael Rubin, and the Winklevoss twins will bless the collection. Michael Rubin is the creator of the All in Challenge, a charity campaign that has collected over $50 million to assist groups combating food poverty.

Nick Rose Ntertsas is the founder of Ethernity. Its website states that it is a platform for worldwide stars—celebrities, sportsmen, and artists—to endorse limited-edition artworks, and the money made from these sales will be donated to the star's chosen charity. Rose states that the artwork they have acquired is complete and ready for sale. An example of recent success in using NFTs is Hashmasks. There is a venture in which digital portraits coexist with collectable NFTs, the appearance of which is both desired and highly sought. They have reached the $10M ETH mark in only a few days.

A unique and ultra-rare CryptoPunk NFT sold in ETH for $762,000. The digital art market cap is projected to surpass the market value of physical art, as digital art continues to grow.

Growing

According to Jehan, NFTs are the main missing link between physical and online publications.

NFTs are transparent and rare. This is because they are recorded in a public ledger, which protects valuable collectibles. NFTs may play a key role in the decentralised finance (Defi) industry, according to some. Alpaca City's Ethereum-based virtual environment offers proof of concept for this.

Alpaca City's November token pre-sale raised over 1,000 ETH in 15 minutes. Owners can "breed" Alpaca NFTs, which will revolutionise the NFT market: NFT loans, interest-bearing accounts, etc. Interoperability is also required since NFT holders wish to send and receive assets from many blockchains.

Tracing and transferring tokens is now possible because to TRON's new NFT standard, TRC-721, which has a defi primitive. All of the stakeholders, both those in favor of NFTs and those opposed to them, are beginning to understand the true worth of NFTs. Secure and accessible NFT protocols are being offered by the companies, while purchasers race to acquire skin in the game. Decentralized Smart Contract Network Decentraland, Hashmasks, and CryptoPunks are all using Ethereum to launch NFT initiatives. Virtual reality is a world similar to a digital land, in which players may connect with others, explore, purchase land plots, and even establish new businesses.

Next Move?

Much will rely on investor interests, the VR/AR game industry's growth and profitability, and the introduction of NFT-specific blockchains to power ecosystems. Finally, assuming gas costs stay constant, it is challenging to estimate NFT market potential (particularly Ethereum). Novel Financing Techniques have yet to show their capacity to maintain value over time, which is why important concerns won't go away for the time being. liquidity of NFTs is lower than that of more liquid financial instruments (but growing). It is quite simple to get one; but, finding a willing buyer who shares your own tastes is difficult.

People aren't excited about having unwelcome NFTs towards the end of the song when they can't play anymore. And right now, the celebration is in full flow. On February 8, a customer bought 9 separate NFT plots for $1.5 million. This transaction, too, set a new NFT record.

Digital real estate has now officially surpassed traditional real estate in price. It may be hysteria, but a growing number of crypto-savvy investors are running with the bulls.

What digitalists have discovered is that selling anything in the cyber realm may amplify the collective power of the public. All of humanity is connected, yet it is likely that tokenization will occur in the near future.

5.11.1 Selling an NFT

A simple guideline will work for all platforms, therefore it's a good idea to start with that guidance.

Setting your wallet

Before you can use cryptocurrencies or non-fungible tokens (NFTs), you will need a digital wallet to hold them. To further secure your transactions, we suggest that you use Google Chrome and install the MetaMask wallet plugin. Use this link to search for the commonly asked questions and suggestions for MetaMask. After you've installed OpenSea, go to the upper-right corner, click the icon, and then select My Profile. The instructions for logging in will be sent after you have your wallet.

Creating a collection

The page where you can view your account balance should be up now, however we are still working on it. Select My Collections, then click Create in the top-right corner. Once you have finished building your collection, name it and add a short description and a picture; we aren't establishing an NFT just yet; you will be able to modify all of this information once you've created your collection. Clicking the Add New Items button will take you behind the scenes and show you what your collection really is.

Fine-tuning your collection

While it's important to get started on the creation of your initial NFTs, there are a few things you should accomplish first. There is a customized banner to the right of the picture, seen above. Click on the "Make Your Own" pencil symbol in the top-right corner to submit your own logo. Aim for a size of about 1400x400, and avoid text. If you look at the Payments page, you will see pending secondary sales payments (which are now going to wait in your bank account) and selecting Visit will take you to the public collection.

Click "Edit" to add social links, images, and change the item's title, description, and picture. Additionally, if you keep the Accepted Payment Tokens option as it is, you will also have the option to set the resale tax up to 10%. If you wish to get 5% of the total sales price for your NFTs (for example), go to the "Receive a Percentage of Future Sales" page and put 5 in the "Commission to Recipients" box. Then, go to the page that says "Sellers Address" and enter your wallet address there. When you're completely satisfied, press the Submit Changes button and you will be sent to your company's back office.

Creating an NFT

The first NFT you'll make is under the Add new item heading. You will find an upload option to photos, videos, and audio files on the following page. In addition, you may name your NFT after selecting the choice from the drop-down menu. The process for adding an external link and a short description is finished next.

The NFT feature is currently limited to one instance at a time, therefore you will have to make several copies of a work and decide whether or not to include the edition number in the statistics area.

The advice provided previously was to make an individual token and then log into the insights to find the authorization number. In the event that you need to make more than one duplicate of a similar work (token ID), rather with multiple tokens and finding the authorization number in the insights, you can add ?enable supply=true to the end of the URL on the peak of the page and press Enter to reload. In order to modify the supply field, you need have completed this step first.

Keep in mind that you'll have to construct 100 individual sales lists (each with the amount set to "1") if you change the supply to, for example, 100.

At this time, it isn't feasible to have suppliers make 100 individual deals, and allow customers to select the amount of they would want to buy. Until this changes, it is not possible to modify the stockpile in the creation process.

Adding properties and levels helps streamline the exploration of your work by making it easier for collectors to locate your pieces. For example, "Year of creation" could be property of "2021".

Add unlocked material that only the owner of the item may see. Higher quality files, contact information for actual objects, and access keys are all examples of unlocked material.

Once you have obtained a sense of contentment, click the Create button and fill in the message in your wallet. You will not have to pay any petrol taxes to create an NFT (transaction costs). You'll see that your first NFT is neatly positioned beneath your search bar after you click the "Create" button. Click the pencil icon in the top-right corner of each NFT to alter it.

Announcement of items for sale

The easiest way to upload your NFT is to visit a publicly available property page and click on "Sell" (you can access it via your account page or by clicking on the property in the search bar you see above). Instead of a price-based auction, choose a fixed-price advertisement. When you are in a good mood, follow the directions in your wallet and then click on Publish your ad.

You will need to pay a petrol tax before you can list on OpenSea if you have never sold it before. Once the Ethereum blockchain becomes less congested, the trade should be simple. You will also be requested to verify the token in a non-ETH currency, which will incur a different (but lower) gas cost. So you won't have to pay anything the second time around.

If you accept a bid for an unlisted item using WETH, you will be requested to verify the WETH and pay a gas charge to accept the offer. When buying fixed-price listings, buyers pay a gas charge. When selling, sellers pay when accepting bids.

Since there are a lot of other users, don't be concerned if the transaction takes a little time to complete. When you return to re-enter the posting process, our framework will know that your wallet has completed the exchange and won't prompt you to pay costs when you set up the next posting.

5.11.2 Step-by-step procedure to sell an NFT in OpenSea.com

1. Download Metamask (https://metamask.io/) and install it. It is a Google Chrome extension.

2. Create a portfolio on Metamask. The following images are in Italian, but it easy to understand what is the right

choice in English: start, create the wallet, I agree, create a password.

Benvenuto nella Beta di MetaMask

MetaMask è una cassaforte sicura per identità su
Ethereum.
Siamo contenti di vederti.

Inizia

Nuovo su MetaMask?

No, ho già una frase seed

Importa il tuo portafoglio esistente usando la tua frase
seed a 12 parole

Importa Portafoglio

Si, iniziamo!

Questo creerà un nuovo portafoglio e frase seed

Crea un Portafoglio

METAMASK

Aiutaci a Migliorare MetaMask

MetaMask vorrebbe raccogliere dati di utilizzo per capire meglio come gli utenti interagiscono con l'estensione. Questi dati verranno usati continuamente per migliorare l'usabilità e l'esperienza utente dei nostri prodotti e dell'ecosistema Ethereum.

MetaMask..

✓ Ti consentirà sempre di rimuovere il consenso tramite Impostazioni

✓ Invierà click e visualizzazioni di pagina in modo anonimo

✗ **Non** raccoglierà chiavi, indirizzi, transazioni, bilanci, hash, o qualsiasi altra informazione personale

✗ **Non** raccoglierà il tuo indirizzo IP completo

✗ **Non** venderà i tuoi dati per profitto. Mai!

No Grazie	Acconsento

Questi dati sono aggregati e sono quindi anonimi per le finalità del Regolamento generale sulla protezione dei dati (UE) 2016/679. Per maggiori informazioni sulla nostra politica sulla privacy, vedi Politica Privacy qua.

 METAMASK

< Back

Crea Password

Nuova Password (minimo 8 caratteri)

Conferma Password

☐ Ho letto e accetto i Termini di Uso

Here is the view of Metamask by pressing on the Chrome extension.

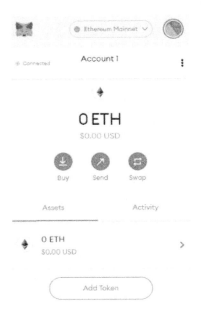

3. Move 0.1 ETH from your crypto wallet to your Metamask wallet.

   This amount of Ethereum is necessary to validate the upload of your first item in your account).
   It can vary due to the congestion of the blockchain.
   If you do not have a crypto wallet, you can press "buy" in Metamask and buy your ETH here.

4. Go to Opensea.com, log in with your Metamask wallet, and create a Create/My collections collection.

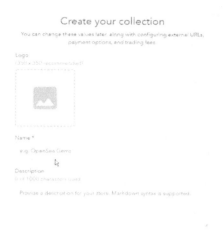

The following image is an example:

5. Create an Item:

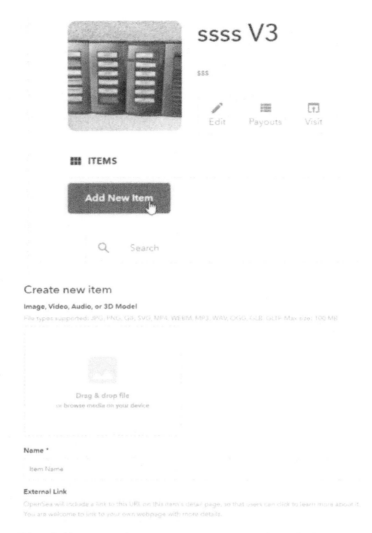

The following features are optional and depend on the type of NFT you are going to upload.

It is important to leave the number "1" because the item is unique and therefore NOT FUNCTIONABLE.

6. Sell your NFT

It is possible to choose a fixed price, put it on auction or bundle it.

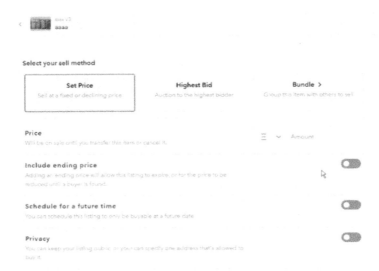

In the auction, we have to set the price. The minimum for sale is 1 ETH. We also need to set the end date of the auction.

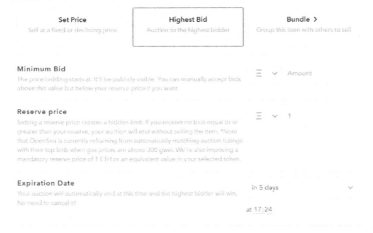

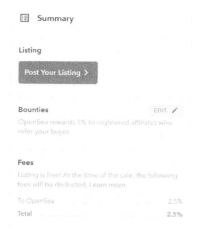

Summary

Listing

Post Your Listing >

Bounties   EDIT ✏
OpenSea rewards 1% to registered affiliates who
refer your buyer.

Fees
Listing is free! At the time of the sale, the following
fees will be deducted. Learn more.

To OpenSea   2.5%
Total   2.5%

7. Press "Post Your Listing" and pay the gas fees in ETH (around 0.1 ETH). These fees fluctuate a lot as it depends on how congested the Ethereum blockchain is.

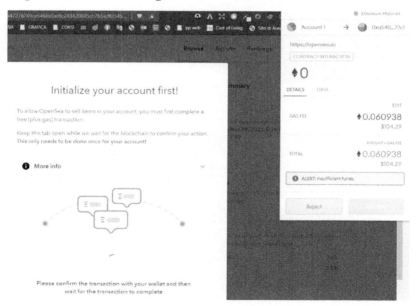

8. Sign with your Metamask Wall, and your NFT will be on sale.

5.11.3 Step-by-step procedure to sell an NFT in Rarible.com

As discussed earlier on how to create a Metamask wallet, you will also need a Metamask wallet to sell on Rarible website (https://rarible.com/).

1. Create your crypto wallet with Metamask: https://metamask.io/

2. Go to https://rarible.com/ and create an account. After creating an account, click in "Connect wallet"

3. Click in "Metamask" tab and sign in to your wallet. It's necessary to have at least 13 years old.

4. Click in "Create" and select the collectible type that you want create

5. Fill the form with the details of your NFT and click in "Create item"

6. Pay the gas fees and your NFT will be on sale

5.11.4 Step-by-step procedure to sell an NFT in NFTshowroom.com

- Go to https://hiveonboard.com/ and click "create an account"

- Click in download backup, click in the blank box and then in "create hive account".

- Download and install the chrome extension of Hive Keychain:https://chrome.google.com/webstore/detail/hive-keychain/jcacnejopjdphbnjgfaaobbfafkihpep?hl=it

- Click the extension and then click in use keys/pwd and enter the data from the username and password in the file downloaded in hive on board.

Username: aaad
Password: Qycvja1dr7bUzrBHM7K66m6wvXYUr49s

Now your account is active.

- Now you have to buy HIVE coin. You have two possibilities:

- Buy in an exchange market, like Binance (https://accounts.binance.com/it/register?ref=52159529) and then move in your hive wallet.

- Buy directly with a credit card https://www.moonpay.com/ . This solution is a little bit more expensive than the first one.

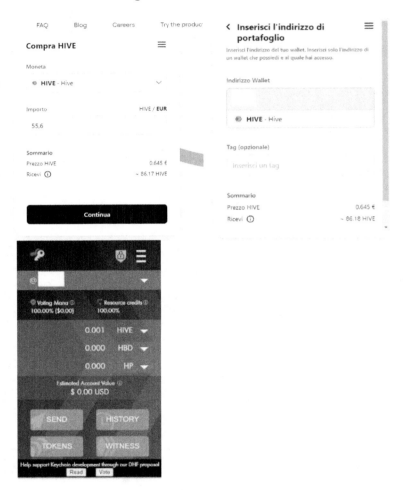

- Go to https://nftshowroom.com/ and login by entering your Hive wallet username, clicking in "Login with Keychain," and Hive wallet password.

- Click on your username and complete the profile's info. It's necessary to fill every field to be approved from this marketplace because the approval is manual and the team will check that you already have at least 5 images/videos in your website (you can create it for free with www.sites.google.com/new) or portfolio (7 days trial with www.portfolio.adobe.com) or Google Drive open link.

- Click apply to whitelist and wait 5-7 days (https://www.notion.so/NFT-Showroom-artist-guide-FAQ-and-whitelisting-3551e5437e0b443cb040a833750f6acb). The NFT Showroom teams will contact you in direct message in Instagram to validate your account. If you don't have an Instagram account, you have to create it. There isn't any other solution.

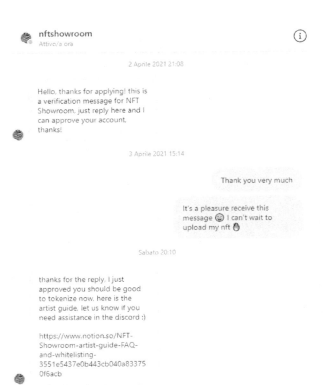

- After your account has been approved, you can start to upload your first NFT, going in nftshowroom, login in and click in "Tokenize".

- Choose what type of art you want upload; it's necessary a light version less than 1 Mb as a thumbnail and the normal size file of a maximum 30Mb.

- Complete every field. Mark NSFW (not safe for work) only if you upload inappropriate content.

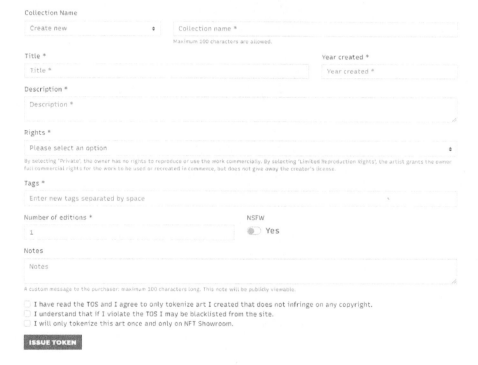

- Approve the uploading paying the 5 HIVE fee for the first NFT + 1 HIVE for every duplicate.

- Then wait for someone to buy your NFT.

5.12 TOOLS TO CREATE NFT FROM AN IMAGE

5.12.1 Goart Fotor

http://goart.fotor.com.s3-website-us-west-2.amazonaws.com/

5.12.2 Wordart

https://wordart.com/create

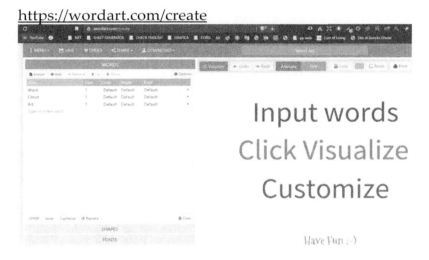

5.12.3 Night Café

Creation Settings

Input Image

Image Source
Preset: Image uploaded by user

Colour Settings
Using colours from the style images

Resolution
Low

Fidelity
55%

Smoothing
0%

Style 1 Image

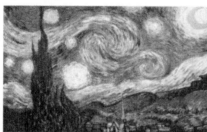

Style 1 Source
Preset: Starry Night

Style 1 Weight
43%

Style 1 Mask
No mask applied

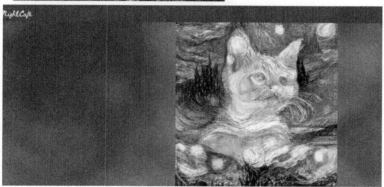

Untitled Creation ✎
Created a minutes ago
This creation is private. Make it public

✎ 1 Style 🖼 Low Res

This artwork was created with the help of Artificial Intelligence. Create your
own AI-generated artwork using NightCafe Creator

BUY A PRINT

DOWNLOAD

DUPLICATE

NEW CREATION

226

5.13 COMMON QUESTIONS WE GET ASKED IN CONSULTING.

This chapter summarizes the most common questions people have about NFTs.

Some of the topics covered in this portion of the Q&A have already been discussed in previous chapters; however, a review helps connect the information learned.

5.13.1 How do NFTs work?

These can be created on Blockchain contracts that support non-fungible tokens. NEO, EOS, and Ethereum were the first extensively used. Now also has a standard NFT-tokens, or NFT is a unique crypto asset that can be used to represent tangible and intangible goods. Real products are physical objects that can be touched, such as buildings, gadgets, etc., while intangible products can only be felt indirectly. Fungibility is the ability of assets that will be exchanged for the same items such as gold, dollars, etc. Non-fungibility is an irreplaceable or unique asset capability for art, etc.

Non-fungible tokens are a digital proof of authenticity and trustworthiness known as the blockchain. It keeps your transaction history record. NFT opens a creative platform for the items that are underestimated and provides collectors with easy ways to gather art digitally. Non-fungible tokens (NFTs) evolved with time and industry growth. Beeple is a popular name that appears in the world of NFTs.

NFTS can be created and issued in a variety of ways. For example, ERC-721, the Ethereum blockchain's standard for posting and trading non-fungible assets.

ERC-1155 is a newer standard. Tokens can be loaded into one contract, opening up additional possibilities. Interoperability is improved by standardising NFTS issuing. So assets may be moved between platforms very quickly.

If you want to save money while still admiring your NFTS, choose a reputable wallet. Your NFT will be at the address. Notably, NFTs cannot be duplicated or transferred without the owner's authorization.

NFT can be traded on the OpenSea. They connect sellers and buyers, with each token having its own worth. Naturally, NFT prices fluctuate based on market supply and demand.

But how is that valuable? As with all valuable goods, the value is assigned by those who value it. The value is mutual trust. People believe in the value of fiat money, precious metals, and vehicles. Every valuable thing gains value the same way, so why isn't it stored digitally? Money does not exist for the purpose of having an exchange value. People think that money has worth regardless of whether it is fiat money, precious metals, or automobiles. In the same way, precious items everywhere rise in value, and that's why a digital library doesn't exist.

5.13.2 Where to Buy Digital Art

There is probably no better indication that anything is happening than a lack of knowledge and frustration, as well as specific inquiries and readily available responses. Until recently, the majority of high-priced art was purchased through a gallery, a trade show, or an auction house, ideally after viewing the item in its original form.

Consider how eloquently online viewing rooms are being deconstructed by galleries and trade fairs as a step in the wrong direction, as a substandard replacement for trade fairs that will be unable to take place during the outbreak of the epidemic. All of a sudden, people are buying artwork in the name of anonymity on online marketplaces that have no connection to the art sector, and in many cases, do not even have permission to serve the traditional art audience. Contrary to this, even the largest and most popular markets, even those with auction records that are increasingly being read, rely on the followers of digital artists and new media artists to generate revenue. For example, if you scroll through the drops on Nifty Gateway, it quickly becomes apparent that the artists featured here are clearly chosen depending on the number of followers they have amassed.

The followers become collectors, and the art is dropped like sneakers and hoodies; there are unique items and open collections. Most of the time, the artists drop unique items and open collections; this is how the high sales sums come about. Open collection means that the art can be bought within a certain time window, five minutes, seven minutes, nine minutes; the number of sales is then the edition's size. The price per available collection is usually between $ 550 and $ 990. More than 100 works per edition are sold for $ 990. And that adds up.

Every day, there are drops on Nifty Gateway, the site launched by the twins Griffin Cock Foster and Duncan (name jokes have already been made), which are publicised in the platform's newsletter. Afterwards, it states: "TONIGHT'S drop will be available in 15 minutes!"

A few days ago, the server crashed during a drop because there was a lot of traffic. Of course, you can dismiss this as a sophisticated marketing strategy, complain about the loss of quality and say that none of this is art. And what is Christie doing with the Beeple NFT? Should the people who got incredibly rich with Bitcoin and Ether really get into art and shop at Christie's?

Kenny Schachter, the "Artnet" columnist, collector, gallery owner, curator, and artist, says in interviews and on Clubhouse time and again about digital art in the marketplaces that they are all just screensavers, gifs, and video game stills. "Like object on the back of a van," he said in an interview with "The Art Newspaper." Ne, like something from the internet that is now being sold on the internet. And the internet is full of memes and gifs, animations and renderings that relate to the context in which they are created.

At Clubhouse, it is explained by artists and experts like Lady Pheonix: "Bad art is what people collect and enjoy." And: "Memes are going to".

5.13.3 What does an NFT look like?

You can't touch NFTs because pretty much anything digital can be an NFT - a painting, music, videos, or even a cat GIF. A few days ago, the auction house Christie's sold the work Every day: The First 5000 Days by Mike Winkelmann, aka Beeple, for almost 70 million dollars. He posted a picture every day for 5000 days - now he has put them all together into one digital work. The buyer now receives the image file and an associated non-fungible token. The proceeds catapult Winkelmann into the top 3 of the best-paid artists still alive. And that with a digital work of art that can never hang on a wall. The band Kings of Leon is releasing their new album When You See Yourself as NFT. Six of the NFTs will have a golden ticket that will give you front-row seats at the concerts for the rest of your life. Art activists bought a picture of Banksy, digitized it, and then burned it. This image is now only available in digital form as NFT; it will be auctioned on the OpenSea site.

OpenSea is the eBay of the NFTs, and it is very successful. In February, the platform had sales of $ 86.3 million, up from $ 8 million in January. Other sites that offer auctions include Rarible and Nifty Gateway. If you are interested in the Kings as mentioned earlier of Leon album or one of the Golden Tickets, you have to be able to dig deep into your digital pocket. FynnKliemann is also experimenting with NFTs. He auctioned 100 jingles for 250,000 euros.

Once again, people and organizations that can afford such experiments are in the lead. Investor Mark Cuban is one of them. Also, the NBA basketball league and FC Bayern Munich. The fantasy football platform Sorare can be described as a digital Panini album. The tickets of the individual footballers are extremely limited.

The enormous increase in value. The most expensive trading card so far was that of the player Mbappé from Paris Saint-Germain. It changed hands for $ 57,000. Because the card is registered via the blockchain, it cannot be counterfeited.

5.13.4 After Cryptocurrency comes to the crypto art

Crypto art is the new catchphrase that haunts the media landscape. There's a lot of this "art" on OpenSea. This digital art can still be duplicated, copied, and distributed, including NFTs. You don't have the image rights. NFTs only have one thing that cannot be copied: ownership of the work. Artists continue to retain all rights to the work, just like a real painting. As with art, anyone can buy a Banksy poster - but you can only own the original once.

5.13.5 What is the point and purpose of NFTs?

For artists, it is an opportunity to see money for the work and the work finally. Likes on Instagram are all well and good, but you don't earn anything with them. The artist can receive a percentage share in a resale of the NFT. FynnKliemann's jingles bring him ten percent of every resale. As a buyer, you see it more as an opportunity to appreciate digital art, much like a museum honors physical art. In any case, it is an investment that should pay off at some point.

5.13.6 There is also criticism of the hype.

NFTs are climate killers. A brief technical digression is necessary to explain this. The Ethereumblockchain, on which NFTs are based, uses a mechanism called Proof of Work. In so-called mining, the computer solves complex puzzles to be allowed to add new blocks to the blockchain. The difficulty of these tasks is artificially increased in order to prevent too much 'money from being generated too quickly. So, there is an arms race. Faster computers solve the puzzles in less time, new puzzles slow down the computers, so more computing power is needed, which in turn is slowed down with more difficult tasks. It should be clear that this principle hardly wins any sustainability award.

5.13.7 Are NFTs still worth it?

Suppose you have the necessary Cryptocurrency: of course. It is a business where supply and demand determine. The crypto objects can be bought and potentially profitably resold, just like classic art. Or maybe not. Every art market fluctuates; the market for crypto art is no different. Nobody can say when the hype will end.

5.13.8 Crypto Hype: What Are NFTs Anyway?

Before we get into NFT, we should briefly recap what a blockchain is so that it can be seen how non-fungible tokens fit in there. The most famous blockchain project is certainly Bitcoin. However, the Bitcoin blockchain is limited to use as a cryptocurrency platform. This is not the case with all blockchains.

This is how data storage works in the blockchain.
In general, a blockchain is a kind of database made up of blocks that are strung together like pearls on a chain. On the one hand, each block contains the actual data that is to be stored in it and, on the other hand, a unique hash value that ensures that the data content is unchanged.

In addition to its own hash value, each block on the chain knows the previous block's hash value. In this way, the blockchain authenticates itself in a kind of chain reaction. If a hash was changed anywhere in the chain, the chain would break.

In this way, the data in the blockchain is more secure from manipulation than in ordinary databases. The so-called NFT makes use of this aspect.

Non-fungible tokens

The term token is most closely linked to its use as an asset. A token can also represent an asset or an economic good or be a digital equivalent of a real good.

In relation to a cryptocurrency, all tokens are fungible, i.e., interchangeable. This means that each token represents an equal asset; it does not matter what specific token you have. It is worth the same as any other holder's token. This is how our money works too. It doesn't matter which specific ten-euro note you use. You can also use two five-euro bills or five two-euro coins or any combination. The means, in this case, means of payment, are exchangeable.

This is precisely not the case with the NFT. Non-fungible, i.e., non-exchangeable tokens, represent a very specific asset and are therefore unique. They only have the technology of storage on the blockchain in common with currency tokens.

This makes NFT ideal for assets of which there are only one or a few. These are currently digital trading cards, game characters, virtual stretches of land in virtual worlds, or so-called crypto art. However, identity cards, vaccination cards, or other important documents could also be stored and secured via the blockchain.

Crypto collectibles and NFT art as dominant use cases - currently.

The most important or at least widespread use cases of NFT at the moment are crypto art and digital collectibles. Let's start with the collectibles.

Anyone who has ever played Magic the Gathering or Yu-Gi-Oh or Pokémon with real cards knows that success lies in owning the right cards. There is also a collector's aspect, i.e., the desire to own particularly rare or popular cards. So, a market has developed in which individual cards are sold for thousands of euros.

With NFT, this model can be transferred to the blockchain. A car manufacturer would create 20 copies of a particular trading card as a digital asset and store it on the blockchain. Now 20 potential buyers could buy this asset and later prove their ownership.

Anyone who thinks that this is theoretical should take a look at OpenSea - one of the largest of the now quite numerous marketplaces for NFT. OpenSea contains all kinds of collectibles and digital art objects or assets that can be used in virtual worlds such as Decentraland.

In early March 2021, BTC Echo reported the sale of a virtual area in the collectible monster game Axie Infinity for 1.5 million US dollars, or around 890 ethers, the Cryptocurrency on the Ethereum platform. This transaction replaced the previous record holder, the Cryptokitties Dragon, for what is probably the most famous blockchain game Cryptokitties. The kitten, which looks more like a hamster with a dinosaur tail, changed hands for 600 ether.

More and more artists are also relying on NFT to sell digital works with a guarantee of uniqueness. The Canadian singer Grimes had made around six million dollars in sales within 20 minutes with an NFT sale on the Nifty Gateway platform. The German artist FynnKliemann is currently auctioning 100 specially made jingles as NFT. Leon's band Kings is selling their new album "When You See Yourself" on Open Sea in a 14-day auction.

Twitter CEO Jack Dorsey also wants to participate in the NFT hype. A few days before the microblog platform's 15th birthday, Dorsey is auctioning an automatic copy of the Valuables website's first tweet. The current highest bid is $ 2.5 million.

11 projects build a strong foundation under the DEFI and NFTS marriage

Meet team makes the NFT market almost equally complex, flexible, and liquid as the rest of Crypto.

The digital collection on Blockchains moves retail mania for higher Crypto now, partly because they are cool and partly because the market seems to arrive at this consensus finally: the ownership of digital goods that can be proven can obtain real merit.

When there is genuine merit, there is money to be made. In recent years, it has been demonstrated that this collection of tokens, also known as non-fungible (NFTS) tokens, has a very high value.

Currently, a new fund for NFTFI is being established as a data point in the storey of the union of NFTs and Decentralization Finance (DEFI). This technology enables borrowers to deposit digital things as collateral on their credit reports. Among those who contributed to the $ 890,000 round were RoehhamGhehamlou, Dapper Labs Coinfund, Lao,1kx and others. NFTFI announced the investment on Thursday.

NFTFI is one of various companies that make it more easier to obtain money, get results, and get money back from the digital collection room by partnering with third-party vendors.

How does it work?

Ave and Defi Giants Compound are basically similar in that they are both money markets, but they both use fungible guarantees, like various stable coins or ET, to operate. NFT is not viable, because they are markets with a lack of liquidity, which makes it more difficult to locate prices in these markets.

When more items are introduced to the market, it changes more quickly, making it easier for liquidity to flow through a greater number of creations. And keep in mind that this is Crypto: In our industry, rapid change means quite different things than it did in the old era of social networks and Pokey phones, which is a good thing.

Several press releases have said that "NFTs begin to conceptualise new financial service categories when they foresee how we establish and recognise digital content's ownership online," according to MitraLasse Clausen, a partner at 1kx venture capital business.

The following 10 initiatives, which are separate from NFTFI, function to almost similar extents to complicate, adapt, and liquidate the NFT market, as well as the rest of the Crypto space:

Nintex.

The startup, the platform, is working on a new edition with numerous additional features. The government over the underlying NFT is for holders of tools and fractions that allow more delicate ownership. A DAO will also run the entire app. "This is a no-brainer. Uniqueness reigns supreme "Joel Hubert told Coindesk in an email.

Ark Gallery.

As a result, NFT pioneer lava labs become more fungible. Ark then established additional mechanisms to increase liquidity for non-fungible original tokens, which may be credited for the current crypto punks boom. We're working on the blank. "We will start the NFT project," Roberto Ceria Ark told Coindesk in an email.

Mintbase.

Mintbase makes it easy to create non-fungible tokens. It recently had a Sino-led funding round. Mint base permits sales royalties to be distributed to up to 1,000 persons. COO CAROLIN told Coindesk, " "It's really a part of the fractional ownership discussed by everyone".

NFTX

This allows public index funds to own many NFTs with one token. It features tokens for NFT categories and the market spectrum. "Many people do not have the knowledge or time to trade individual NFTs but desire market exposure.

5.13.9 Defi

A hot new trend is well underway in the crypto community: Defi. Although Defi is not exactly new, the YFI crypto token's success has sparked new interest in Defi and its associated cryptocurrencies among traders and investors. Even if you are only trading the bigger cryptocurrencies like Bitcoin and Ethereum, it is worth keeping an eye on the Defi boom as it could be affecting your assets. Here is a brief guide to what is going on at Defi, YFI, and the wider crypto market.

<u>Nice increase at YFI</u>

Cryptocurrency prices have been in a superior advantage, as cryptocurrency stole the show from everyone else when its value rose 165% to $ 38,682. This token is YFI, the governance token for decentralized finance (Defi) of the yearn Finance platform.

Yearn aggregates the various yields through the Defi logs. The users generate income by lending their coins to various protocols or by storing them in "vaults." Governance tokens such as YFI can also be purchased by users who provide liquidity for the process known as "yield farming." As the name suggests, the holders of these governance tokens can also vote on the network's proposals.

YFI-like coins also jumped on the Defi bandwagon and reached higher prices. The price of YF Link rose to $ 581 (328%), that of YFFI to $ 84.14 (465%), and that of YFV to $ 56.62 (201%). YFII, an offshoot of YFI, rose from $ 935 to $ 5,076 in three days.

Governance tokens are becoming a popular speculative asset as their supply is limited, and investors want to get in before it is too late. The range of YFI tokens is limited to just 30,000 pieces, with 29,962 tokens already in circulation at the time this article was written. One of the reasons there are such dramatic price movements is because these tokens are highly liquid, and a single large transaction can have a huge impact on the price.

5.13.10 Invest in Defi

It seems like everyone wants to get into Defi, but what does this term actually mean? Defi stands for "Decentralized Finance" and aims to replicate our traditional financial system's application areas with high-tech and little bureaucracy and without intermediaries. This means that issuing and borrowing, trading derivatives and securities, taking out insurance, investing, etc., is all done through a decentralized open-source network rather than banks. Smart contracts, which the participants in the blockchain verify, automatically execute the terms of the financial agreements. Defi smart contracts are currently valued at roughly USD$8 billion.

Defi and Ethereum

This should sound familiar to anyone interested in Ethereum. In fact, the vast majority of these applications run on Ethereum. Other platforms with opportunities for smart contracts should work for Defi as well, but Ethereum is currently leading the field. In theory, DeFi's popularity should give ETH a healthy boost too.

Yearn Finance's core products are "safes" that offer yield farmers the best returns while pooling money to reduce users' workload. The crypto community already expects the upcoming launch of Yearn's ETH vaults to increase demand for ETH and decrease supply as more Ethereum tokens are locked in the vault for yield farming.

5.13.11Boom or bubble?

While some investors are quick to jump at the chance of impressive returns that yield farming promises, following the latest trend is not always the right step. Long-time crypto enthusiasts will still remember the 2017-2018 ICO bubble well. Many Defi projects are still speculative and involve both risks and rewards.

Yield farming, which is really driving the Defi rush, has also been criticized by industry leaders.

Ethereum co-founder VitalikButerin has warned investors to be careful when it comes to Defi. He compares the business model of yield farming (which drives inflation in the supply of governance tokens) to the Federal Reserve's printing.

Invest in the crypto future with StormGain

As always, the savvy trader will do his research on particular investments. But as soon as the dust has settled concerning the Defi boom, Cryptocurrency will win across the board as the areas of application of the blockchain become more and more apparent. That is why we recommend a diverse and flexible crypto portfolio on a platform that offers you high rewards for your participation.

Stormin is the most effective cryptocurrency trading platform on the market. Stormin is available on the Internet or as a smartphone app and offers the opportunity to trade the top 6 cryptocurrencies with a leverage of up to 200x around the clock - on a user-friendly interface available in several languages. Stormin also offers the best customer bonuses on the market, including up to 15% annual interest on cryptocurrency deposits.

5.14 HOW AUCTIONING WORKS IN THE MARKETPLACE

NFTs are part of a $250 million industry that is rapidly growing.

According to a 2020 study by L'Atelier BNP Paribas, the market for non-fungible tokens, or NFTs, has grown to $250 million. As cryptocurrencies like Bitcoin continued to rise in popularity, investments in NFTs surged 299 percent in 2020.

NFT manufacturers and resellers made millions. After paying $67,000 for the Beeple project, an art collector made $6.6 million on a 10-second video artwork.

NFTs include digital trading games, virtual real estate, art, and cards. Here's how to buy and sell NFTs.

NFTs, unlike common cryptocurrencies such as Bitcoin and Ether, cannot be directly traded and distributed through a variety of platforms.

Most NFT platforms allow buyers to have a digital wallet and use Flow, WAX, or Ethereum.

Here's how to buy and sell NFTs.

For both designers and sellers, digital art has taken in millions of dollars.

On Nifty Gateway, "Crossroads" by Mike Winkelmann was resold for USD$6.6 million.

The majority of digital-art trading platforms allow artists to collect royalties. Some of them cater to a select few, while others encourage everyone to create and sell their work.

NFTs gave a windfall of benefit to professional digital artists. Digital-art trading platforms, according to NFT artist Trevor Jones, may prevent the need for more conventional art markets. NFTs have also attracted the attention of several traditional auction houses. Christie's, a 1766-founded auction house, auctioned a Beeple piece in February, marking the first foray into digital tokens. Currently, the painting is valued at $9.75 million, with two days left to go until the auction ends.

The work of multimillion-dollar digital artists may be found on platforms such as Nifty Gateway, Foundation, and SuperRare which allow purchasers to choose from a carefully curated collection of work.

It is great because Nifty Gateway allows artists who have only lived on Instagram and Twitter to showcase their work. Following the adoption of crypto currency, they started selling crypto art and are now enjoying the benefits and growing fame.

On sites like Nifty Gateway, SuperRare, and Foundation, artists such as digital comic artist Chris Torres and Grimes have found homes. These websites compensate artists with a royalty of approximately 10% of any potential sales of their work.

The use of credit cards by buyers is intended to make Nifty Gateway's site more accessible to buyers, but other platforms lay a stronger emphasis on decreasing the entrance barrier for developers.

In contrast to Zora and Rarible, which are invite-only sites, Mintable and Rarible let anybody to publish, sell, and trade images and text as non-traditional assets.

Artists can still earn royalties on these pages, but the content is considerably less carefully regulated than on the other pages. Users of Rarible can submit anything they choose, from blank photographs to their own adaptations of well-known pieces of art.

Robert Martin, an NFT developer on Rarible, believes the sites need to strengthen their security, but he praises the ease with uploading content to Rarible.

These websites offer NFTs for sale at various prices from $10 to hundreds of thousands.

5.14.1 OpenSea

With everything from trading cards to sports, virtual reality and art, OpenSea bills itself as the world's largest non-financial-transaction (NFT) marketplace. On the internet, there are over 200 categories and 4 million things to choose from.

Ether can be used to purchase common NFT products such as CryptoPunks, CryptoKitties, and virtual real estate on OpenSea.

OpenSea is used by a number of marketplaces, including Decentraland, which is a popular virtual real-estate platform. The NFTs sold by OpenSea have generated approximately USD$24 million in revenue, according to DappRadar.

Opensea requires you to fill out a form on MetaMask as (https://opensea.io/).

5.14.2 NFT and sports

NBA Top Shot distributes sports footage for a variety of prices ranging from $20 to several thousand dollars.

The popularity of fantasy sports has also had an impact on NFT revenue. A unique fantasy soccer platform is available that allows users to create, sell and manage virtual clubs using digital player cards.

This site was launched in 2018, it has only just begun to acquire popularity among users. The cryptocurrency news site CryptoSlam reports that Sorare just sold almost USD$13 million in ether.

CryptoSlam requires you to fill out a form on MetaMask and Google (https://cryptoslam.io/)

5.14.3 Gamers and trading-card collectors

Axie Infinity produces NFTs for the gaming environment.
Axie Infinity produces NFTs for the gaming environment.
Axie Infinity is a fictional character created by Axie.
Axie requires you to fill out a form on google as (marketplace.axieinfinity.com/login?)

CryptoSlam says that Axie Infinity, a company that offers cartoon animals designed to fight in a Pokmon-like way, is one of the top ten most popular websites on the web for crypto-collecting.

The expansion of non-traditional gaming is projected to continue. Combat Racers, a blockchain racing game developed by Altitude Games, was released on the Arkane Market, which currently has over 100,000 players.

Myth is another famous trading card and memorabilia website. Market and Treasureland are two of my favorite places in the world. The growth of NFT gaming is expected to continue.

5.14.4 Virtual real estate market

On Decentraland, users may purchase and trade virtual real estate. Janine Yorio, who is the co-head of Republic Real Estate, foresees a role for digital real estate to emerge as the next major investment industry in Decentraland.

Using virtual reality and real estate, Decentraland, a non-fungible token (NFT) platform built on the Ethereum blockchain and owned and operated by individuals, makes use of the Ethereum blockchain. It's a multiplayer game to play roles, allowing players into a networked first person shooter to build a virtual world (NFT). According to Yorio, the game resembles a more advanced version of "SimCity," "Minecraft," or "Fortnite."

It has been reported that Atari, the firm that created Pacman, has ambitions to build a bitcoin casino on this platform.

The price of the platform currency named "MANA" has increased by more than 321 percent in the past 12 months and now this currency has a capitalization of $225 M.

Decentraland requires you to fill out a form on google as (https://market.decentraland.org/)

The site's very first tweet is auctioned off as a non-financial transaction, stated Twitter CEO Jack Dorsey (NFT). The digital asset now is 2.5 million dollars, depending on its market value. Valuables is a platform that lets users to sell their tweets in exchange for ether, which is a cryptocurrency. The website is solely dedicated to the sale of tweets in the form of NFTs. Another platform on trend is Glass Factory.

You can create digital art like holograms and sell them as tokens on the secondary market.

The artist Peter Rudwall sold his personal information as NFT, including his social media profiles, weight, and birth date.

5.15 FUTURE OF NON-FUNGIBLE TOKENS

Since the inception of NFT, the popularity of NFT games has skyrocketed. As of January 2019, Dapper Labs, the company that created CryptoKitties, has begun collaborating with other NFT providers in order to facilitate interoperability between game platforms. This means that a native NFT from one platform can now be used on another platform without modification. NFT projects have been created by a number of major organisations, including the video game producer NBA and Ubisoft.

In recent years, the potential for NFTs has extended dramatically beyond the gaming industry. Organizations and organisations are investigating the potential of non-fungible tokens as a means of establishing identity as well as for certification, ticketing, and fractional ownership of both digital and physical assets. Any situation in which there is a requirement for traceability and clear ownership falls under the purview of NFT use cases.

The future of NFTs will heavily depend on the progress of the Ethereum network and wider blockchain technology.

It's safe to assume that as blockchain technology continues to grow, NFTs will follow – whether it's on the Ethereum blockchain, another public network, or a private network.

Crowdfunding a non-fungible token

Non-fungible tokens are still relatively new, and most game developers have had to figure out how they can be made as they go. This means that many NFTs are built using existing smart contracts or by creating their protocol. In some cases, the founders of an NFT will also create a game to showcase its features and utility. This allows users to purchase the game and give it a level of credibility.

5.15.1 The NFT Approach to Crowdfunding

Funding for a new company by using crowdfunding is a relatively new concept. NFTs (Non-Fungible Tokens) have been accessible on the Ethereum network since 2015. But among game creators and a broader audience, they are still relatively obscure. This means that many developers may not have the tools or resources to create an NFT. This is one of the reasons that the NFT Approach to Crowdfunding was created. This approach makes it possible for NFTs to be created, hosted, and distributed on any platform (including mobile devices and web browsers). In addition, game developers can also build their own crowdfunding campaign using the "NFT-Crowdfund" standard. It provides developers with the tools and resources they need to create their own NFT. This allows them to create their own ERC-721 token — which is an NFT that can be used as a crowdfunding campaign.

5.15.2 Creating NFT-Crowdfund

Here is how you can potentially build your own NFT-Crowdfund:

1) Create your colored token for crowdfunding on a platform (Ethereum Wallet, Metamask, etc.) or via a command-line interface (console).

2) Use NFT-Crowdfund protocol for creating and distributing the NFT.

3) Use ERC 721 to describe your game items.

4) Use ERC – 684 for creating pre-order items with a discount. These will not be fungible after the Crowdfund ends. Unsold pre-order items are burned.

5) List your rare item(s) on a marketplace for selling post-crowdfunding using the NFT registry, or create your own marketplace. Rename your NFT if needed to reflect the marketplace name. All pre-order items must be re-categorized to match your new marketplace category.

1) Create your colored token for crowdfunding on a platform (Ethereum Wallet, Metamask, etc.) or via a command-line interface (console).

2) Use NFT-Crowdfund protocol for creating and distributing the NFT.

3) Use ERC 721 to describe your game items.

5.15.3 Hype Art NFT Marketplace

Finally, I wanted to introduce you to this revolutionary project named Hype Art. I am developing with a team of art and cryptocurrency lovers.

Non-For-Profit (NFP) projects began to gain widespread notice. Although crypto was going through a downturn at the time, the industry saw significant growth because of it. The most used marketplaces for NFT (Superrare, Niftigataway, Rarible) are presenting their platforms in a way that is more similar to Amazon and eBay than to an art gallery: collectors don't feel any artistic experience when browsing these platforms.

The artist is not at the center of the discussion. No space is given to the vision and the thought behind its work.

5.15.3.1 What do we want to create?

We think the artistic vision of the NFT creator needs to be placed at the center of the narrative. Each artist will be able to share the creative idea behind their work through a live interview (hosted by Koinsquare) together with a curated description of the work presented.

We aim to create a 3d virtual gallery that allows the collector to replicate the same feeling of seeing works displayed in a real gallery.

We want to stimulate the community of our collectors by using gamification; therefore, auctions will be made in parallel to airdrops to our followers.

5.15.3.2 Where?

Hype.art will use Opensea (ETH blockchain) and FAN (Tron blockchain) as platforms where the auction will take place, to access a bigger market.

Hype.art will instead provide the artistic promotion towards the community and a structured team to allow artists to customize their "online exhibitions".

5.15.3.3 Key players

There are 3 key players: Zulu Republic, Koinsquare and Satoshygallery.

The **Zulu Republic** is a place that exists on the blockchain where people, businesses, and organizations can thrive on their own terms. Our purpose is to help advance the development of decentralized technology, which is likely to have an enormous impact on the advancement of human rights and empowerment throughout the world, as well as the mitigation of the digital gap.

Koinsquare is a project that aims to promote and disseminate information and knowledge in the field of blockchain and cryptocurrency technology.
With our commitment, passion and professional approach, we present and analyze different topics such as Cryptocurrencies, Smart Contracts, centralized / decentralized Exchanges, ICOs, Fintech Industry, Market values of the major crypto assets, Mining systems and much more.

Sathoshy Gallery was born in a very early stage of cryptocurrency history. Since 2013, it is using iconography and art to fill the gap between technology developers and the general public and spread the crypto culture to a larger audience. Satoshigallery has provided art paintings to various private collectors worldwide, illustrated books for

Andreas Antonopoulos, and drew some of the most iconic logos in the crypto space (Bitfinex, Tether, etc.).

5.15.3.4 When will the project launch?

- March 2021: Hype.art was born

- April 2021: Platform and artistic development

- May 2021: Marketing development

- September 2021: Launch of platform for public

5.15.3.5 Do you want to partecipate to AirDrop?

Artist exhibition will include thousands of Airdrops and a premium Auction, ready to scream out the first Artist with the launch of Hype.art. You have been one of the first to get an invitation to view the Exhibition and to bid in the Auction. We will be providing a date announcement to the subscriber as soon as possible.

Subscribe to the newsletter to not miss any news: **www.hype.art**.

6 CRYPTOCURRENCY

The Metaverse was meant to be more than a typical game environment governed through the use of a singular narrative that does not allow the user to do much. The Metaverse was meant to replicate the aspects of our physical world within the virtual world, and central to the functions of the Metaverse in this instance would be the existence of a virtual economy When we speak of the virtual economy, this goes beyond the microtransactions that take place when we purchase certain features in an app to gain advantages. Let's place several examples of what the virtual economy is believed to be:

- 34,356 parcels of land were sold between December 2017 and January 2018 in what is believed to be the single, largest, real-estate auction in the world. Before we bring up issues of foreign ownership of real properties in countries, it must be noted that this real estate auction sold parcels of virtual land, that were meant to constitute a digital city that existed within a particular Metaverse platform. This Metaverse, had its own digital economy, with its own Cryptocurrency.

- On a smaller scale, users are able to win prizes and incentives if they are able to complete specific objectives throughout various platforms in the Metaverse. These incentives range from approximately $125 to $3 million.

Before we delve into the intricacies of Cryptocurrencies, it becomes necessary to define what the Virtual Economy is. The Virtual Economy is described as a combination of platforms, markets that are established, beginning and dubious at the same instances, and those entrepreneurs that bravely ventured into the virtual world and sought to make a living from it.

There are certain structures that must be defined in the virtual economy, that the transactions that result from it are safeguarded by the same protocols that ensure the safety of Cryptocurrency transactions. These include:

- Distributed Ledgers which are defined as an approach to record and share data across several data banks (which serve as the "ledgers" of the virtual economy. Like a physical ledger, this allows each transaction that takes place within the virtual economy to be recorded, the data of these transactions are then stored, and the stored data can be shared among various participants who are in the shared network. Unlike the physical ledger, the virtual ledger does not exist in a single location. The virtual ledger exists in multiple copies all over the virtual world, and constantly updates themselves on each transaction that takes place within the Metaverse.
- We have touched upon Virtual Reality and Computer Vision so we will not go into the details of this once more.
- Ray Tracing, which forms part of the visualization process in the virtual economy. This consists of the computer which generates an image through the tracing of individual light rays from a camera to the objects that are within its field of view. This is useful in the creation of photorealistic images that are needed to fuel the virtual economy.

- NFTs, which have been discussed in Chapter 5, are central to the virtual economy, and are described as uniquely digital items constructed upon the Ethereum blockchain. From the description of Non-Fungible, the value of these tokens cannot be substituted in any form, unlike Cryptocurrencies, which make these NFTs a prized commodity within the virtual economy.

6.1 What are Cryptocurrencies?

Cryptocurrencies together with the Non-Fungible Tokens perhaps form the backbone of the Virtual Economy, in the same way that our coins and paper money have their value backed by the bullion of precious metals that exist in our respective country's reserves. The presence of the Non-Fungible Token in the virtual economy ensures however, that the there is a decentralized, digital representation, that is universal in nature and allows for ownership of digital assets that are scarce (limited in their quantity), unique in the codes that make up these tokens, and authentic, where these tokens can be readily managed. Because these are such an important aspect of the virtual economy, it becomes necessary to establish an economic standard and a series of protocols that regulate how virtual items are moved and transacted with in the Metaverse,

A more technical definition of the Cryptocurrency defines it as an asset specifically created to operate as a means to digitally exchange products. The crypto aspect in the Cryptocurrency emanates from the use of cryptography, which prevents the free generation of the credit units equivalent to the Cryptocurrency used, and allows the monitor of the exchange of the currency between the parties who exchanged their services. The Cryptocurrency is simply a decentralized currency within the Metaverse that is not regulated by any form of a centralized banking system. Rather, the exchange of Cryptocurrencies are regulated through the use of blockchains.

While Cryptocurrencies exist within a slightly dubious hold – and this is solely because it is digital, and is subject to the weaknesses of digital components, and has nothing to do with its inherent value- the presence of the Cryptocurrency becomes the basis for a financial infrastructure, much in the same way each country has a basic monetary unit that becomes the basis of its entire economy. There are various types of Cryptocurrencies which we have touched on in Chapter 2, such as the ubiquitous Bitcoin, and we have the Ethereum and SOL Cryptocurrencies that become the basis of a flourishing virtual economy in their own rights. Because digital assets are the future, it makes investments in them worthwhile despite their lack of tangibility. The Cryptocurrency then serves to anchor the virtual economy and provide a basis where economic transactions can safely take place that would protect the interests of users and developers as these exchanges take place within the virtual economy of the Metaverse.

6.2 How does Crypto work in the Metaverse? Why Choose Cryptocurrency?

Cryptocurrencies, whether they are Bitcoin, Ethereum, Sol or the other Cryptocurrencies that were recently developed provide a more secure basis for the exchange of goods within the Metaverse. Subsequently, the existence of Cryptocurrencies can be compared to the presence of the gold reserves that back our currencies in the physical world, and provide more value to the other content such as NFTs that are present within the Metaverse economy. Cryptocurrencies and the investment developers and other interested individuals make into them ensure that the economy of the Metaverse as well as the Metaverse itself is able to expand through the incentives provided to developers.

It would not be remiss to compare Cryptocurrencies to our actual money that we use in the exchange of goods and services in the physical world, and as a result, we could engage in virtually any form of service that people would pay money for. At this point, we have rehashed all the aspects of how Cryptocurrency is money, yet how did we go from paper money to digital money? With the rise of the Internet and the presence of authorities that centralize the issuance of money, there came the idea of the conversion of money into a digital form. How can the general population make the most of the money that was converted into a Cryptocurrency and how can these authorities regulate the issuance of money in the same way our federal reserves and banks control the value of our currencies? How can we keep a single person or a group of people from amassing untold shares of this digitized money in a clandestine manner that ensures that they retain all the power and the ability to dictate what goes on within the Metaverse? This is not as outlandish as you may think it is, since there are several tech companies that control the internet, and these people decide what can happen within the Metaverse, which directly contradicts the democracy the Metaverse can be.

More importantly, the transition towards a digitized form of money has been familiar to most, especially with the pandemic shuttering banks, and causing us to convert our finances into a digital form such as those employed by Paypal, that we may pay for goods through the use of Digital Wallets which we have touched upon in Chapter 3. Considering Cryptocurrency is a digital form of money, who is to say one cannot simply employ a means to duplicate the amount of money and ensure that we would never have to work another day? This is where the centralization of the Cryptocurrencies comes in, where in this model, centralization causes the functions of a bank to be enacted within the economy of the Metaverse. There are ledgers that record each transaction that takes place within the Metaverse, and this ensures that there are no duplications, frauds and mistakes made when two parties come to terms and exchange money for goods. The digital ledger in this case, predates the existence of the blockchain that is now used to safeguard each Cryptocurrency transaction. The centralization of money has a flaw, in that it vests in a single person the power to make decisions on how money can be regulated, which in the wrong hands, can have severe economic repercussions, especially for those who have invested into Cryptocurrencies. Then there can be mismanagement where a single error in judgment can cause effects like deflation (where the currency loses its value). Centralization gives an authority the capacity to control what happens to your money, and we have seen this happen over and over in the physical world, needless to say, this is not a good idea within the Metaverse.

Where do Cryptocurrencies come in? When it comes to our money, we have established that the value of our money is dependent on the quantity and value of our gold and silver reserves in our country's central bank. However, the flaw with this paper currency is that these are unable to reflect the current value of the gold and silver reserves that are present. Cryptocurrencies on the other hand, are able to approach the value of gold closer than paper money ever will, and this makes it the more valuable option, despite its lack of tangible form. Cryptocurrencies are the base economic unit of the Metaverse, and are unlikely to be disrupted unlike economic shutdowns (recall the 1997 Asian Financial Crisis and the 2009 Economic Crisis), as the only way that Cryptocurrencies can suddenly be devalued and left vulnerable would be to shut down the entire internet – an entirely inconceivable concept considering how essential it is now.

Cryptocurrencies are ideal within the Metaverse as these are able to be ported from one platform to another, and can be used in any platform as long as you have internet access. Within the Metaverse, the Cryptocurrencies allow you to engage in investments and businesses of any amount as these are unconstrained by the limitations imposed by countries with regards to the amount of foreign currency that you bring into their borders. Because of this added portability, Cryptocurrencies provide a safer means to store your finances safely within the Metaverse. As Cryptocurrencies are decentralized, they remain unaffected by decisions made by our national governments, and are untouched by policies that allegedly control finances. Needless to say, Cryptocurrencies are able to affect the way business takes place in the Metaverse, as not only does it serve as the entire economic structure of the Metaverse, its digital aspect allows any transactions that utilize it to be recorded in real time, which makes the

Metaverse a safer place to perform all sorts of business transactions.

The presence of the blockchains that are paired with the Cryptocurrency, regardless of Bitcoin, Ethereum, SOL or other units, ensure that financial information is perpetually protected. An added advantage is that Cryptocurrencies are unable to be turned into counterfeit bills, as blockchains continually update themselves to prevent such an occurrence from ever happening to investors of Cryptocurrencies.

In the interests of the democratization of the Metaverse, here is where Cryptocurrencies come in. One of the main concerns with these currencies is that it could allow a single person to amass enough wealth that they can control the value of the currency in accordance with their whim. That cannot happen, as illustrated in this example: To capitalize on Bitcoin, its approximate average capitalization value is pegged at USD 50 billion. To be able to even manipulate the value of Bitcoin, you would need USD 10 billion, and it is highly unlikely that anyone in the world has that kind of money ready to be used in such a capricious manner. It would take several billions of dollars to even make some form of impact into the value of Cryptocurrencies, which contributes to its stabilizing factor within the confines of the Metaverse economy. From what can be gathered, it would take a lot of people to invest in Cryptocurrencies to make some form of impact, and thus it would not take a lot of money to be able to invest in Cryptocurrencies and, thus in the Metaverse. This lets anyone with the finances sufficient enough to invest would be able to take part in the expansion and investments. This has an added benefit, too many investors in the Metaverse and in Cryptocurrencies also prevent a single person from manipulating the

Cryptocurrency market. Investments in Cryptocurrencies are generally safe, but would greatly benefit from the movement of these currencies into investments which would serve to protect your Cryptocurrencies from being manipulated. These are what blockchains prevent.

6.3 Make the most of the Metaverse with Crypto Investments

There are two ways to invest in the Metaverse with the use of Cryptocurrencies. These are differentiated into long-term and short-term investments. Short-Term Investments would be familiar ground to stockbrokers as this is simply trading – where one can buy and sell financial assets within a period of time that ranges from days to weeks. A long-term approach employs the same tactics, however, the investment time takes approximately a year before you decide to trade in your investment for another asset. Holding is the term used to refer to investments in Cryptocurrency, and this is classified as a long-term approach to investment, and thus you would want to make the most of it.

Though this practice lends itself to long-term approaches, specifically a buy and hold strategy, this can safely be applied to short-term approaches as well. However, this requires you to think like a stockbroker so you would be able to divest and invest your shares at the most opportune time. This is a mentality that is ideal for investments that are volatile in nature, such as Cryptocurrencies – volatile that is, because they are in digital form. The long-term approach on the other hand requires you to carefully research the type of investment you would want to take part in, and from here, amass the amount needed to purchase your investment, and literally forget about it (though you should not really forget about your investment- this is more figurative, in that you don't mess with it, but you know that it is still there). It would be prudent however, to keep tab on the investments, so that you would be able to keep track of the value of your Cryptocurrencies, but at the most, this type of approach requires minimal intervention on your part.

A short-term holding would also cost more, as there are necessary transaction fees that you would have to comply with before you can complete a transaction. When compared with a long-term approach, your transaction fees are minimal, as you do not necessarily trade your assets all the time. This translates to savings in the amount of fees you would have to pay.

At the core of it all, before you begin to invest in the Metaverse and in Cryptocurrencies, you will want to ask yourself what your motivations are. Why would you want to risk your finances on an intangible asset? College Education? A Retirement Nest Egg? Though money is ultimately at the core of it, this is a superficial reason as to why you would want to invest. We're not in the business of armchair psychology however, as your motivations would ensure that you make the right decisions to invest and divest your investments, especially when Cryptocurrency prices in the market are at their bearish stage.

Investments are a risky venture, but the rewards that you can obtain from it are worth the risk provided you manage to exercise the requisite amount of patience needed before your risk pays off. Patience is a virtue that you as an investor must have with regards to Cryptocurrencies, as though there are Cryptocurrencies whose values may skyrocket, when compared to the steadier form of

Cryptocurrencies that exist, like a rocket, they eventually fizzle out and disappear. A more impatient investor would have immediately jumped in, and though the gains are fruitful, the losses are greater. A steadier, more established Cryptocurrency may have its value slow, but it is better to be slow and steady, rather than go fast and crash harder.

Investments in the Metaverse are rarely cut and dried in their approach as these require some form of risk. Contrary to what was established in the previous paragraph, slow and steady approaches may not necessarily be the best approach with regards to investments. The best investments with the use of Cryptocurrencies involve those that are not entirely safe, nor unprofitable, or investments that are not too profitable themselves but also carry the added element of risk. To determine the type of investment that you would choose, it would be essential to identify the minimum rate of return. This is best done through a projection of how much money would you need at the end of a certain period? This can range from 5 to 15 years. From this, you can determine how much of your finances can you set aside to invest in a particular currency. You can compute for the rate of return through the use of your expected future value (the money that you project having at the end of your chosen time period), and the money that you have at present value (the money that you could invest in your chosen business). Once you have made the necessary operations, the amount that results is what your minimum rate of return becomes. From here, you can choose which Cryptocurrency on the market has the closest approximate rate of return to your minimum rate of return or more than what you computed, for you to invest your funds in.

Another crucial aspect in the investment process, and this does not only apply to investments within the Cryptocurrencies, is the Risk Appetite. We all have heard that some of the more appealing aspects in life carry a certain element of risk, and while this can be applied to adrenaline junkies, this same concept can be carried over through the use of investments in Cryptocurrencies. Here, your patience would be put to the test as the risk appetite determines how much loss are you willing to shoulder in the event that your investments do not pan out? Investments in Cryptocurrency do not necessarily remain steady, as because of the volatility of the digital environment, it carries a high level of risk. The higher you expect your return of investments to be, the higher the risk that these could devalue at a certain point. Sometimes, the investments that you envisioned may not give you the returns that you had envisioned. The worst part of investment is that sometimes, you may not be able to recoup the amount that you had originally invested into the Cryptocurrency. Risk appetite then will help you come to the realization that if you really choose to invest in Cryptocurrencies, you would be able to determine how much money you can invest in your chosen Cryptocurrency.

How can you estimate how much money you would want to invest In the Metaverse? You would have to ask yourself some hard questions, such as how much money are you willing to lose? Before we go into the mantras that this is negative thinking, investments are always risky, no matter what form they are in, and no matter what you choose to invest in, there are always ups and downs, and there are no certainties, except that at some point, you would lose money when your investment goes bearish. Knowing how much you are willing to lose eases your mind and allows you to safely project about how much to invest without much sacrifice to your way of life. This way, your financial health does not go down the drain if your Cryptocurrency goes down in value. While investments in Cryptocurrencies carry a certain amount of risk, a foolhardy move would be to concentrate all your investment money and life savings into a single Cryptocurrency. This would leave you with very little room to maneuver your life, especially since all your assets have been tied up with investments in the Crypto market. Knowing how much you are willing to lose also lessens the pressure, as in your mindset, you have projected how much you can lose and you would still be able to live with that. This also increases your chances to successfully weather the storm that your investments have found themselves in.

Other methods to determine risk appetite would be to identify the amount of money you would not need to use within the next five years – maybe a few treasury bonds gaining interest over time, extra savings, and so on. Investments are a long-term approach, and you would need to ensure that your investments remain intact to ensure that you do get the returns on your investments that you had originally planned.

Initial Coin Offerings are your gateway to start off your investment in Cryptocurrencies, and if you are not new to the investment business, you would know that this is like the Initial Public Offerings that are in the stock market. If you are a fledgling investor, then, this is your initiation into the realm of investments. Before you do plan on investments into a Cryptocurrency, you would have to read about what you choose to invest in. These entail reading the white papers of the Cryptocurrencies that you can choose. But first, more insight into the ICO, because though it is similar to the IPO, there are certain distinctions that one must consider. An Initial Coin Offering is a means where the creators of a Cryptocurrency (Bitcoin, Ethereum and SOL to name a few), generate the funds needed for them to create a new Cryptocurrency. Because of the decentralized nature of the Cryptocurrencies, these ICOs are unregulated by authorities – unlike IPOs which are regulated by some equivalent of a Securities and Exchanges Commission or other federal authorities involved with investments. ICOs unlike the IPO, because they are deregulated and decentralized, these are easier to perform when compared to an IPO.

A proper ICO will offer their prospective investors their White Paper, which in itself is similar to a prospectus used by companies who wish to start with an IPO. A White Paper is now defined as a document that narrates the procedures of the fundraising activity done by the creators of the ICO, and includes the rationale as to why an ICO is conducted. Because you are a prospective investor, it is the best practice, or make it imperative that you read through these white papers to ensure that you are putting your money where it will become a worthwhile investment. The white paper would help you determine if the Cryptocurrency you are about to invest in is a legitimate enterprise, and if it would be able to compete with other established Cryptocurrencies on the market. These white papers are written by those who have an extensive knowledge of what the Cryptocurrency is about. These can include a variety of professional who have contributed their knowledge into what the Cryptocurrency actually is. The main job of the white paper now, is to convince you, as the prospective investor, that it would be worth your while to invest your money into this currency. White papers are generally the main means by which creators of a Cryptocurrency are able to legitimize their Cryptocurrency, and the best practice is to invest in a Cryptocurrency that has issued their white papers to you, all you would have to do then is to choose which one would you like to invest in. An ICO that offers no white papers to its investors is a practice that should be flagged and avoided.

What can you expect to read from a white paper- since we have established that this is a prospectus, this will contain the visions of what the creator expects their Cryptocurrency to be, and the technological aspect that makes this Cryptocurrency unique from the other Cryptocurrencies that are already on the Metaverse market. The unique selling proposition of the Cryptocurrency should highlight what problems in the virtual economy would this form of currency be able to resolve, and why this particular problem should be addressed, and why this Cryptocurrency can perform that task rather than the Cryptocurrencies that are already there in the first place. The white paper should also contain details on how this Cryptocurrency token will be distributed to those who have chosen to invest in it, and elaborate on the details on the creators of the said Cryptocurrency. The white paper should contain a timeline as to how the ICO will eventually lead into the launch of the Cryptocurrency. From the content, the language and the content of the white paper should be your main focus, and lastly, the white paper should elaborate on the development of the Cryptocurrency and the credentials of the developers behind it.

This is a crucial step in the determination to identify if you banked your money into the right investments. The white paper may be one of those that are professionally written, but key areas that you should focus your attention on relate to the vision of the creators, the people who have organized the ICO (where they have the necessary backgrounds on Cryptocurrencies or business), and the quality and language of the paper which is reflective of the content that it wishes to convey to the potential investor.

6.4 Conclusion

Investment in Cryptocurrencies, as with all other investments are not to be taken lightly despite their lack of tangible form, as their value is inherent to the success of your investments within the Metaverse. Given their critical role in the establishment of the virtual economy, it becomes necessary for the potential investor to ensure that the Cryptocurrency that they choose to finance is able to fill a necessary void within the marketplace of the virtual economy. The Metaverse was not only meant to be created for the sole purposes of entertainment and socialization, but a universe where transactions can be made without the processes of regulation by a central authority, and there are no centralized decisions that limit the transactions that are made. It is necessary then to determine the legitimacy of the Cryptocurrencies that anchor the virtual economy as this underlies the entirety of the structure of the virtual economy and helps the Metaverse flourish as a business entity, aside from its roles in the gaming industry.

7 INVESTMENTS IN THE METAVERSE

Investments in the Metaverse are governed through a series of codes embedded in Blockchains and Cryptocurrencies that ensure that each transaction that is contracted to the benefit of both parties, where these transactions are recorded in the form of a ledger that contains the details of these transactions – similar to how one would fulfill the obligations for a contract enacted in the physical world.

Before we delve into the investment and business aspect of the Metaverse, we need to touch on the impetus that fueled the growth of the Metaverse and made it a hotbed of economic growth in the present times. At the heart of the economy, whether virtual or physical, it was money. We were told repeatedly by our parents and teachers that we have to work hard that we may be able to prosper in our chosen careers. While this may have been true in the past, nowadays it becomes more onerous and near impossible to amass the finances needed to secure a home and be able to retire comfortably. With economic downturns that occur, it proves more difficult now to start a business unless you happen to be born rich, or win the lottery.

The virtual economy then became the proving ground for entrepreneurs and skilled individuals would be able to amass the resources needed without the need to sink a large amount of money that would serve as their start-up funds. There are several ways to earn within the virtual economy, and these include the more popular streaming sites, eSports (a rather lucrative business), skin designers (for games and other socialization sites, where some skins net you several advantages over ordinary skins that may be found in game), and level boosters (to gain more advantages as you play through a particular level). You may have interacted with the virtual economy at some point, especially if you are fond of games, through the use of various microtransactions that you have paid real money to purchase premium currencies so you can buy specialized items in the game. This is just an example of how the virtual economy actually works, but from the perspective of the layperson. More entrepreneurial individuals however, have a more complex means to invest and earn within the Metaverse, and content creation is just one among the several methods employed to carve out a niche within the digital world.

7.1 Business Areas of the Metaverse

It would be remiss to have a discussion on the virtual economy if we fail to include the catalyst that made it possible for developers to think that it is possible to earn within the virtual world. Yes, we are speaking of the game industries. When we speak of games, this is not in reference to the milder, yet completely solitary Solitaire and Hearts among other games. These are the games that are preferably known as dungeon crawlers, which, when paired with the use of the internet and the ability to interact with other players in real time through the game platform, it became possible to trade items, and currencies to different players across servers in the virtual world. These games, properly called Multi-User Dungeons became one of the earliest iterations of the virtual economy as this allowed the exchange of items in a virtual environment. From these Multi-User Dungeons came the dawn of the Massive Multi-Player Online Role-Playing Games such as

Warcraft- which allowed players from all over the world to interact with each other in a virtual space. Within this virtual space however, it became possible to engage with other players to trade weapons and other items in a virtual setting – although at this point it was not explicitly permitted by game developers, but the trades went on nonetheless. From here, more possibilities arose for creators to develop virtual goods to take advantage of the spike in the demand for various virtual items that can be used in games.

At this point, the creation of virtual goods (albeit still centered within games) rose to a billion dollar industry where not only was the creation of the virtual goods essential to the virtual economy, but also the troubleshooting of these virtual goods, the purchase of these virtual goods (especially if these are premium items), and the brokerage of virtual goods, became the forerunners of what would be the transactions within the virtual worlds then.

In 2003, the business applications within the Metaverse in its form then, diversified from the game industries and moved on to social platforms. Second Life became the pioneer social platform and retains some popularity until today, as one of the earliest forms of the Metaverse where people can interact outside of a game environment and where the population of the world in Second Life were able to transact businesses with other members of the world. Because of this, it became possible now to diversify the business applications from the game industries, to include collectible virtual items, virtual gambling, and even purchase real estate in digital cities that would serve as the nucleus for a virtual metropolis.

The possibilities within the virtual economy have experienced an increase, what with the pandemic that forced developers to conceptualize novel ways through which the average citizen would be able to earn in a virtual world. Not only did this include a variety of online transactions, but other transactions that are normally done in person (such as bills payment and food delivery) became part of the virtual economy through the use of digital wallets that hold a digitized form of our local currency.

Other business applications within the Metaverse take place in a variety of arenas. The first one would be the Closed Centralized Marketplace. From what we can gather in the earlier forms of the virtual economy, the earliest types of transactions took place between players of the same game within the same server. The same concept can be applied towards the Closed Centralized Marketplace where the rules are laid out by game developers as to the types of transactions that can take place within the marketplace. The presence of a singular developer that identifies the rules creates the centralized marketplace. Here, the creator has no say in the economy, and it is the discretion of the developers that allows the amount of an object that can be traded, and the price that other players are allowed to pay for it. Here, Cryptocurrencies do not form the backbone of the encapsulated virtual economy – it is the in-game currency such as gold, silver, diamonds and so on. These in-game currencies are the sole means to pay for virtual goods and services that take place within the server of the game, and are subject to the variations similar to our physical economy- inflations, deflations, economic bubbles and recessions. The virtual assets that can be traded in this type of marketplace include weapons, vehicles and real estate. The content created can come from either the game developer, t third-party developer, or even the players themselves. Because these assets are meant to be used within the specific environment of a game, a general rule in this marketplace is that these assets cannot be traded outside the marketplace, at least from a legal standpoint. There are black markets for these types of goods, but we will not touch on those.

Open Centralized Marketplaces provide another opportunity for businesses to take place within the Metaverse. Because this is open, the sale of virtual assets that were mentioned in the previous paragraph allow players and other users to trade game assets for actual currency, and allow users to exchange in-game currency for real money. These transactions usually take place within the platform of the game itself, where the marketplaces are still under the sway of the game developer, but it is more permissive in the types of transactions that it allows to take place. In this type of marketplace, game developers have realized the increased potential to earn if players had a more open environment where they could trade goods and exchange real money for in-game currency and vice-versa. This type of marketplace then fostered an improvement in the variety of virtual goods that are able to be sold, and created the need for financial institutions that enable these transactions to be recorded. Within the game platform of this type of marketplace, the purchase of virtual assets would be easily accomplished, and there are entrepreneurial purveyors who make it a business to acquire premium items within the game for a higher resale value. Virtual goods remain a key commodity here, however, unlike game transactions in the past, and in other platforms, these currencies do have an expiration point which compels the user to purchase more, or use the currencies to fuel the virtual economy within this type of marketplace.

Distributed Open Markets are described as decentralized in their organization and are not owned or controlled by a singular digital entity. Because of the lack of restrictions that were present in the closed and open centralized marketplaces, this allows content creators to have more freedom in the creation of the virtual assets that they wish to create. These assets have the added advantage in that they would be able to exist anywhere in cyberspace, where when compared to the assets made in the centralized marketplace, the assets created there are strictly used within the confines of the server. The virtual assets created in this type of market are able to be bought, licensed and distributed as one would do in the physical world, within decentralized markets.

What makes all of these markets run at its core, are the virtual assets that make for the tradable commodities within the virtual economy, and the tokens that represent these virtual assets. A token Is symbolic of the variations of virtual assets that exist throughout the Metaverse, and these carry specialized features such as access to premium services for a specific time period, which increases their value among the population of the Metaverse.

7.2 Metaverse Marketing

It would be an oversimplification of matters when we reduce the virtual economy of the Metaverse to the type of market economy that becomes the basis of economies in the physical world. The Metaverse itself for it to be marketable has to be composed of several distinct areas, which have their own inherent economies that are able to overlap with each other to form the entirety of the Virtual Economy that the Metaverse can be. As a result of these areas, there are several key points to invest within the Metaverse, where investors can go beyond the investments in Cryptocurrencies, and beyond the trade of the NFTs and Virtual Assets between players. To be able to understand key areas of investment within the Metaverse, it is important to approach this from the ground up, and we deal with its most basic structures needed to create the Metaverse.

The first and perhaps the most critical investment area in the Metaverse would be its infrastructure. In Chapter 2, we have touched upon the necessary requirements needed to create a fully functional Metaverse, and these include the need for a sustainable power source needed to keep the servers of the Metaverse active; the presence of internet speeds higher than what is already available; the use of micro-engineering to enable the creation of these components on a microscopic scale to let the Metaverse technology be available and affordable to the population, and the use of a variety of other servers that would link the most far-flung areas of the world to the Metaverse. We noted in Chapter 2, and it is reiterated here, that investments are needed to ensure that our current digital capacities are able to sustain the creation of a virtual world. Though the technology needed may be perhaps a decade in development, investments would enable the continued experimentation needed to create a more worthwhile product.

The next section of investment within the Metaverse refers to the Human Interface, and it is here that it becomes varied in its structure, as we go back to Chapters 3,4 and 5 to lay out the variety of hardware needed for the user to experience the completely immersive experience of the

Metaverse. These can include investments in the improvement of the sensory technology such as haptic technology, and the improvement of the HMDs that allows for an improved VR and AR experience for the user. Under the Human Interface aspect are the gadgets needed by users to access the Metaverse.

Decentralization is a necessary concept intended to make a free Metaverse for all users. This removes the restrictions and regulations for certain aspects such as the Virtual Economy mentioned in the previous section, and thus, it would enable more users to be freer with the content that they create and their ability to transact within the economy of the Metaverse. In line with the democratization of the Internet, decentralization of the internet ensures that everyone has a say in how the Metaverse is developed, and prevents a monopoly on the type of transactions and content that may take place within the platforms of the Metaverse.

Another area for investment involves the use of software, and this is another critical point in the structure of the Metaverse. When in reference to the software, this does not refer to the platforms through which the user can access the Metaverse, but rather, the software that allows the developer to shape the Metaverse such as the use of Modelling Tools, Video Recording, Artificial Intelligences to heighten the interactive experience and the recognition of gestures and language to ensure a more comprehensive interaction within the virtual world. This section is referred to as Spatial Computing, and this defines the parameters of the Metaverse, and allows the virtuality of the Metaverse to be experienced by all users.

The Creator Economy can be the backbone of the virtual economy, and these include investments in the creation of

NFTs, Cryptocurrencies and Virtual Assets, all of which can be traded and mined throughout the Metaverse. Aside from these, the creator economy includes the technologies needed to design assets, animate objects and monetize their creations. Because these are essentially assets that require some form of promotion within the Metaverse, another key area of investment is in the Discovery process.

Discovery is a truly simple process, and is key to the marketing process in the Metaverse and all other aspects of life. Take for instance that you have developed a revolutionary new app that addresses a problem that you feel that the world has. The first thing you would want to do is to craft a marketing strategy to let others know about your app. Investments in discovery can be as simple as the use of the Facebook Boost ads to allow your app to be promoted for a specific period of time to a certain number of people. This eventually transitions to the use of App Stores such as the Google Play Store that allows would be users to access your app. This is just a simplified version with other key players out there such as the use of Steam, Discord and Unity among other business solely devoted to the discovery process of the Metaverse.

Lastly, the key area for investments in the Metaverse would be the Experience Aspect. This involves the variety of platforms that allow the user to access the Metaverse, and these can include platforms such as Facebook, Zoom and Twitch, to more elaborate ones such as Fortnite, Blizzard and Meta. Here perhaps, is what allows the creator economy to flourish as these provide the platforms where the virtual economy can be truly engaged in by other users within the Metaverse. Aside from the trade in virtual assets and Cryptocurrencies, it becomes possible to trade digital services as well within the confines of the Metaverse and can heighten the customer service experience for business conglomerates for example, to be more interactive with the purchasing population.

7.3 Best Means to Invest in the Metaverse

It would be remiss to say that more attention has been allotted to the Metaverse ever since Facebook rebranded itself as Meta in 2021. The Metaverse has always existed as a universe alongside ours, with a variety of factors that hinder it from the fully realized Metaverse envisioned by the digital developers. Forbes magazine notes that investments in the Metaverse would revolutionize the way consumers do business and interact with other people. While it would not necessarily entail the purchase of shares from existent brands such as that of Facebook, there are other means to ensure that you are able to join in the investment processes that take place within the Metaverse. In Chapter 6, we have discussed how to properly invest in Cryptocurrencies, and you would have to carry over the same mentality with investments in the Metaverse. In the previous section, we have outlined the various sectors wherein you would be able to invest in the Metaverse, if Cryptocurrencies and other virtual assets don't really appeal to you in their current form. Blockchain platforms are more popular areas of investment due to the security afforded to every transaction that takes place between interested parties, and these allow for the continued trade of NFTs and Cryptocurrencies across platforms, which allow users to earn a lot of money, without the need to leave the computer. We have also touched on the importance to invest in the VR and AR Software needed by the Metaverse, so these are safe investments for you to invest funds in.

We go back to Cryptocurrencies, and we have touched upon the use of white papers as a means to safely gauge the legitimacy of the Cryptocurrency and the stability of the Cryptocurrency that is under development. This would be the safest practice if you invest in Crypto. Within the Metaverse however, a concrete strategy would entail the purchase of numerous NFTs. Why NFTs? Non-Fungible Tokens are a unique digital asset that no other inhabitant in the planet has, which make these very unique commodities that would fetch high prices for those who are in the business of their collection. This allows the investor to take part in the Blockchain where the NFT is anchored to.

Another area considered as a worthwhile investment (as much as it possibly can), is the Grayscale Decentraiized Token, but the requisites are quite pricey, as this requires a $25000 investment to be an accredited investor. The safest practices however, without complete reliance on the variations of the stocks on the tokens within the Metaverse include Cryptocurrency investments and investments in the creators of Blockchains such as Ethereum and SOL. More worthwhile investments, and the ones more likely to give you a solid return on your investment would be the infrastructure. After the investment in the infrastructure, you can begin to invest in the NFTs in various platforms and from there, you can invest in social tokens which are unique forms of Cryptocurrencies in themselves. Virtual Real Estate is another commodity that you can invest in, which would ensure that your investment begins to appreciate in its value.

Additional areas that are meant for the consideration for potential investors in the Metaverse have to do with the inclusion of exclusive online shopping. This is vastly different from your online shopping on Amazon and eBay, as this involves the sale of goods that can be exclusively used within the Metaverse. While initially it may seem frivolous and somewhat vain, we must take into account the importance of our virtual avatar within the Metaverse. As we are unable to physically insert ourselves within the Metaverse, our virtual avatars become the main means to establish our physical presence within the Metaverse, and thus appearances in this case matter.

Remote work was not initially thought of as a mainstay until the pandemic made it necessary to adapt to the available remote work options that were available online. As the pandemic continues to progress, remote work remains one of the areas where you could potentially invest in, as it is unlikely that It would disappear, as more and more businesses gradually transition from physical set-ups to a remote work environment. Key developers that focus on the creation of the virtual workspace include Facebook and Microsoft Teams which begins to implement the use of digital avatars in its application, expected to happen within the first half of 2022.

7.4 The Key Players of the Metaverse Domain

Now that we have identified the key industries where you could invest your earnings in, and the best practices to keep in mind as you mull over your investment options, you will need to keep your pulse on the most important developers, since, as of this writing, these are the major developers that every investor must keep an eye on as the Metaverse begins to develop and mature in its appearances. If you have watched the news recently, you will recall the attention that Facebook had gotten as it rebranded itself to Meta – which signified its intention to take part in the development of the Metaverse. This aside, there is a catch to be considered, in that with the wide variety of fields that are within the Metaverse, which developers can be truly considered key players as each developer has their own specialized niche within the Metaverse.

Take for example, the development of NFTs that contain virtual assets and other forms of unique, virtual content, OpenSea is believed to be considered as a key player in that it was able to secure the necessary funds for its continued operation in the development and trade of more virtual assets as NFTs. In the realm of Telehealth as it relates to the Metaverse, there is Virtuleap. It can be said that both Meta and Microsoft are the more prominent developers of the Metaverse. There are other developers however, that investors may consider as integral to the development of the Metaverse. Active Theory is a Metaverse developer that focuses on accessibility and inclusivity of the Metaverse to all consumers as it promotes the use of websites, wherein the Metaverse can be accessible through the use of a URL which does not require the need to download potentially heavy apps, or an extensive tutorial to start interactions within the Metaverse.

Amazon Web Services (AWS) is integral to the Metaverse as this engages in the cloud platform needed to store the data of users as they access the Metaverse. It is believed that AWS would be able to cope with the increased internet speed required to run the servers of the Metaverse. While Microsoft Azure was meant for the use of enterprises, AWS would be able to sustain the infrastructure of platforms that are able to withstand high risk environments.

Decentraland is a virtual platform sustained by the Ethereum Blockchain where content creators can develop the virtual assets that are needed by users that they would be able to interact with it and be able to earn from the creation and sale of these assets. In its current state, it becomes possible for the investor to not only purchase the NFTs that are present, but also obtain the virtual real estate that we have touched on, as well as the tokens needed for the premium content within the platform, three prized commodities that form excellent investments.

Dapper Labs specializes in the creation of NFTs that are comparable to sport memorabilia. Beyond this however, this same developer provides investors who wish to invest in a particular niche to have a say in how their shared niches can be developed. Additionally, aside from sports memorabilia, the NFTs can also consist of virtual items that can be used by our virtual avatars to facilitate interoperability across different Metaverse platforms.

Epic Games is best known as the developer of Fortnite, and as we have reiterated, Fortnite can be considered a proto-Metaverse, and thus, it is no surprise that its developer is a key player in the development of the Metaverse as one of the platforms that comes closest to the simulation of the actual idealized Metaverse. Investors should know that though Epic Games is well known for Fortnite, it aims to diversify its environments to allow for shared virtual experiences (such as their virtual concert), and it allows its users to create digital avatars, customize their environments and create their own content. Another aspect relates to the software needed to run the Metaverse, as Unreal Engine allows for the creation of other applications and visual effects that can be added to the Metaverse.

Madeium is an independent ecosystem that functions on multiple blockchains that is suited for businesses that focus on the creative industries. A Peer to Peer System allows content creators to flourish in an environment where there are no mandates imposed by a particular authority, or a corporation. This is best suited for those who wish to take part in the creation of the Metaverse for the sake of the expression of their creativity, not from the amount of money that could be obtained from it. This allows creators to access the tools needed to empower them to create all that they want.

NVIDIA is known for the manufacture of computer parts, and needless to say, it forms part of the infrastructure of the Metaverse, as well as the hardware needed to let the user interface with the Metaverse to promote interactions with it. What makes NVIDIA a key player is the development of the NVIDIA Omniverse Platforms which links three-dimensional, virtual and augmented realities. This allows for the creation of a photorealistic environment and enhances the quality of collaborations between engineers and developers to develop a Metaverse that is entirely similar to our own physical world. NVIDIA also has stakes in the promotion of interactions, streaming services, and workstation sharing. The avatars which it has dubbed Omniversal allow interaction through speech, computer vision and the processing of natural language. NVIDIA perhaps can be considered as one of the heavier key players in this section due to its importance in virtually every aspect of the Metaverse.

Synthesis AI is a key player in the Metaverse in that it focuses on the enhancement of the virtual experience through the use of tools that allow for realistic interactions within the Metaverse. Human API in particular remains worthy of consideration in that this allows for the creation of advanced AI models that heighten the quality of the virtual interactions to the point it creates the illusion of physical interaction.

These are just some of the key players in the Metaverse, and investors should keep a close eye on these, and see which of these spark their interests. This list was not meant to be a constant since as the Metaverse develops, the importance of each player may rise and fall in proportion with the rate of development of the Metaverse.

7.5 Where you should invest your money?

As to where you can safely invest your money, this is entirely up to your discretion, though a basic rule is that it would be safest to invest in the infrastructure of the Metaverse, and the companies that begin to develop the needed hardware and software for the Metaverse. These are considered solid investments and would guarantee at least, that the particular feature that you chose to invest in, would always be needed in the Metaverse. If this does not pique your interest a more prudent approach would include investments in various NFTs, or in the creation of NFTs. The purchase of NFTs, Tokens and unique Virtual Assets would provide you with the highly prized commodities sought in the virtual marketplace. A look through the guides established in the previous sections would help you narrow down the best path for your investments. All that needs to be done now is to determine which section of the Metaverse are you most comfortable with, where you feel that your money would work for you, and where you feel you would be able to weather the ups and downs of the prices of your investment. We spoke in Chapter 6 about the requirements you would have to undertake before you commit to investment, and ultimately, the investment you would choose has to be one you are comfortable with, and where you feel your money would be safest. If you prefer a more constant investment, you would never be wrong with investments made in the infrastructure of the Metaverse, and the hardware and software companies. If you have a lot of extra cash to invest, you could take the risk and invest in Cryptocurrencies.

7.6 Other methods to earn in the Metaverse

What fuels the Metaverse, and its unique economy involves the creation of virtual assets. In recent news, you may have read about the student who has managed to support his college studies through the conversion of his daily selfie pics into NFTs which managed to net him approximately a million dollars-worth of earnings through the sale of his pictures. This is just one of the numerous ways you can earn within the Metaverse if you choose not to go through the investment route, but you would have to be of a creative or highly technical bent, as though you would not dabble in the investment of stocks, you may consider investments in the experiences of the Metaverse. Part of the experience aspect include the ability to create virtual items, which makes content creators, especially the really skilled ones, able to monetize their passion and create unique items that can be sold within the Metaverse for high prices. As these assets can be converted into NFTs, which increases their price and value among the population of the Metaverse, it would be a lucrative business opportunity for would be creators to create distinct and rare digital assets that would be unique to each person who purchases these. NFTs are among the safer investments and you can consider investments in these.

Another way to earn would be through the participation in activities within the Metaverse. Gamers in particular, as well as eSports fans would be familiar with this concept, as several developers have created environments where various participants in the Metaverse can congregate, and complete several tasks to get the chance to win a lot of prize money. Some of the earnings have reached up to a million dollars at the most, and a hundred thousand at the least. If this tickles your fancy, and you want a chance to let loose and at the same time, earn big, then this is one of the ways that you can earn.

A less spoken of option would be the purchase of virtual real estate, similar to how real estate developers would purchase large tracts of land and develop these to create condominiums that they can resell. While virtual real estate has yet to integrate the construction of similar structures, virtual real estate is one of those concepts that begins to gain ground as time passes by. Virtual real estate can be compared to physical real estate in that it would appreciate in value over time, which makes it a good way to earn – if you choose to sell your parcel of land, or a worthwhile investment – if you choose to hold on to it.

7.7 Conclusion

The Metaverse, similar to our physical world, is a place rife with business opportunities for investors who wish to earn from it, or be able to earn in it. Multiple avenues exist for business within the Metaverse, and this chapter would provide a guide on how to best use the investment opportunities that exist within the virtual world. There are other ways to earn within the Metaverse, and while this has been detailed in the preceding section, eCommerce begins to evolve while in the Metaverse, and the next chapter would narrate how this changes the way we would do business online.

8 E-COMMERCE AND THE METAVERSE

We have touched upon the creation of the Metaverse, as well as the various infrastructure needed to sustain its structure, and the hardware and software that permit us to access it. Throughout the chapters of this book, we have touched upon the games that became the forerunners of the Metaverse, and how from these games, we have managed to create a semblance of a virtual economy that led to the possibility of expanded business opportunities in another universe altogether. The importance of investments in the NFTs, Virtual Assets, and Virtual Real Estate, as well as the Cryptocurrencies that populate the Metaverse now have become the impetus for the growth of the virtual economy. As with all businesses however, it becomes necessary to go into the necessary sales talk to permit the expansion of the Metaverse. We have briefly glimpsed the importance of sales in the Metaverse when we have reached the topic of white papers, which serve as the briefer for the investor, and convinces the potential investor to take a chance on the Cryptocurrency that was written in the White Paper. Now this aside, this has opened up a plethora of opportunities where marketing becomes an essential part of the virtual economy, and allows the expansion of options for what can be done, business-wise, within the Metaverse.

While we may have seen numerous virtual ads and boosted Facebook posts as we scroll through our timeline, this is just a fraction of what eCommerce within the Metaverse is all about. The Metaverse aside, there are reasons why certain cities such as New York, London and Tokyo became known as business hubs, and you would be able to find a lot of businesses and industries with their headquarters there. These are cities with business hours that take place at virtually any time, as they would have to communicate with other businesses across different time zones. Subsequently. Because the Metaverse operates on the same basis, this becomes one of the main reasons why the Metaverse is an ideal area where marketing, and those engaged in the business in marketing, would be in their element. To marketers, the Metaverse is a constantly active hive of activity, which co-exists at the same times with our physical world, where each user is able to function independently. The Metaverse is a self-contained environment, which is able to generate virtual assets created by a variety of content creators.

8.1 Sales in the Metaverse

How did the Metaverse become the latest hotbed for economic growth? We have mentioned that it is decentralized, it allows for a more democratized approach to the use of the internet, and allows for the free creation of more content by users, aside from those content generated by developers. Marketers of the online variety have flocked to the Metaverse as they view the Metaverse as a new environment where several marketing ploys would prove to be fruitful and expedient as they can take direct advantage of the high speed internet infrastructure that forms part of the Metaverse. Subsequently, this allows the marketers to boost their product within the Metaverse, and they would be able to interact with interested parties in real time. More importantly, the digital aspect of the Metaverse aside, the marketers would be more in tune with the pulse of the Millennials and Gen Z population, who are the likely purveyors of the content within the Metaverse, and also are the ones who show a marked interest in the products that are sold in the marketplaces of the Metaverse. The Metaverse, in this instance functions not only as the environment where sales can take place, but it is the very tool that fuels the sales needed by marketers. It can be said that the Metaverse sells itself, and that would be important if it wishes to expand. While we know that the internet can lead to a multitude of connection to various individuals, where brand awareness – important to online marketers and therefore, crucial to sales, can be readily done. If you have seen the sequel to Wreck-It Ralph, you can perhaps, gain an inkling of how interactions with marketing could potentially take place, as it would be possible that within the Metaverse, you would be able to see various brands everywhere, like a billboard in Times Square.

The Metaverse has transcended its association with the gaming world and has begun to progress into a more diversified portfolio that focuses more on real-life situations, to include the development of a diversified economy beyond game microtransactions. The Metaverse then becomes a place full of potential to garner the sales that are actually needed by businesses who wish to remain relevant to the successive generations that are able to access the Metaverse.

8.2 The Future of Sales in the Metaverse

Contemporarily, it is necessary to retain the importance of brand awareness in sales, and the use of the Metaverse as a marketing tool in itself. Because of the novelty of the Metaverse, and it has yet to be fully developed, businesses that are more avant-garde in their marketing approaches can take advantage of the Metaverse and launch digital ad campaigns that would be able to reach a large population. However, to flourish in an innovative environment, it is necessary too, to be innovative in the way you approach potential customers for sales. The standbys of past ads must be done away with, and the marketer would have to develop a wholly unique concept that users in the Metaverse can automatically associate with the brand that is marketed.

There are other opportunities for the promotion of eCommerce within the Metaverse that do not rely exclusively on the sale of Cryptocurrencies and NFTs. We touch on several key areas where marketers may employ the full brunt of their marketing abilities.

Virtual Reality is the key to the Metaverse, and it would be essential to the success of the marketing campaign to harness the use of the Virtual World. It not only becomes an instant platform to raise brand awareness among your potential customers, but it also allows them to engage on a level that remains unprecedented, where they would be able to take part in the promotion of the product and determine the final form of the product that is marketed and under development. Needless to say, this type of approach would best appeal to the Millennial and Gen Z crowd, as they would be more likely to take a hands on approach with the development of products – as evinced by the number of surveys in apps for instance, that take into account suggestions from its users.

Augmented Reality, which we have touched on earlier in this book, provides another marketing opportunity in that, through the virtual overlay that is added to the physical environment, it becomes possible to enhance the interactive experience of your customers, where they would be able to learn more about a particular product if they interact with it. As we have mentioned that augmented reality would be the more affordable option due to its interoperability with other hand held devices, this would be a marketing opportunity that would reach a greater portion of the population. How would this work? If the customer used their phone's camera to scan a store for instance, the items would be overlaid with virtual versions of themselves that provide additional information that allows the customers to experience the item without actually touching the item. An immersive experience that would increase the likelihood of purchase by the customers.

We go once more into the concept of Brand Awareness, and this can include the use of virtual billboards, and even the virtual items that our virtual avatars wear, similar to how we would wear items with a brand logo, except that this would carry more unique options. Here it is unavoidable that we have to integrate the use of the NFTs as these are more likely to integrate the specialized virtual content that increases the value of the product that is marketed. Through the use of NFTs, it becomes possible for the marketer to launch their products into niches that their products would not be ordinarily present at, such as through the use of digital artworks that form a large percentage of NFTs.

Marketers can also enjoy the use of the Virtual Popup, which is similar to a physical pop-up store in that it permits the marketer to interact and network with their customers in the Metaverse. Because of its virtual nature, the marketer would be able to reach a wider audience that is not limited to their locale, and can theoretically reach every person who has access to the internet. This would be a more cost effective measure as this lessens the need to create the physical aspect of the store, cuts off the need to pay rent, hire people and decrease overall expenses which can make the product sold more affordable to customers, now that the overhead has been substantially decreased.

The Virtual Boardroom and Classroom have become a staple of daily life ever since the pandemic hit, and the more astute marketer can see this as another opportunity to market items within this section of the Metaverse. Here, the virtual boardroom and classrooms become a focal point where you can immerse potential customers into the capabilities of the marketed product. Marketers at this stage would be able to teach customers about the product and give them a test demo as to how this product would actually work. This provides additional marketing opportunities as this would be the ideal platform for an employee onboarding process, particularly if the marketer would need to add additional personnel to help get the word about their product out there.

Concerts are prime marketing opportunities, regardless of their location, and as a result, concerts and other virtual events within the Metaverse provide a wider opportunity to raise brand awareness and provide perfect sites for product placement. Much like virtual classrooms, marketers and other companies can host their own events and ensure that their product becomes the more prominent focus of the event- much like Tupperware parties focused on the sale of the product for instance.

8.3 Conclusion

The Metaverse is an entirely new concept wherein companies and marketers have a whole new area to spread awareness about their particular brand. Because the Metaverse is a universe that never sleeps, and that never rests, this provides a prime marketing opportunity to reach customers on an unprecedented level. Subsequently, while the Metaverse is still in its developmental stages, it becomes necessary to seize advantage of the environment where others are hesitant to enter. This would allow marketers and other business to get the drop over other competitors who would be hesitant to use the Metaverse itself as a marketing tool, even though it lends itself well to the use of eCommerce and sales. The longevity of the internet, bodes well for marketing opportunities, as you would be able to place your product no matter where you are in the world, and that you would be able to reach the greatest possible amount of customers at the lowest and most cost-effective prices. All it takes, to repeat what was said in Chapter 7, is the determination to take a certain amount of risk, for an end result that will potentially pay off for the company and marketer who take that risk.

9 LEGALITIES AND REAL WORLD ISSUES

At the beginning of this book, we have mentioned that the Metaverse was intended to function similarly to our physical world, with the key institution of decentralization that removes certain restrictions in the operations of businesses. However, the removal of all of these regulations can potentially raise some legal issues with regards to the transactions that take place within the Metaverse. Earlier, we have also stated that the Metaverse was intended to democratize the internet and shift control from the technological giants into the hands of the general population. This prevents a group of entities from the ability to impose a set of restrictions that could potentially curtail the creative freedoms of those who take part in the Metaverse. However, the idea of too much freedom would pose several issues, particularly legal issues.

In the physical world, legislators have crafted laws and constitutions that outline what the citizens of each nation are permitted to do, and what they are forbidden to do. While certain freedoms are allowed, this also restricts certain aspects within the physical world, such as the ability to open up a business (what with all the bureaucratic red tape), the amount of taxes that must be paid to advertise (which in itself is restricted in the name of fair competition), and the methods that can be employed to market certain items. There are too the impositions of tariffs and other forms of tax in the exercise of the power of taxation of the government, and the regulation of certain practices which serve as the exercise of the police power of our national governments.

The Metaverse in this instance would permit an increased sense of freedom. However, freedom itself must be regulated to ensure that the Metaverse remains a wholesome and completely legal environment for the remainder of the users of the Metaverse.

9.1 Potential Snags in the Metaverse

Among the foremost legal issues that will be prevalent within the Metaverse have to do with intellectual property rights, due to the increased accessibility afforded to various users within the Metaverse. If you go through the internet, you would be able to find areas where you can obtain free access to virtually anything that you would search for. However, while it would be great to get items for free, rather than to shell out funds, there are issues which would deprive the creators of these items from the royalties that they are entitled to as the creators of these items.

Patents are one of the legal snags encountered within the Metaverse. Federal Law of the United States provides that the first person who creates a novel, unobtrusive invention where the patent is granted is entitled to have a monopoly for that type of creation for two decades. The issue with the Metaverse, is that, other versions of a particular product, or indeed, other platforms of the Metaverse itself, would remain subject to patent and intellectual property disputes, regardless of the developer, as at this point, due to the continuous evolution of the Metaverse, it would be difficult to identify who would be the first person to have come up with the idea, as each idea presented in the Metaverse would be unique in itself. A landmark case adjudged by the United States Supreme Court noted that the implementation of a software that related to escrow arrangement could not be patented as this was an abstract idea. With due consideration to the Metaverse that it is an abstract idea, this could prove to be a potential pitfall on the patents that protect the Metaverse.

Copyright Law is another concept that would continue to be infringed upon regardless of the various legalities that would secure the intellectual property rights of the affected party. The question that relates to the Metaverse is whether or not the copyrighted software that forms part of the Metaverse was infringed by another software.

Contract law is one of the messier parts of the laws that relate to the Metaverse. Smart Contracts would fall under this legal concern, as this would entail the need to identify the parties who have rights to certain parts of the Metaverse. Contracts in this instance, have to be clear in their construction to allow legal issues of ownership to be clearly resolved. In the Metaverse particularly, this would help relieve issues of interoperability between various Metaverse platforms to ensure that users would remain unaffected by the legal tangles that prohibit the use of certain components purely because they are the subject of a litigious process.

Copyright Act serves to protect the unique content of the Metaverse from unauthorized duplication by a third party. The construction of the Copyright Act provides protection for the owners of original creations from third parties who would seek to copy the copyrighted creation. However, fair use policies are often utilized as a defense for these parties who seek to use copyrighted software. This defense is not absolute in that this would immediately absolve the liabilities of the party that copied the original work. As with other defenses, this is dependent on the circumstances that govern the fair use policy and the copyrighted material. Another area of concern with regards to the copyright act, are the digital twins, such as iconic landmarks. Though these form part of the structure of the Metaverse, these can never be copyrighted under the provisions of the Copyright Act, as the likenesses of these buildings have been copyrighted by the original owners of the buildings themselves.

The liabilities under the copyright act as it relates to the Metaverse function differently. In a case sample, a person who inserts a copyrighted material into a particular section would be liable for the breach of copyright law. The Metaverse developer into which the copyrighted material was inserted would bear no part in the liability incurred, and would not be a party to any lawsuits that result from the copyrighted material. The Digital Millennium Copyright Act, provides the defense needed by the Metaverse developer, under the safe-harbor provisions outlined under the said act. Takedown notice provisions under the same Digital Millennium Copyright Act allow third parties to remove the copyrighted material within the Metaverse.

Trademark law safeguards against the unauthorized use of trademarks in such a way that a reasonably prudent consumer would be the subject of deception that leads them to think that the owner of the trademarked material was the point of origin for the defective or counterfeit item, or that the owner of the trademark endorsed the production of the said defective or counterfeit material. Within the Metaverse, where it becomes extremely likely to create exact replicas of luxury items for instance, this may result in losses for the company who have never given their assent for the use of their product in such a manner. In the event that an enterprising user manages to insert a copyrighted and trademarked material into the Metaverse, and that they were able to sell this particular item for a high price and successfully pull off the deception that the item sold was part of the genuine trademark, then this scenario would create a question of fact. Though the Digital Millennium Copyright Act has a safe harbor provision that would prevent the liability of the Metaverse developer; the Metaverse developer would also be protected from copyright infringement claims filed against them if they could prove that they were unaware of the insertion of the copyrighted material into their domain, or if they have exercised their due diligence and have taken the steps needed to remove the copyrighted material from their domain once they were made aware of its existence. The issue that arises would be whether or not the use of the imported trademarked item by the user within the Metaverse constitutes trademark infringement, which in itself needs to be sufficiently proven.

The Federal Trademark Anti-Dilution Act is an area of concern within the Metaverse, allows the owners to trademarks to sue if the trademark that was used in an ad campaign or product brand was tarnished by a third party. The act becomes applicable whether or not there was confusion that resulted among the consumers as to the origin of the trademarked items, or other items that bear the trademarked insignia. This however, makes it more of a copyright claim rather than an issue of trademarks. To forestall this, it would be a prudent practice for the developers of the Metaverse to exclude distinctive and well-known trademarks within their advertisements, especially trailers, online advertisements and the landing page of the Metaverse developer's website.

The Right of Publicity is another legal concern within the Metaverse, as this allows the existence of a prima facie case against anyone if they use someone else's name or likeness while in the Metaverse. This is an issue because this can encompass a large population as liability is attained on the grounds of the alias of the complainant, or a look=alike, or a voice imitation. One concern with this law is that its application is not concise, and Is heavily dependent upon the interpretations of each state that chooses to invoke the right of publicity. What can be done however, is to ensure that the online persona is transformative in nature, as it will be protected by state legislation that protects works of expression, and the states that provide protection for transformative works. A legal issue would be, whether or not the Metaverse developer would be liable if the user imports the persona of a third-party into the Metaverse? We go back once more to the use of the safe harbor provision of the DMCA, as this provision does not protect companies that function as online hosts. There is some debate on the implication of the Communications Decency Act as to whether or not it protects these online hosting companies from lawsuits that arise from the right of publicity. The safest practice would be to assume that the Metaverse company could be held liable for lawsuits that involve the right of publicity, and this involves the precaution to prevent the use of online personas that are similar to celebrities in particular.

9.2 Legalities of the Digital Domains

Personal injuries are among the main issues that could relate now to the domain of the Metaverse. Recall that in Chapters 3 and 4 that the Metaverse was meant to be a wholly immersive experience under VR, and a partially immersive experience under the AR Technology. Now, take for instance that the environment was sufficiently altered in such a way that you forgot the layout of your home and fell down a flight of stairs while wearing your HMD. Another scenario would be, if the user was currently engaged in a horror game (try not to test this out), and if the jumpscares were of such a horrific (in this case – it was really convincing) that the user suffered some sort of heart problem, who would bear liabilities for injuries that resulted from this use of the Metaverse?

Physical injuries are not the only potential area for concern within the Metaverse as it is entirely possible that there would be invasions of privacy. In 2021, we have read in the news about breaches into the data security of several sites, which include the sites related to social media, which in turn created an outage of their services. Take this scenario, and apply it to the data obtained in the breach, and if it was sold to a third-party. While our constitution guarantees our right to privacy, the true question here now, is are we truly afforded that right within the Metaverse? There are damages to be awarded, there is no question about it. The question that is present now, is who would be liable for the damages to a user, if their personal data was among those obtained by hackers in a data breach, or if the developer or platform sold the information to these advertisers? Recall that to be truly active in the Metaverse, it would require a certain amount of invasion in that certain aspects of your body would be scanned, and your mannerisms adopted. This is more than just data, this is your life that has been reasonably mimicked with the help of computer software, and this would prove dangerous for you as well. While this should not turn you against the Metaverse, as the developers have exercised a prudent amount of caution with the protection of your data, this should at least allow you to be careful as to what you do share in the Metaverse. There are class action suits after all for violations of privacy and the unauthorized use of personal data. This would give you some food for thought particularly since the internet in our smartphones for instance, seems to be able to adapt to our thoughts.

On the part of the Metaverse developer, it is entirely possible to protect themselves from such class actions suits and other potential lawsuits that may arise from a variety of causes of action. While this will not completely extinguish the liability of the Metaverse developer, it can limit the amount that they can be held liable for. The terms of service that we agree to prior to the use of the Metaverse platform would have to be more thorough and exact in its construction to ensure that arbitration and class action waivers on the part of the user are taken into account. Case precedents for contracts that have been consummated online provide that users must agree with the terms provided for in the terms and services of the Metaverse platform before they can engage with its services. This is tantamount to an agreement signified online and would protect the developer from excessive liabilities. On the part of the user, it would be best perhaps, to read the fine print before you engage in a particular platform.

9.3 Lookouts for Future Iterations

Because the Metaverse was developed to be a fully immersive environment, a reasonable expectation to be had is that this environment would be conducive to the same types of offenses that currently exist in the physical world. Theft for instance, takes a whole new definition as the digital world makes it possible for more than your wallet to be stolen, your identity may fall victim to these unscrupulous individuals as well. Perhaps, a more critical concern, would be the occurrence of traumatic events.

Let us take this particular scenario, where, in our virtual avatars, we can look whatever the way we want, regardless of our actual physical appearance. Now, imagine a world, where everyone was in their idealized form, and where everyone feels more comfortable in their socializations. There is the potential for sexual harassment, which has transcended from the sending of rather lewd pictures, to acts of lasciviousness that were actually performed in the virtual world. If you happened to know the perpetrator, that would be great. Chances are however, there are those who prefer to remain masked and use the cloak of anonymity afforded by their persona in the Metaverse, and you would be unable to find who they are immediately. As with rape victims and victims of sexual harassment, it is possible for the person to have some form of post-traumatic stress disorder, which can really disturb the psyche and emotions of a vulnerable individual. The more disturbing question is, if the Metaverse developers knew that such acts were going on, would they have been able to prevent it? Or would they simply turn a blind eye onto such occurrences? Theft for instance, with regards to NFTs, can also be considered. Blockchains may protect Cryptocurrencies from such an occurrence but who is to say that other virtual assets may not have been subjected to theft as well.

Where the Metaverse seeks to replicate the good in the universe, in our world, and encapsulate the beauty of it; it is also another world, where offenses such as those in the preceding paragraph may find themselves in with an advantage of digital anonymity. Suffice it to say that when developers create the Metaverse, they not only create what is beautiful, they can also bring in the nastier elements of the real world such as the opportunities for crime. Therefore, it would be expected that users would be able to file lawsuits against each other. The question now lies, as to whether or not the Metaverse would share in the liability? And a question of jurisdiction of these law suits as well, especially if the perpetrators come from other parts of the world, unacquainted with the aspects of digital law.

9.4 Conclusion

The Metaverse in its inception was meant to be similar to the physical world, but in a metaphysical sense, developers may have captured the good, but there are always the negative elements from the physical world that make their way into the Metaverse itself. Freedom is an ideal which we all could live by, but there are certain regulations that are needed to ensure that the world, and subsequently the Metaverse, remains a safe place for everyone, and for all people. Digital Law that relates to the Metaverse is never constant, as the digital world continues to adapt, and therefore the laws that apply to it must adapt as well, lest they become obsolete in their interpretation and allow for a more lax application that can overlook the occurrence of certain offenses such as trademark and copyright laws, as well as the potential for torts and damages amongst the citizens of the Metaverse. While we do not have to be lawyers to be truly aware of the Metaverse, we just have to be more cautious in our actions within the Metaverse to ensure that we too remain protected under the auspices of our laws.

10 Avatars of the Metaverse

Before the inception of the Metaverse, or indeed, any form of social media, the earliest iteration of avatars existed first in the gaming industry in that these were the virtual representations of the player (ourselves) into the virtual world that was created. For the long-time gamers, there was the initial thrill of choosing which character you would want to play as when you enter a game. Fantasy games could have your avatar be a warrior, a rogue or a sorcerer; First-person shooters can allow you choose from a series of pre-designed avatars that would represent you while you are in a solo level or if you are in a server connected game. These forms of avatars can be considered the earliest iterations of the virtual representation of ourselves in the virtual world. However, the use of these avatars were solely limited towards the use of games, and not much else.

In the first decade of the new millennium, before the conceptualization of Facebook, users of Yahoo Messenger would recall the specialized feature of Yahoo Avatars. While this did not allow for in game representation and were limited in what they can do, they did allow some form of customization to let users customize the appearance of their avatar, and use these to interact in the chat rooms that once populated Yahoo Messenger. At this point, customized avatars became possible not only in the use of games, but also in the earlier iterations of social media, where they functioned merely as your point of interaction within the virtual world.

To tie this with the Metaverse, the use of the virtual avatar, would in essence retain the same functionality in that it is our representation in the Metaverse, through it we would be able to interact with the general population within the Metaverse and take part in all of the activities within it. Because we cannot physically transport our bodies into the Metaverse, the avatar becomes important as our main contact point into how we, as users, interact with the Metaverse. To fully comprehend the potential of our avatars, we must first understand what it means to fully immerse ourselves into the virtual world.

10.1 What it means to Go Virtual

Suffice it to say that we opt for the more virtual representation of ourselves, rather than the physical aspect, as it can be seen that not everyone was built the same, and that's okay. The world would be a boring place if everyone shared the same characteristics, and in the name of diversity, that would always be a good idea. The creation of our virtual identities, stems from the need to be socially accepted.

Time was, the game obsessed person would be picked on, or the secret gamer would have to hide their favorite past time for fear of stereotypes and labels. The virtual world became a portal through which the suppressed can live out their fantasies (the positive ones), and be able to interact with others through virtual personas that are reflective of how they see themselves, or how they want to be portrayed. The virtual world became a place then for social acceptance, where people would be free to interact without the social classifications that would normally bar a person from the usual way of their interactions. When the user, through their virtual avatar, gains social acceptance, then trust begins to build up, and when there is trust, the user would begin to interact within the virtual world and potentially increase the rate of interactions. Even in the contemporary age, where it is commonplace for people of all social classes to virtually interact, the use of a virtual avatar only serves to heighten the quality of interactions within the Metaverse. It would not be strange to see the virtual avatar of a person online, at this point, we have seen some form of virtual avatar on social media, and by this time, we have interacted with this at some point as well.

Yet it would be important to understand the impact of the virtual avatar outside from its applications in games and in social media. It was reported that in the earlier portions of 2022, Microsoft Teams would begin the integration of virtual avatars into the meeting rooms on their MS Teams App. This entails that the use of the virtual avatar would gradually expand into the education and business sectors, and become the focal point of interaction between teacher and student, employer and employee, and other relationships in between. Thus, the virtual avatar would gain several advantages (in a more humorous note, if the roll out of the virtual avatar does become fully implemented, it would save the morning rush to put on a business top or a uniform and allow you to gain a few more minutes of sleep), in that it would enhance the quality of the virtual classroom and the virtual workplace, to increase the types of interactions that can take place in these rooms. The main flaw in this in that, for these experiences to be fully realized, it is essential that the users would have to have the necessary peripherals to execute the experience.

Yet with the advantages, we must also draw attention to the greatest disadvantages. If you have an avatar, you will understand that with customization, it becomes possible to be virtually different from who you actually are. You can be any person, of any race, and of any gender, and this gives any user a certain degree of anonymity. The virtual world is not necessarily a wholesome place, and where avatars in the right hands could be the focal point of virtual interactions, avatars too can be the weak point that allows cybercrimes to proliferate within the Metaverse, and unless the appropriate safeguards have been implemented, this anonymity may be an opportunity for other crimes to be committed within the Metaverse itself. As a result, it must be impressed that with the development of the virtual avatar within the Metaverse, while it can allow for customization of appearances, it should not allow for absolute anonymity to ensure the continued safety of the Metaverse.

This aside, it would seem that regardless of the current state of the Metaverse, the virtual avatar would remain a quintessential part of socialization, as through our virtual avatars, we can fully enjoy the virtual experience, and take part in more shared experiences with other people. It would take some time for the virtual avatar to transcend its aesthetic usage, and become an instrument that allows us to exist in another universe altogether. It is the use of these avatars then that allow the monetization of the avatar within the virtual economy setup in the Metaverse.

10.2 The Effect of the Avatar

While this may sound like a movie sequel to Avatar: The Last Airbender, or James Cameron's Avatar, we cannot deny the effects that a virtual identity has afforded to users. There is an increase in the amount of time that we spend online, and perhaps in a digital environment, one can sometimes forget the rest of the world when fully immersed into the virtual world. While the activities in the Metaverse remain the main draw for most users, the length of time that they stay in is a different idea altogether. With a virtual identity that allows you to customize your appearance, and allows you to explore a world on your own terms, perhaps the allure of the Metaverse and the virtual avatar is in its appeal to our instincts, where we can shape ourselves, and be exactly who we want to be. This is not one of those metaphysical ideas where we discuss the potential of our existence, but a more superficial approach where the user takes on their idealized forms.

A certain effect attributed to the use of the virtual avatar is called a Proteus Effect, named after the Greek sea god, Proteus, who was famed for his ability to change shape (if you have read the Odyssey, you definitely get the idea). The Proteus Effect narrates the effect of our avatars appearance into how we would actually behave in the physical world, which entails that there is a blurred definition now, into how our interactions in the virtual world spillover into the physical world. Some studies into the Proteus effect detail that more physically attractive virtual avatars could lead to a more confident, and more intimate reaction in the user as they interact in the physical world. Additionally, avatars with a height advantage result in users who are more dominant and assertive in their interactions. The ability to customize appearance is not solely limited to the physical characteristics of the user, but rather, can expand into the clothing. Studies into the Proteus Effect have noted that with the ability to adapt a more professional look, ideal for their real world profession, this has led into a productivity boost, as well as a confidence boost that leads into the idealized stereotype for that profession. Physicians for instance are able to make decisions faster when clothed with a more professional look, and the typical office worker gains a productivity boost when their virtual avatar is suitably attired.

The Proteus Effect is important in that it determines the quality of the interactions within the Metaverse. This means that if we are more confident or self-assured in our virtual persona, we may be more likely to integrate these characteristics into our actual behavior. Because interactions are what fuel the growth and expansion of the Metaverse, developers of virtual avatars can expect that a large chunk of the virtual economy would be devoted to the improvement of the interactive quality of the virtual avatars, and, this becomes a point where the customization of the virtual avatar becomes part of the virtual economy through the development of limited edition content by various content creators. A more important aspect is that, because it allows the user to experience various perspectives through the ability to alter their appearance, this can result in an enhanced shared experience that heightens the interactive qualities of the Metaverse.

10.3 The Monetization of the Virtual Avatar

We go back into the uses of Cryptocurrencies, Game Currencies and NFTs in the Metaverse. In the later iterations of games, we have seen how it was possible to accumulate in game currency and spend it on premium weapons and skins that would boost the attack and defense of our character in game. Now, if we apply this concept onto our virtual avatars. It is observed that many users of the internet have shown that they are of the mind to spend real money for virtual characters, then it follows that they would carry the same mentality if they want to purchase features that would allow them to develop the full capabilities of their character.

This is where monetization comes in, and perhaps, if you are in social media that uses an avatar, then you may have engaged in these types of interactions, where you spend currency native to this game, for features and customizable options considered as premium options. This is the monetization within a closed centralized economy, where the developers still have a say in how the virtual assets are created, and thus, accumulate what premium currency is spent for their own benefit. Now, if the same concept were applied towards a decentralized, open market, this takes the customization and creation options out of the hands of the developers and allows individual creators to develop features and clothing that still manage to conform to the aesthetics of the platform, and allow the users of that platform to purchase specialized content from these creators.

Here, NFTs become an important element in the virtual economy that surrounds the virtual avatars, as NFTs assure the purchaser that the content embedded within that NFT is wholly unique when applied to their avatar, and this increases the value of the purchased item, and subsequently increases the demand for the content developed by that creator, which fuels the creation of more NFTs. Dapper Labs is an example of a platform that allowed users the ability to create their own avatar, and after its creation, spend in game currency and actual currency to purchase the desired features and outfits for their avatars. A closer look into the businesses would show that some designer labels indeed have joined the monetization aspect of the virtual avatars. In the same way that you would stroll down a designer district and purchase luxury and designer items, you could spend real currency to purchaser designer label virtual items for your avatar. Thus, if you do make your way to the Metaverse at some point, do not be surprised to see avatars clad in designer wear. This only goes to show the economic potential of virtual designs and outfits, and how this would catch on to the greater audience.

The customization aspect at this moment can only be experienced through the screen of our mobile devices. Until Virtual Reality Technology becomes more portable and more advanced in its interactions, perhaps then we could appreciate the entrance of physical businesses as they enter into the Metaverse, and expand the possibilities of what our virtual avatars can be.

To go further into the potential of the monetization aspect of the Metaverse, it would be prudent perhaps to explore the impact of the Metaverse upon the fashion industry. IN the physical world, we are more familiar with the concepts of designer labels such as Gucci and Prada to name a few, but there are those who have the potential to create the most avant-garde designs, but are hindered by a lack of financial capital and the lack of connections that are vital to break in to the fashion industry. Realistically, if one does have the connections and they managed to land into an established fashion house, it is the name of the fashion house that gets recognized, and not the individual creator, and all the creative aspects of the designer are not fully realized at this point. Some designs which are ideal in the creator's mind are often rejected for the tried and tested barometers of the fashion world, and anything unusual would certainly be quite scandalous to use the fashion expression.

In the interests of democratization, the Metaverse can provide an alternative path for the would be designer to be able to showcase their creativity to a wider audience, without the need to spend for materials (except perhaps the digital software), the labor (think of all the time it would take to sketch out those intricate outfits), and more importantly, the connections needed to thrive in the fashion world. Additionally, the would-be designer would not need to create several outfits for the sake of the New York, Milan and Paris Fashion Weeks. This would also aid in the savings of the designer, as well as contribute to the sustainability of the fashion world. Metaverse and digital constructs aside, we have seen advertisements that describe the waste produced in the fashion world, and while we are familiar with waste in the form of discarded items, we barely pay attention to the scraps of cloth that are littered from the latest runway designs. The provision of a digital platform allows the creator to showcase the best of their imagination without the need to contribute their own carbon footprint on the planet. Besides, with the use of several types of software, impossible designs are now possible, and the digital platform of the Metaverse can now be a digital runway for the sale of custom creations that can be paid for through the use of NFTs, Cryptocurrencies or Actual currencies.

The shift in the paradigm of the fashion world has allowed it to center its focus, not on the sales that it generates, although this is still an essential part of the fashion industry, but on the creativity of the designer. Thus, it is possible now to earn from the creation of customizable features, as users of the Metaverse would now be able to purchase unique content from these creators in the form of NFTs or through the use of premium currencies in several platforms to be able to customize their avatar. The fashion industry now, that if you have seen several social media platforms, have some of their designs available, and thus, it can be assumed that they have come to the realization that the fashion industry has realized the potential of the Metaverse in the search for its clientele, to make their names more relevant to the millennial and Gen Z population, aside from the other generations that populate the Metaverse.

Among the models thrust towards the Metaverse population include what is called the Direct to Avatar, where within the Metaverse, it becomes possible to sell items directly to a user's avatar. This business model, beneficial to the purveyors of the fashion world, reduces the dependence on a third party for the delivery of the goods. Because the item is digital in nature, and thus can be transmitted digitally as well, this does not require the need for physical delivery to the purchaser. You may have encountered this type of business model in games and virtual social media platforms where the purchase of a skin or item goes directly into your avatar's inventory, without the need for any form of shipment or bill of lading. This form of business model would find itself useful to the millennial and Gen Z populations as these are what comprise majority of the population within the Metaverse, and are representative of the consumers who are more likely to purchase the goods within the Metaverse. In a way, the demand produced by this section of the population has resulted in the need for the fashion industry to adapt sustainable practices and cutting-edge technology to create fashionable pieces that would greatly appeal to the digital native. Digital outfits in this instance, are the newer trend in the fashion world, as world of design shifts from cloth to pixels.

The benefits of this form of technology within the Metaverse however, are not solely limited to the clothes that one wears, as the versatility afforded by a digital environment has expanded to include designs such as those for cars, houses, and in some social media platforms, these can include rooms where you can mix and match pieces and be your own interior design. Within the Metaverse, because it is a pixelated environment, and as long as you are tech savvy, it becomes possible to hone your design chops, earn from it, and create all you want without the physical limitations imposed in the physical world. If you have read the comics of the Fantastic Four, you can gain a glimpse of how versatile the concept of digital items could be. Just as their Future Foundation uniforms are able to adapt to their mood, or design, digital clothing could also gain the ability to adapt to the user's surroundings in the Metaverse.

What fuels the sale of the items? It would seem far-fetched to think that people would actually spend real money for the purchase of items that you cannot even physically wear. You might even think that it would be a ridiculous notion that you would purchase designer items that you could not even show off (you know you want to if you had them), or even wear as tangible proof that you have the financial capacity to purchase these types of goods. The fuel for this lies in a psychological approach, where the Millennial and Gen Z population are more concerned with social issues and sustainability. Thus, the use of digital fashions, are then viewed by this specific population as more of accessibility concern rather than one of vanity. Aside from this, there is the concept that the purchase of this consumer goods, which leads into consumption which circles back to the idea of accessibility. It is the belief of this generation that if one is able to purchase these types of items, then these items would grant them access into more select cliques and associations not accorded to those intrepid enough to enter. Thus the fashion industry, in this aspect, retains the cliquishness associated with the users of designer items. The creation of digital designer items and other designer retail goods then, would serve as the main enticement for those who want to be socially accepted in the Metaverse, to purchase these items, to be accepted into the Metaverse. Another idea to be considered in the monetization of the digital avatars, and subsequently the monetization of content created for these digital avatars leads to the expressiveness that the Millennial and Gen Z generation often find relatable. Thus, the creation of various items that would cater to the expressive freedom afforded in the Metaverse would greatly appeal to this population as the avatar is basically the main means through which they can express themselves. This provides more opportunities for designers, fashion brands and content creators in the way to institute constant brand awareness to ensure that their brands remain in the loop with regards to the Metaverse.

10.4 Virtual Avatars, Virtual Economies and Games

From the virtual runways of the Metaverse, we head once more into the gaming industry where the trade of customized skins, armor, weapons and the like fueled the initial foray into the sale of customizable items for avatars used within the gaming world. However, in this instance, it must be necessary to view the gaming industry from a different perspective. Gone are the traditional games where there is little room for freedom of movement, and more adherence to a quest-driven narrative. In the current games, such as that of Roblox and Fortnite, it became less about the game and more about the experiences that are available through the games themselves. We have narrated about the concerts that took place within the game industries, and thus, this may open the market for limited edition content that users of the game can purchase within the game. This aside, it also becomes possible to purchase licensed digital content that can be applied onto our avatars in these games. Games in this instance should be considered not only purely as games, but as a form of social media, as it is possible to socialize with other people in the game platform. Marketing strategies are then necessary to include the option to provide alternative fashions to users within the game. For instance, aside from the sale of armor and weapons, there could be the sale of more casual (yet perhaps more theme-related outfits) that would still appeal to the users of the platform. The demand to customize avatars within a game platform would still carry the same demand over from the mere customization of avatars for the use of social media use.

To generate the need for the virtual item, games and other designer brands need to create a new market strategy that allows the customer or user to experience what their brand would be like in the environment of the Metaverse. It would seem that brands that have adapted to the use of virtual reality generate more sales than those brands that resolutely adhere to the non-adaption into the digital age. If one would recall, one of the changes wrought by the pandemic included the adaptation of the customer into online shopping. As it is, now that customers no longer need to drive themselves to a bricks and mortar store, they are more likely to indulge in impulse purchases just because they can. As a result, designers and creators can take the opportunity to generate smaller items that would entice the customer or user to purchase these. Think retail therapy, but in a digital form, and not through the excessive use of eBay. You can actually purchase items that make you happy, at the drop of a hat. That is the convenience afforded to the designers and creators that populate the Metaverse.

Going back into the fashion industry and the games, the two industries have begun to reach an accord where it becomes possible for the user to be aware of the brand – such as Balenciaga or Ralph Lauren, whilst in a game environment. While we do not expect to see Project Runway in the Metaverse (who knows, it may happen), it does allow the user to experience what it is to have a luxury commodity and a designer item. Ralph Lauren in particular has made great use of the Augmented Reality in that users can scan the logo to gain additional accessibility to features that would enhance their shopping experience. Levis is another brand that has accommodated shopping with friends through their virtual platform, so it becomes possible to shop and socialize in the Metaverse, as though you were in an actual mall. This heightens the need for brands to collaborate more with developers to ensure that their brand continues to remain relevant to other users in the Metaverse.

10.5 The Assurance of Identities

One of the bigger concerns with the use of the digital avatar is the anonymity that gets associated with the creation of the avatar throughout various Metaverse platforms. Remember that we mentioned that with the creation of a customizable avatar in our chosen Metaverse platform, we can look like our idealized fantasies. In essence, our avatars may not even resemble our physical characteristics whatsoever. Now, if you have seen any movie that involved a shape shifter, you may know where this leads to. With the ability to virtually change our appearance at will, who is to say that we can just easily shed the identity of our avatars of our own volition? Customization is a double-edged sword, in that, where it allows us to be expressive through our avatars, but this afforded customization allows the user to change their appearance should there be any untoward incidents. Now, cloak of anonymity aside, any other regulations would contravene the freedom that the Metaverse champions, yet, it would also run contradictory on an ethical perspective. Any more restrictive practices on the need to control the identity of a person would be considered invasive and violative of the user's right to privacy.

This does not mean however, developers would allow users to easily switch. As the Metaverse is meant to resemble our physical world, there are certain limitations that are imposed in the ability of a person to change the appearance of their avatar, or change the entire identity the user behind the avatar. Blockchain Technology and the use of Biometrics would ensure that no matter which platform is utilized, the developers would still be able to control the singularity of personal identifies, while at the same time, be able to ensure the continued privacy and security of the users within their platforms. The use of Identity Management Systems are touted as a solution that would ensure that the identities used within the Metaverse are regulated and maintained. It becomes necessary however, to define the concepts that are associated with the use of digital avatars.

Identities can refer to the unique attributes that are found in a person, which is a composite of all the experiences, cultures and attitudes that have been inculcated within their person. Identities can be applied in two different means, where we users are referred to as an actual natural person. The other application consists of the identity attributed to a corporation or abstract entity- remember we have spoken of brand identities in the past. When all of these ideas are taken in the context of the Metaverse however, it is necessary to know that identities are unique attributes that remain constant regardless of the conditions to which the person is subject to. However, the development of a true identity, physical or in the Metaverse would take some time. Earlier, we have written about the Proteus effect where the user would manifest characteristics similar to that of their avatar, in that they begin to imbibe the characteristics of their digital persona while entrenched in the physical world. This aside, the philosophical context of identity when applied to the Metaverse has no strict interpretation, save perhaps, when the identity of a person, through the avatar used, retains the same level of constancy that they have throughout all the platforms of the Metaverse. Because of the complexities in the creation of identity, the use of blockchains and biometrics would find difficulty in the distillation of a user's identity into a simplified category. This issue must be addressed before identities can be truly systematized.

Personas are a more familiar term, as users in the internet have developed identities that they call their "art-sona" for artists, "fur-sona" for animal enthusiasts, and a host of other names for a variety of situations. While identities are attributed to a single person, and it remains consistent throughout the use of the avatar, the customization of the avatar in several ways can lead to the development of various personas which can coexist within a single user. An example of this would include say, a professional by day and later a glammed up version of themselves outside the professional setting. Personas may act differently, but at their core, they still maintain the same identity that the person who created these personas has. Personas then, when applied to the validation of identities in the use of the Identity Management System

Attributes, under this concept are what allow a user to qualify within a specific class in accordance with the organization of the identity management system. Here are the more conventional forms of attributes such as age, gender, country of origin, height and weight and hobbies. It must be noted however that the categorization of the users into these attributes are arbitrary in nature, particularly with issues of race (a dilemma that may be encountered by bi-racial users), hair color (some shades of brown, blonde and red may transition in between each other on the color spectrum), and gender (while we have male and female categories, we also have genders that can be non-binary, or even within the LGBTQ spectrum).

Identifiers within the Identity Management System refer to the markers that are used to designate a person from a specific category or a specific locale- such as through the servers or IP addresses used to access the Metaverse. These identifiers do not utilize the physical characteristics of a person, but are able to mark a specific avatar to be from a particular area in the world. Identifiers are assigned to the user by a third-party in an arbitrary manner, where the identifiers may range from the name of a user, their social security number, or the chosen username of the avatar, to more sophisticated identifiers such as the use of biometric data. These data are converted into strings which are meant to authenticate the identity of a person, as well as distinguish the data of the user from the other users who share the same categorized attributes under the Identity Management System. With the commonality of names however, this may become an issue with identifiers whose data strings are reliant on the use of the first name of a person. Thus, future developers need to address the need that developed identifiers must be able to distinguish a person in a unique manner to ensure that there is no such ambiguity as to the identity of the person. No one in the Metaverse must have the same identifier, and no person should have more than one identifier, which highlights the concepts of unicity and singularity within the Metaverse, and these are the precepts by which identity management systems should abide by.

In lieu of an identifier generated by the physical characteristics of a person, there are identifiers that are generated through the use of random numbers. You may have encountered a similar form of technology when you sign up for a particular service, and the browser asks you if you would like to use a randomly generated password that comprises a series of alphanumeric characters and symbols that it will automatically associate with the site that you have visited, as well as the email address that you have used to sign up for the services on the internet. While this concept may apply to the Metaverse in that no one would have the same identifier, because you can sign up to multiple platforms, especially if issues of interoperability have not been addressed, then it would be possible to have more than one identifier which defeats the purpose of the unique identifier. Thus, this form of identifier generation would be ineffective in that it does not guarantee that a single person could maintain a single identity throughout the Metaverse, bar the inception and implementation of the interoperability of all Metaverse platforms.

Other identifiers are unique in that these are arranged in such a manner that they are distinctly identified to be associated with a particular agency. Take for example, if you remember your school ID Numbers, there may be identifiers there that ensure that you were enrolled within a particular year, and that you were the nth student to have completed their enrollment for that year. These types of identifiers are not randomly generated by any site, but are originated from a particular agency or entity such as a government office, or a company. These identifiers include the likes of your social security number, your bank account, or even your company email address. These ascertain your identity within the agency or company. Identifiers issued in such a manner are considered ideal as these ensure that you alone carry this identity, and you could not obtain any more identifiers within that particular agency. It would be impossible to have say, two passport numbers or even two social security numbers.

A more idealized form of identifier rests on the use of biometric data and the conversion of this biometric data into data strings that are absolutely unique and singular to a particular person. This can later expand into the use of fingerprints, as well as iris and retinal scans to ensure that the identifier of the person remains on that person, and no other person can potentially duplicate this (save the scenarios seen in various action and sci-fi movies). The technology needed to scan the biometrics to the precise configuration in the body however, may be the point of contention for this form of technology, as current biometric scans only take an approximate measure of the biometrics of a person. Thus, if developers need to use the biometrics of a person as an identifier for an avatar, then it would be necessary to integrate other forms of the biometrics such as fingerprint scans that complement an iris or retinal scan, that lessen the chance of a shared or similar biometric signature, and ensure the platform that the user is indeed who they say they are. This form of data capture however, may be misconstrued as rather invasive in its conception, as this does require the use of wholly unique identifiers from our person.

Through the use of identifiers in the sense of our avatars, we have touched upon the identifiers that rely on the person, but one should not discount the identifier that was used throughout all these years. The use of the IP address remains a unique way to identify a user through their device as IP addresses are unique to the model and computer they originate from. The benefit with the use of IP addresses is that, through the use of the Internet Service Provider, it is possible to trace the locale of the user through the triangulation of the IP address in a particular area, around the world. The best part is that this does not completely become an invasive process as identifiers do not transmit personal data from our computers, but only the approximate location of the unit that the user had used to access the Metaverse platform.

The user name and password of a person can be used as identifiers in the app, as it would be unique to each person. Recall how you would sign up for your email address, at its most basic form. You would create an email address, a unique password, and before you can create it, you have to add other identifiers such as a backup email, your real name, and a mobile number through which you can access your data in the event that you do forget your password. Recall though, the discussion on what constitutes the identity in the Metaverse. There are two kinds, where the natural identity refers to a person, whereas a legal identity invests an abstract concept such as a corporation with the identity it needs to be able to perform legal tasks such as the capacity to sue or be sued in turn. Legal issues aside, it is also possible for these corporations to have their own email server, and if you do work from home, you will know that you have identifiers that originate from a particular company as well. The use of the IP address is no assurance that the user is a person, as it is now possible for bots to reply in lieu of a person.

The use of the Blockchains would depend on the type of identifier used, which are typically composed of key pairs, which are both public and private in their classification. These key pairs are encrypted in a manner that they uniquely identify a particular feature – such as a digital wallet, but do not disclose any personal information attributed to the generation of the key pair. It is possible for one person to have a multiple key pairs, such as your keys for multiple Cryptocurrency investments if need be. The private key needed as an identifier to help in the execution of the transactions from the blockchain which is in turn identified by the public key. The transactions that take place in this instance are not limited to the transference of Cryptocurrencies – as we have touched on previously, but also the transactions that involve the sale of a token through the obligations presented in a smart contract. Permissioned blockchains, unlike the permissionless blockchains of

Ethereum and Bitcoin, can be attributed to a particular identity, as the key pairs used by the Bitcoin mining permit the regulation and subsequently the punishment of these users should there be a violation of the terms and conditions for that Cryptocurrency. Despite the decentralization of the Cryptocurrency transactions, there is a centralized authority that governs at least the activity of the Proof of Work and Proof of Stake protocols, and polices the permissioned blockchains of the Cryptocurrency.

10.6 The Importance of Identity in the Metaverse

This may carry certain political implications, as to the use of identity throughout the world. Statements from the World Bank state that every individual must be furnished with an identity as this is the access point through which socio-economic benefits can begin to accrue with a person. Given that the Metaverse was intended to replicate our society from the physical world into the virtual world, it would be reasonable to assume that the provision of an identity is a fundamental right that is afforded to every inhabitant within the Metaverse. When the idea of identity is taken into the context of a human right, it then provides the benefits that follow to the person who has been thusly furnished with an identity:

- Access to health care services and education are provided for, along with the right to suffrage, the ability to gain access to financial services to accumulate and earn money for their needs, and the ability to benefit from social welfare programs in accordance with the policies of their respective countries.

- An identity would allow a person to access the necessary government services, such as those afforded with the use of a social security number or a national health insurance number. Policy decisions would be made more transparent as a group of identified individuals would be able to experience the benefits of a particular policy, and an improvement in the way the population is run, as there would be no duplication of the identity of a particular person.
- Lastly, the identity of a person would enable the centralized authority, such as the government, to monitor the status of the general population through the measurement of vital statistics, the conduction of census, and other measures which the government feels are necessary to ascertain the quality of life experienced by each member of the population.

The Metaverse aside for now, we must impress upon you the importance of an identity. For most, much as we hate to say it, we barely think of our identity as a basic human right. Since birth, from the moment our parents have taught us how to speak and write our names, we have been born with the idea that that is who we are, and our birth certificates confirm that. Now in countries that are comparatively less developed, there are numerous individuals who are unable to benefit from the programs implemented by various supranational entities purely on the basis that they have no identity. While it cannot be said that they are not persons – that is a matter of anatomy and genetics altogether- they belong to no nation, and belong to no specific group. These marginalized individuals are denied the basic services that are often accorded to us, regardless of the quality of the services rendered to us.

In the quest to address the issues of identity among stateless individuals, the United Nations has opted to join in the quest to provide every person an identity. This program, called the ID2020 Alliance, was created to foster collaborations between various organizations to ensure that each individual and all peoples are able to obtain a digital identity that would prevent their exclusion from the provision of basic human rights. Because of the scope of the implementation, it is necessary for the United Nations that the digital identity created for these people would not be compromised by any means. This program outlined by the United Nations aims to ensure that the creation of a digital identity would be able to stay within reasonably defined parameters, be part of an ethical digital system, and be able to use these digital identities for the promotion of a social mindset. There are four criteria which would be used to measure the capabilities of a digital identity system as provided for by the UN in that the digital identity and its attached system must be portable – it can be used in other identity systems as well; persistence- in that it remains constant and fixed despite its portability into other digital identity systems; privacy- in that the digital identity would not compromise the data of the person it identifies, nor will it convey any personal information in its code; and user-control- where the user would have a say in what kind of data is made available through the use of the assigned digital identity. The protocol to which this digital identity is attached to is referred to now as a proof-of-concept, where this would allow institutions, public and private, to be able to assign user-specific identifiers to a person. What developers of a digital identity system should keep in mind however, given the security risks involved with the creation of a database that would figuratively hold all the identities of every person in the world, is that the data should not be held in the hands of a single person, or a group of persons. This way, the privacy of the data would remain uncompromised. Once this issue has been addressed, it is envisioned that the implementation of the digital identity system would aid in the provision of a digital identity to the refugee to ensure their eligibility for social welfare programs and cash aid among other benefits. To take into context with the Metaverse, once these groups have been identified as such, it would streamline the processes needed and ensure that these people would be able to link with the authorities that they need to seek help from.

While the allegiance of the ID2020 Alliance is noted to be on the side of international usage, it does revert back to the idea of the Metaverse, with the use of blockchains to ensure that the identities of the users within the Metaverse are correctly validated, and the blockchains would be able to trace the identity of the user, and ensure that the identifiers associated with that user cannot be changed or altered in any form. As much as possible, the creation of a digital identity system within the Metaverse, to be linked with the avatars of the user, must not be under the control of a single person or entity; it must be portable and be usable in other platforms that can access the Metaverse, and that the user has the discretion to choose what kind of data may be shared with the digital identifiers. Despite the precautions developers may take, there is still a singular weak point in most forms of the Metaverse, in that the identity of the users are all contained within a single entity. If one would recall the world wide Facebook, YouTube and Instagram outages in the late months of 2021, there was an accompanying data breach which leaked the personal data of several users – from which Facebook opted to rebrand itself as Meta. Thus, in the creation of this type of system, it must integrate the Metaverse precept of decentralization to minimize the risk of data breaches from a single platform. The flaw with a centralized structure is that, once the safety precautions that have been undertaken by the system developers has been breached, the data leak would be of such enormity that it would completely compromise all the digital identifiers and identities that were created for the users involved.

A solution designed to counter this to ensure the development of a consistent identity for a person has to start from the moment the child comes into this world. In the context of the Metaverse however, this does not mean that a virtual avatar should be developed for a child no, but in the future, such as if the need for education has shifted to the use of virtual classrooms, then it would be easier for the child to obtain the accreditation and verification needed by the school authorities that they are a bona fide actual person, and thus may take part in the advantages afforded to those who were bestowed with identities from the moment of their birth. Thus, the identifier needed from the child at this point is biometric data. We have touched on the flaws of biometric data where the current software only obtain an approximation of the unique features that it can detect. However, later developments may permit scanners to obtain a more comprehensive data scan and allow for a more complex set of data strings associated with the said biometric. That said, the current state of biometric data may be used in conjunction with other forms of verifiers to ensure that the data that is under verification is indeed that of the user. The biometric hash that results, the term used to identify the unique biometric data obtained, would undergo a form of encryption to ensure that the identity of the person involved remains singular – in that it can never be used anywhere else and the person cannot register the same set of biometric data under a different name; and their data that is included in the biometric has does not disclose any personal information as to the user. The biometric hash can theoretically be compared with other biometric hashes to ensure authenticity, but it would never be able to draw the information about an individual.

A second flaw that can be obtained from the use of biometric systems, aside from the problem of centralization, is the problem of storage. Since centralization is an issue, the biometric data cannot be stored in the phone of the user, otherwise it would be easier to breach by unscrupulous individuals. To head back into the application of this system in the Metaverse, developers who intend to use a biometric verification system to ensure that the user is the one whose data is encoded within the virtual avatar must ensure that the blockchains that are needed to verify the user can utilize the public and private keys effectively. It must be important that the blockchain remains decentralized, which minimizes the risk of a data breach. The blockchain in its current state, cannot securely store the private keys of the data of a person. It can only record the transactions that have taken place within it, and because of this, the use of blockchains as a security measure can have flaws that are exploited. Biometric data then, should never be used as the basis to unlock the private keys needed by the blockchain, to ensure that the data contained within the blockchain cannot be readily accessed by the individuals who may have been able to replicate the biometric data needed to access the services.

10.7 Authentication and the Zero Knowledge Protocol

The use of biometric data as a verifier for identity carries certain risks particularly since the capacity to truly safeguard the data contained within the biometric information can be inexact, and at the same time breached if there is an exploitable flaw in the programming, despite the utilization of blockchains. Thus, another means for verification within the Metaverse revolves around the concept of Zero Knowledge Protocol. Summarily, this is a means to authenticate the passwords of a user without the need to exchange any form of data in between the servers. Through the use of this protocol, it is possible for the user to communicate in private, and be able to send files clandestinely, without the knowledge of a third-party.

To truly grasp what it means to authenticate the credentials of a person, we first define authentication within the virtual world. Authentication is an act that confirms the truth of a given attribute that is otherwise claimed to be true by another party. Authentication differs from identification as identification concerns itself with the statement or indication of a claim where a person attests their identity or that of another object. Identification is the mere statement of an alleged identity, whereas authentication goes further and confirms that the allegations made are true. The gist of this type of authentication is that the secret knowledge is the public key of the person who seeks to prove their identity, to the other party- who is known as the verifier. Perhaps you may see a flaw here, as because the one who provides the secret has to provide the knowledge, it is possible that the secret may be intercepted and the third-party who manages to intercept the secret would be able to impersonate the prover and access the data.

There are however, ways to prevent this type of interception to ensure the perpetual security of the data such as through the authentication of the public keys. These keys are unlike passwords, which you could speak over the phone or merely exchange as written notes. These are cryptographically enhanced keys that ensure that only you and the verifier would be privy to the information that is kept between yourselves. This type of authentication requires the management of the keys, where these can include the revocation of the key, or the creation of a trust chain.

The next measure that can be undertaken would be to encrypt the layer that transports the information. This ensures that the use of the authorization of the public keys would work, and thus this would require the use of shared information between the two parties, or the aforementioned authentication process to access the data.

Zero Knowledge Proof, which we have touched upon, requires no exchange of keys or passwords between the two parties. This form of encryption allows for the creation of temporary keys that allow the secret key to be communicated to the verifier after the authentication process has taken place. The main drawback with this solution however, revolves around its cost, as it is quite expensive to use.

Data leaks can be prevented through the protection of an authenticated database where the access to the database is limited, and the storage itself has undergone a form of encryption with another secret that only the user would be privy to. Indirect Secret Storage is where the verifier avoids the storage of the secret within their database, but allows the storage instead, of a replicative derivative of the secret, which the user would have to provide to the verifier before they can access the data needed.

10.8 Conclusion

Throughout this chapter, we have begun to lay the foundation of our personas within the Metaverse in the form of the digital avatar, and the various risks involved with the creation of our persona within the Metaverse. While this chapter has initially focused on the superficial aspect, that related to the customization of our appearances in the Metaverse, and how content creators can monetize the digital avatars as an economic opportunity within the Virtual Economy, we have focused on the other uses of the digital avatar, as a representation of ourselves within the Metaverse, and how it can help simulate functions that we would normally do in the physical world. Subsequently, it is of prime importance too, to learn, to protect our avatar- as it is our digital identity, from the various ways identities can be exploited throughout the Metaverse. Thus, it becomes necessary to delve into the social implications of the digital avatar, a symbol of our identity in the virtual world, and how it can be protected through the use of blockchains, biometric data, and authentication processes to ensure that everyone can be held accountable for their actions within the Metaverse. This ensures that the

Metaverse remains a wholesome place, with its restrictions, to protect the interests of all of its inhabitants.

11 The Game Economy

When we speak of the Metaverse, we would be remiss in our discussions If we did not include the idea that sparked the existence of a virtual world in the first place. While the earliest forms of the internet favored more on the communications aspect, given that the internet was originally developed to transmit documents across long distances, one cannot deny that it was the advent of video games that made developers conceive of the possibility, that there is a world out there that can be constructed entirely of pixels.

The world of games has certainly come far, from the likes of Pong, simplistic in its design, to the more complex worlds of Minecraft and Roblox, just to name a few worlds that have created the essence of what the Metaverse can be. The entertainment factor that one derived from these games belies the complexities of the codes that are needed to enable these worlds to exist, even in the simpler games that we probably have played with in the past. Now one could think that games are for sure one of the ways that one can earn within the Metaverse. Even outside the Metaverse, the entertainment industry manages to earn a lot, despite the presence of the pandemic that severely limits what we can do. But what makes some games better than others? We can always say that it is a matter of taste, but that would be an oversimplification of the capacity of the game industry to enrapture the attention of the world, and generate the newer form of competition referred to as eSports. The fact that these games, such as Warcraft for instance, can be used to earn real money, as evidenced by the numerous tournaments that have taken place in the past few years cements the idea that the game industry continues to evolve in such a way that it perpetually manages to gain the attention of a few people. At the crux of it all, we know now that the true capacity of the game industry, and by extension, the Metaverse, would be reliant on its ability to capture the attention of its audience, and enrapture themselves in the wonders of the game environment. On a parallel note, the development of the game industry can be said to run concurrent to the interests of the developers of the Metaverse, as their ideas often coincide given that the Metaverse and most game environments use the same software to enable the increased functionality in the game.

11.1 Attention Economy

The beauty with the game industry, and the Metaverse, is that it has the potential to sell itself. All it has to do is to capture the attention of the audience it intends to earn from. The marketing chapter of this book goes into detail as to how the Metaverse can sufficiently sell itself through the use of demos that allow the potential customer a glimpse into the gameplay, or at least, the virtual environment within the Metaverse to ensure that their interest is sufficiently piqued. If we could take a trip down memory lane, what would be the earliest memory that you have of a video game? For the older generations, perhaps it would be the video arcade. Remember those times when you would play PacMan, Sonic or even Donkey Kong, just as a reminder. What captured your attention then? The graphics? The catchy sound? The experience? Your competitive streak? Or simply the time that you got to spend there? Regardless of the reason, people took the games seriously enough that they spent time to learn how to play it, and though they may not have stuck to it, it did prove that if you could capture the attention of the audience, or customer, long enough, you would be able to earn from it.

The game industry continues to exist in forms where you would be able to access the game through the use of a video game cartridge (for the really old-school clientele), or through the use of CDs (for the millennial crowd), and these games were originally sold at a fixed rate, which remains a constant in the game industry until today. The appeal of this type of game is that for the fixed price of the game, you would have unlimited access to the game, that you can access at any time. This is perhaps the more economical option, if you are the type of gamer who plays the game only in certain times such as your free time, or if you are a hardcore gamer, intent to complete the game at all stages (completionists – we probably have been one of these at some point in our gaming lives). The problem with this type of game however, is that if you do not like it, you have wasted money; or if you have completed every part of the game, then you would get bored, then you would just stick the game on a shelf to be forgotten.

There are other ways to monetize from the game industry, which have their own flaws as well. These can include games where you pay by the hour to access them, although this approach remains quite unpopular due to the limited time that you have to even achieve the objectives of the game. There are also games where you pay by the month, where you would be able to access the features for a month until such time that you have to renew your subscription. However, these types of monetizations are flawed in that they cannot entirely capture the attention of your customer, and subsequently, can result in the cancellation of the subscription, and cause the game to fall out of popularity. World of Warcraft is one of the few games that manages to earn from this type of business model. There is also the fact that these games can result in losses for the developers as they can be pirated in turn. Older versions of games however, because the copyright on them has expired, can be legally downloaded, but for the most part, most games that originate from cartridges and CDs are prone to piracy.

In recent years, the game industry has focused on a newer aspect of what is called the attention economy, and this is referred to as the Free to Play system. You may have experienced games of this type when you checkout the games through Google Play Store, and some of these games have features where you would be able to access all the game's features and be able to take part in the quests, side quests, tasks, events and so on. However, within these free to play games are premium currencies as well such as gems, keys and crystals, which allow you to unlock more features that would otherwise be ordinarily unavailable to most players. Aside from the use of real currency in the game however, it is entirely possible to farm for these premium currencies as special events, log-in rewards and other features allow the user to accumulate these special currencies over time. Dedicated players, because it is now possible to earn the premium currency without the need to spend actual currency, become enthralled with the process and gameplay, and as such, are more likely to be engrossed with the features of the game, if only to level up their character(s), to accumulate these premium currencies, engage in microtransactions and unlock more features or an enhanced game play feature. With this ability to capture the attention of other players, it is of no surprise that this form of business model to engage audiences is the most profitable and most common among mobile games, and with the use of android emulators, for PC and Console games as well.

The beauty of the free to play model is that it allows a multitude of users to take part in the game without the need to spend actual money to be able to experience the proper gameplay. Second, this type of business model does not compel the users to spend premium currency to progress to the next stage of gameplay. This type of business model encapsulates the idea behind attention economy, in that there are periods where there are fewer opportunities to gain premium currency, which then compels users to engage in as much content as possible to either gain more premium currencies, or to unlock features through other means. Some free to play games have no cap on how much of a resource each user can accumulate over time – not all games employ this feature- which then heightens user engagement with the game. This then captures the attention of the users long enough that they take part in the game at random times, before they give up on the game altogether. Regardless of what takes place, free to play games tread the balance between free access, where user attention is captured through the use of "farming" techniques for currencies, or it can also provide options for users to spend currency and unlock premium content without the need to tediously go through the motions of gameplay. This type of business model however, is heavily reliant on the marketing principle, and as such, developers who wish to integrate this into a Metaverse platform must be ready to spend as much in the marketing as they did in the development of the platform. This way, customer engagement is acquired as early as possible, and this would attract more users to try out the game or app.

Within these free to play games however, you may have encountered a lot of advertisements. Some of these ads talk about other games which you can download for free. The better and more interactive ads allow you to try out the game initially before it tries to get you to download the game if you enjoyed the free demo. Ads that do not provide you with any incentive are referred to as interstitial advertisements, as they appear at random times, or as the game or Metaverse platform transitions between areas. The other type of advertisement is referred to as rewarded advertising, and while these ads vary as to the type of content, interactive or not, users do get a reward for watching the ad, whether it is limited amounts of premium currency, a boost in stats for the next level, extra keys, users are more enthralled by the prospect of extra rewards to be obtained from the ads, and thus, this would capture their attention more in the free to play business model.

On the physical aspect, we cannot deny the impact that the pandemic has had in the world, and with the economic downturn experienced by several business sectors, there became the need to earn extra cash. A business model that has cropped up lately has included the play to earn business model, as well as skill-based games. Here, we enter one of the earlier examples to earn from the Metaverse, and this is through the foray into the eSports arena, where more experienced users of a particular game are able to utilize their game experience and defeat other players to earn a monetary incentive, which can often rise to significant amounts. In a less intense, but equally competitive alternative, Skillz, is described as a platform that allows users to compete for cash incentives regardless of the skill level of the user. A ticket purchase would gain admission to a particular game, and if the user manages to win, they would be able to earn from the ticket sales, and the developer would earn as well. However, the downside with this business model is that it heavily relies on the ability to capture attention, and users would have to invest large amounts of time to gain the necessary skill level, and this often causes the player to revert to the free to play model.

11.2 Application of Games into the Metaverse

This section does not mean that the Metaverse will be similar to an open world game, ripe for exploration. Where games often rely on the accomplishment of an objective, or a quest which often initiates the user to begin with the gameplay process, the Metaverse, does integrate several elements from the game industry. It must be recalled that the Metaverse does not rely on leaderboard systems and points. What the Metaverse takes from the game industry are the elements of interaction, the ability to experience emotion, a fully immersive experience and where the user can be what they want themselves to be, as we touched upon in the chapter on Avatars. It must be recalled at this point that most players frequently engage in the Metaverse not because of what they can do within it, but because of what they can be – and this perhaps is the most important precept when you integrate the need for attention economy into the Metaverse itself. We mentioned earlier that videogames were the forerunners of the Metaverse, as these have made it possible to create a virtual world by human hands, now the use of game technology has made it possible for the Metaverse.

When we discussed the creation of the Metaverse, we have made mention of several elements necessary to the function of the Metaverse that are inherent in the game industry, where developers have the potential to earn more from the development of game technology that would aid in the development of the Metaverse. Attention economy helps the Metaverse flourish, but what helps it grow to become a more expansive economy is now called Creator Economy. Developers have taken the initiative to develop games in accordance with the imagination of the creators, and as such, this can be applied as well into the Metaverse. This veers the concept of game development away from the reliance on codes – though these are still absolutely necessary to help run the Metaverse- and focuses more on the visual aspect of the game that relies less on the code and more on the tools needed to run the game. These tools have now integrated the use of Virtual Reality and Augmented Reality that were mentioned earlier on in the book to ensure that the Metaverse is able to alter and evolve with the spirit of the times.

11.3 Virtual Items in the Virtual Economy of Games

With the various microtransactions that can take place into various games, this opens up opportunities for content creators and designers to come up with unique items that can be traded as part of the virtual economy within the Metaverse. Though we have mentioned that there are NFTs that include unique, limited edition content that users can purchase from the creator, other creators who are disinclined to use the NFT for personal reasons can develop other items that are still just as tradeable in the virtual economy within the Metaverse. There are items however, that carry a certain amount of value, and as such, those who wish to take advantage of the game economy, and the virtual economy in the Metaverse would wish to know what these high valued items are to ensure that if they do choose to earn from the content that they have created, they can certainly maximize how much they can earn from their designs.

Before we go into a discussion on the types of items there are, we speak now of the difference between affinity and utility. It is important to distinguish one from the other as each has a varied appeal to different users in the Metaverse platform. Affinity refers to the quality of an item where it emotionally appeals to the player. These can include limited edition characters – such as those from Marvel and DC based games that just so happen to be the user's favorite character- or uniforms –because of how attractive they make a favorite character look. Utility on the other hand, refers to how useful certain creations can be because they greatly enhance the gameplay process.

When we spoke about the virtual avatars, we highlighted the importance of avatar customization, thus, it should be no surprise that cosmetic content and social content would find themselves among the high affinity items as these greatly enhance the experience of users within the Metaverse. Such items include the aforementioned uniforms, skins, limited edition looks of favorite characters, titles and trophies that users can show off to other players while in the Metaverse. While in the concept of skins and uniforms, we are more familiar perhaps with the mechanics of games where you can purchase the chosen uniform or skin for your avatar or your character through the use of premium currency. However, pricier options in more contemporary games can fetch upwards of five figures, which make the development of these items a very lucrative commodity. Of course, with the price, the skin of course has to present some form of value that would make your avatar in the game, or character in the game, meta- just to use the game language to describe characters with a game changing advantage once they have been equipped.

Aside from the use of the cosmetic alterations that feature high affinity items, we also have the use of emotes, a more dimensional form of emoticons that focus not on the gameplay advantages that it affords the user, but the enhanced quality of social interaction while the user is within the platform of the Metaverse or game. Here, these emotes, transcend our usual emoticons. They enable the avatar to gain a personality through the integration of pre-coded actions. These emotes can be as simple as a pose, or as complex as the integration of dance moves – you may have seen some videos of this on YouTube. Special animations are also part of the price and package, and let's face it, in an open world, where you can be anything you want to be – would you not want to be the cynosure in that area of the Metaverse? What better way to do it than to pay top dollar for the emotes that give your avatar some personality within the Metaverse. After all, actions do speak louder than words, and what better way to exemplify this than through the use of emotes.

Stories are a high affinity item that would be more likely found in games and platforms that focus on a highly quest-driven narrative. A good example of the use of stories in gameplay would be the Diablo III game, where players can explore the world of Sanctuary and interact with objects to gain lore that would flesh out the story and ultimately unlock achievements as you go along the game. This game however, has its stories free. Other games, may require you to pay to unlock additional stories that would mark significant milestones in your game progress, and serve in lieu of trophies.

High utility items are different from high affinity items in that they appeal to the user because of their practical applications, and do not rely on sentimentality on the part of their appeal. It is no surprise then, that practical items such as keys in games would be part of the high utility items. Keys for instance give you the chance to unlock premium content, but also have the probability to give you content that you can obtain for free (RNG really hits hard in this one). Users can unlock more features through the purchase of additional keys with the use of real currency, which can fetch high prices between other users. Most often these keys in games are single –use, to heighten their level of scarcity within the game platform. Other keys in games can have unlimited uses, but can be pricey, so it strikes a balance as to how useful they can be. Consumable items are also part of the useful items. While consumables do not include armor and weapons (except perhaps arrows, bolts and javelins), these include the likes of potions that can afford you continuous healing, or even unlimited usage while in the game. This is just the game aspect, this can extend to social media usage in the Metaverse, though developers can use consumables such as the use of limited digital venues that you can book similar to an events venue.

Resources are another usable commodity that players would often trade or spend for. There are two ways that developers can earn from this, either through the release of limited edition resources, or through the use of limited inventory slots, which then makes the user purchase the additional inventory slots just so they can continue with the game. Resources within the Metaverse are best exemplified through the Minecraft, where you can literally build anything through a combination of resources that users mine in the virtual world. These resources can also include the construction of buildings, which would sometimes cause the user to spend to speed up the construction process, and spend some more if the construction requires a scarce material with a relatively low drop rate. To tie in with resources are containers such as chests, which you can purchase within the Metaverse or game platform. These chests may give you a totally new weapon, a limited edition item, or a new character, and can take several forms. Ultimately, these containers contain limited edition resources, where the purchase of each container would give the user a chance to gain a limited resource to enhance the game play experience.

Generators are a handy item that generates currencies or items for the user in games, but place emphasis on scarcity in that they may have certain caps for the amount of the item that can be generated, or if these items can only be redeemed a certain amount of times. You would find these items in most games, where most fall under the latter description. If generators do not appeal to users, then the next feature certainly will due to its added convenience. This refers to automation, where the user can pay to have certain features automated such as the operation of a generator without the need for the user to initiate the actions, or in other games such as auto-play, auto-purchase, and auto-upgrade features that can free the player up to do other tasks within the Metaverse. It is possible to get items that feature automation for free, but it would take real currency to purchase these items as they are limited in their production.

Deeds, function in the same way as they would in our physical world, where these are representative of your right to inhabit that particular section of land, or in this context, the use of virtual real estate, as we have mentioned in the virtual economy chapter. Deeds, when applied in the context of the Metaverse not only signify ownership over the virtual plot of land, but also serve as a permit that allows you to construct a building on your land. This section is iffy, in that in terms of virtual real estate, as with physical real estate, there are certain limitations as to what you can do with the land, and what can be built in the land, regardless of your creative prowess. This question of fact however, is best left up to the discretion of the Metaverse platform developer and the virtual real estate broker who are the best people to answer this question.

We have written at this point, about items that are either sentimental or useful, but, there are items that carry both attributes where they can be useful and have high user affinity at the same time. These types of items include equipment –especially weapons and armor that not only offer gameplay advantages, but also appeal to the emotions of the player aside from their usefulness within the game or Metaverse platform. However, there are items that not only form part of the story, and are not only useful, but also manage to appeal to the aesthetics. For those who have gone to Comic Con, and Game Conventions, you would have seen how these virtual items, converted into real world replicas, can fetch high prices among hardcore gamers who wish to have certain game memorabilia for their private collection. This is just one of the ways that developers can earn more from these equipment virtually and physically.

Characters are another way for developers to earn from the game economy, where limited edition characters (again such as those from the Marvel and DC Franchises), or other cinematic franchises, where users can unlock interactions with these characters for free for a limited period, or pay premium currency to unlock these (which also make the user shell out real money to spend to purchase the premium currency to replenish their stock of the currency). The purchase of these characters however, can sometimes lean more towards the affinity of the character towards the user, but if they do happen to be useful in games or in the Metaverse, then that would make their value worth the amount of the currency paid for them.

Gifts, we love to receive them, we automatically send them as free options, so you might wonder what makes them prized commodities within the game economy. While gifts may result in you gifted with weapons and armor, potions and the like, what they are more useful for is in the enhancement of social interaction between players in games and social media platforms. You would be able to receive limited edition content through these gifts, and you would gift other equally valuable items in turn. There are options in some platforms where you can purchase a virtual gift basket from a shop which can range from a certain amount of interactions, to completely unique content available only through the use of these gift baskets. So in this case, it would be better to give, that you may receive too.

Collectibles are a unique form of content that range in complexity from the need to amass certain items generated at random within the Metaverse platform, to those that you actively have to search out for a chance to gain these items. Some collectibles would net you several advantages, such as a limited edition weapon, armor, or even a whole new set of content, dialogue and a different area to explore within the Metaverse, hence it would be prudent to collect everything as much as possible, or simply maintain every gamer's strategy in such situations – always loot the area and do item runs. You never know what you can collect in the way of collectible items, and resources that would allow you to enhance your experience within the Metaverse. After all, the beauty in this is that you can explore and experience new stories every which way you can turn.

Content creators within the Metaverse, now have a variety of options to choose from, and all they have to do is choose which appeals to them the most. To pay for these items that developers and other content creators have made, we now transition into game currency, which would often form part of the virtual economy within the Metaverse, aside from the use of Cryptocurrencies.

11.4 Game Currencies

We have mentioned several types of game currencies throughout the chapters of this book, but majority of the attention allotted to these currencies have focused on the use of the premium currencies that require users to spend real money to acquire and amass a large amount of the currency. This theme is almost applicable to all platforms, regardless of their applications as games, or even as social media platforms. There are several types of game currencies which you may have encountered, and in this instance, we do not speak specifically of gold, silver, points, or other forms, which in themselves belong to a categorization of game currencies which are to be discussed here. You may wonder why it is necessary to discuss game currencies within the Metaverse. The fact remains that not every single user has the financial capacity to invest in Cryptocurrencies to use these as the main currency to perform internet transactions. While there are options where you can farm for a particular premium currency, this takes time to do, and this severely limits the interactions that you as a user can enact within the Metaverse. Because of this, it is then necessary to utilize another form of game currency that allows you to perform transactions without the need to physically invest hard currency – though there are options for this- before you can begin to enjoy the other features of the game.

Now, it is no surprise then, to use gamer slang, that the whales would use hard currency as a basis for game currency. Regardless of the type of gamer or user you may be, you have most likely seen options such as these pop-up regardless of the platform. Take for instance, in some games, where you do not have enough of the game currency – therefore, this takes you to a link or separate window where you have the option to spend n amount of dollars for n amount of game currency. Players of Marvel Future Fight would know perfectly well the offers that pop-up every time you move to another window, where you are beset with crystal packages, growth packages and the like for a price set in your local currency. This only proves that real currency is still an important matter to game developers, and that these would be one of the options to ensure the continued hold over the user's attention. This is because the use of actual currency is universal among all games. Each game and social media platform may have its own version of currency, but what they do share is that they all take real currency in exchange for a specific value of in-game currency at reasonable rates. The drawback with this type of currency is that because there are so many players who want to spend real currency to make meaningful progress in the game, then this lessens the scarcity in the game and therefore reduces the value of some items and lessens the amount of attention from the user as they don't have to grind or farm for these items.

Now, real or hard currency as we mentioned earlier, can be used to purchase other forms of currency which now includes soft currency, better known as the coins that you can probably farm for and amass if you are a thrifty spender. Soft currencies generally have low value to a player and can allow the player to purchase less valuable items. These types of currencies can easily be obtained as log-in rewards, check-in rewards, bonuses for the completion of a quest objective, or simply obtained as you wait. Soft currencies are among the more predominant form of currency for the free to play business model we have mentioned earlier, as this allows users to take part in game events without the need to shell out money for the added features. Call of Duty Players will know soft currencies as credits, while players of other games will see this as gold, silver, gems, simoleons, or other easily farmable currencies.

Medium currencies require users to continuously grind for more valuable forms of in-game currency that would allow users to access more features in the platform. Though users can grind for these currencies, the tendency with medium currencies is that they cannot be amasses, as there is a cap as to how much of a particular currency you are allowed to have. This ensures that there is a balance in the game economy as this allows scarcity to be implemented and allows the game or social media platform to retain some of its value. There are some frustrations with this, as once users have spent the medium currency, they would have to continue the grind for these currencies from scratch. If it took you a long time to amass this much, this certainly is not enjoyable and may potentially turn users away from the game. Capped accumulation is one of the peskier yet necessary balances needed to keep a game economy in check. This means that you are only allowed to keep a certain amount of currency in game, and compels you to spend the rest. Players of Diablo II probably remember the gold cap of 2,500,000 gold in the inventory, where any excess especially if you went looting through each dungeon would force you to gamble with the NPCs, or if you are in BattleNet, to trade with players for more valuable items such as runes and class specific weapons. Other ways to limit the excessive storage of currencies would stem from the increased grind once you have reached a level cap – which makes it harder to grind for resources. Acquisition caps are another means for developers to balance the game economy as this ensures that scarcity exists with not only currency but certain resources such as energy. While you can still play, users would not be able to generate more of the currency or resource until the passage of a specific length of time. Limited use currencies allow the conversion of the accumulated medium currency into a more valuable currency that may be used in game. Users may have seen this feature in a few Facebook games that allow you to spend the currency in exchange for boosts, bonuses and extra perks to help you complete a level easily.

Energy currency, is one type of currency most users are absolutely familiar with – Facebook Tetris and

Farmville anyone? Before we go down memory lane, we are familiar with the need to spend to accumulate a large amount of energy especially if there is a quest or task that requires copious amounts of it. While game mechanics would allow you to gift energy in small increments – such as two units of energy as a gift; win larger increments off a prize roulette – 5 energy or 10 energy; or be given as rewards in the largest increments from 30 to 50 units of energy. Energy can also be manufactured such as through the use of energy potions where you would have to farm for the resources needed to make these. But despite all of these options for free to play models, the big spenders would easily shell out at least $5-20 in their local currency to accumulate at least 2000-5000 units or so of energy needed to complete the tasks at hand. While this type of energy would ensure that the attention of the user is completely captured, energy caps at least restrict the amount of time each user spends in the platform –for altruistic reasons.

Featured currencies provide opportunities for users to accumulate more valuable forms of currencies to be used within the platform, or at least allow them the opportunity to gain better and more rewards than what the game or social media platform would ordinarily award to them as they play. However, because these featured currencies entail a different game style, the main drawback is that they can affect the attention of the players whose focus is ultimately divided from the need to gain the reward, or to obtain the currency.

Social currencies are those that users would gain from social interactions, and would be the best type of currency to implement within the Metaverse, though this would be disadvantageous to the naturally shy individual.

It is possible however, to gain points in social currencies if you gift items to other users.

11.5 Conclusion

Game economies are a more complex form of virtual economy that would underlie the structure of the Metaverse, and provides additional options for users of the Metaverse to interact with the various elements in their chosen platform. This area narrated how the game economy focuses on the need for attention and the need to provide alternative means of currencies to increase user participation, essential to the function of the Metaverse.

12 THE FUTURE IS NOW

When authors conceived of the future in the new Millennium, there were futuristic visions of the world completely run by computers, and everyone would be able to travel by the power of flight through fancy jetpacks. While there are jetpacks now, and though computers automate certain processes and have become part of our daily lives, we have yet to fully realize the potential of the digital age within our contemporary period. The development of the Metaverse has a long way to go before It can be the Metaverse that was fully envisioned by its developers, where everyone can be fully immersed in a universe that has been grafted onto our own. However, with the proto-Metaverses that are now present, it becomes entirely possible to live in the future, if but briefly, that we too may experience the future encapsulated by the digital age.

12.1 Opportunities for Furthering the Metaverse

With the recent rebrand of Facebook into Meta, more talks about the Metaverse have portrayed it as the future. This implication means that the Metaverse itself has to evolve beyond its current iteration of games and socialization and into a more similar replica of our world, to integrate business, and education aspects as well.

To some companies, games and social media companies in particular, the Metaverse is the best opportunity for them to diversify their portfolios wherein they could expand beyond the microtransactions that fuel their virtual economies, and instead contribute and play a bigger role in the virtual economy of the Metaverse. Thus, this opportunity requires the development of assets, such as the increased use of NFTs and other virtual tokens to be able to take part in the virtual marketplace of the Metaverse itself. The economy that these developers have to take part it, has made them realize that within the Metaverse, the population would actually shell out real and virtual currency for virtual items, and as such, this would compel them to diversify their assets, which serves as their impetus to take part in the expansion of the virtual economy of the Metaverse. This then aids in the transition from the gaming aspect into a more business oriented aspect, and allows the integration of both, to increase the business and earning opportunities within the Metaverse.

For many however, the future of the Metaverse lies with investments in blockchains and NFTs as these are deemed to be the most lucrative assets that are in the Metaverse. Thus, an increase in the values of these blockchains and Cryptocurrencies become the backbone of the future expansion of the Metaverse. Similar to how cities are built around the presence of an abundant resource, a Metaverse that is built around a highly valued Cryptocurrency and blockchain would cause that particular area of the Metaverse to expand, and open itself to a variety of businesses all over the Metaverse. For instance, where the Metaverse was oriented towards stocks, it can now focus on the fashion and entertainment industries. As it flourishes like a city, it has the potential to expand like a city with the integration of several brands into its domain.

Online work remains another opportunity to expand the Metaverse. Work from home opportunities have provided a means for families to be able to reorient themselves with a work-life balance, and in view of that balance, it becomes necessary to adapt to the work from home scenario. Ideally, the Metaverse can become a workspace too, that could replicate our office spaces and provide more opportunities to earn within the Metaverse, and cultivate the need for virtual real estate which would prove another area of expansion for the Metaverse itself.

12.2 Evolution of the Metaverse

The Metaverse can evolve in accordance with the limits of human imagination, ergo, the imagination of the developers. As of this moment, the development of the Metaverse and its evolution is dependent upon the existence of its infrastructure, which only allows a limited, synchronic experience among the users of the Metaverse. As it is, investments, creativity and ingenuity are needed to further the evolution of the Metaverse into the true universe that it was meant to be. The Metaverse in this context, would call for the evolution of our technology, that it too, may partake in its changes and adapt.

CONCLUSION

Throughout all the Chapters in this book, we have described the Metaverse, and how it would play a central role in our lives. It would be prudent to say would, as its use would eventually become inevitable, and as the economy shifts towards a virtual aspect, it becomes necessary to orient ourselves with this new world, that is both strange, and familiar to us. The internet, made more substantial, the physical world, replicated in code. Thus this book would serve as a guide on how to navigate the streams of data that make up the Metaverse and subsequently, allow you to make the most of its opportunities.

Thanks for buying my book. Here is my **gift to you**, two free online **courses about NFTs** that you download for free from this link:

https://dl.bookfunnel.com/5265zz3f4i

Please remember to **leave a review of this book on Amazon**, even if you obtain the book on other platforms.

Please remember to **leave a review of this book on Amazon**, even if you obtain the book on other platforms.

REFERENCES

- https://coinmarketcap.com/alexandria/article/what-is-a-non-fungible-token-nft?cv=1
- https://www.forbes.com/sites/lawrencewintermeyer/2021/02/12/non-fungible-token-market-booms-as-big-names-join-cryptos-newest-craze/?sh=57
- https://academy.binance.com/en/articles/a-guide-to-crypto-collectibles-and-non-fungible-tokens-nfts
- https://opensea.io/blog/digital-art/the-beginners-guide-to-creating-selling-digital-art-nfts/
- https://www.investopedia.com/non-fungible-tokens-nft-5115211
- https://www.maxfosterphotography.com/gallery/what-is-an-nft-how-can-photographers-and-artists-benefit/
- https://www.businessinsider.com/nft-marketplaces-where-to-buy-sell-non-fungible-tokens-online-2021-3?r=US&IR=T
- https://influencermarketinghub.com/nft-marketplaces/
- https://beincrypto.com/top-10-most-expensive-nft-sales-globally/?cv=1
- https://observer.com/2021/04/five-things-artists-should-know-and-do-before-getting-into-nfts/
- https://www.gemini.com/cryptopedia/nft-non-fungible-token-crypto-collectibles
- https://www.esquire.com/entertainment/a35742083/what-are-nfts-explained/
- https://cointelegraph.com/news/five-of-the-most-expensive-nfts-sold-in-2019
- https://petapixel.com/2021/03/12/what-is-an-nft-and-why-should-photographers-care/

- https://gadgets.ndtv.com/internet/news/nft-non-fungible-tokens-what-are-they-blockchain-cryptocurrency-assets-unique-digital-physical-2382693
- https://www.coindesk.com/how-to-create-buy-sell-nfts
- https://www.britannica.com/technology/photography/Into-the-21st-century-the-digital-age
- https://www.wibbitz.com/blog/infographic-video-production-evolution-timeline/
- https://www.nbcnews.com/think/opinion/what-are-nfts-what-could-they-do-music-industry-artists-ncna1261205
- https://news.slashdot.org/?issue=20210305
- https://pixelplex.io/blog/non-fungible-tokens/
- https://decrypt.co/resources/non-fungible-tokens-nfts-explained-guide-learn-blockchain
- https://art.art/wp-content/uploads/2021/03/NFT-YEARLY-REPORT-2020.pdf
- https://www.coinstaker.com/uk-government-storage-evidences-on-blockchain/
- https://www.businessinsider.co.za/nft-marketplaces-where-to-buy-sell-non-fungible-tokens-online-2021-3
- https://www.tandfonline.com/doi/abs/10.1080/03610910802680880
- https://forkast.news/nft-art-nba-top-shot-crypto-collectibles/
- https://tokenbank.co.kr/coin/310/view/
- How Legal are Non-Fungible Tokens (NFTs) in Singapore: https://singaporelegaladvice.com/legal-non-fungible-tokens-nfts-singapore/

- Non-Fungible Token Definition: Understanding NFTs. https://www.investopedia.com/non-fungible-tokens-nft-5115211
- How to Create an NFT Marketplace Platform? | by Linda John https://medium.com/the-capital/how-to-create-an-nft-marketplace-platform-b3dad5ae1ecc
- What are NFTs – and why is the whole art world talking .... https://vr-nft.com/what-are-nfts-and-why-is-the-whole-art-world-talking-about-them/
- An article from 'The New York Times', sold for 478,573 euros. https://newsrnd.com/tech/2021-03-26-an-article-from--the-new-york-times---sold-for-478-573-euros.HkJNgDoEu.html
- How to Make, Purchase, and Sell NFTs? – NFT Hours. https://nfthours.com/how-to-make-purchase-and-sell-nfts/
- NFTs: What Are They and How Can You Create Them?. https://techmepro.com/how-to/nfts-what-are-they-and-how-can-you-create-them/
- What makes NFTs go?. "Twitter CEO, Jack Dorsey sold his https://pdiwan.medium.com/what-makes-nfts-go-fcf07d3e3c6c
- Non-Fungible-Token Market Booms As Big Names Join Crypto's https://www.forbes.com/sites/lawrencewintermeyer/2021/02/12/non-fungible-token-market-booms-as-big-names-join-cryptos-newest-craze/
- 11 Projects at the Nexus of DeFi and NFTs - CoinDesk. https://www.coindesk.com/defi-nft-projects

- Top 5 Best NFT Marketplaces For Artists - NFT's Street. https://www.nftsstreet.com/best-nft-marketplaces-for-artists-2/
- Unreal Real Estate Makes Its Curious Debut. https://www.premierhomesearch.com/blog/487/Unreal+Real+Estate+Makes+Its+Curious+Debut
- Collinson Crowdfunding-Your Gateway to Innovative Investments. https://www.ccfl.co.nz/raising-capital/key-benefits
- NON-FUNGIBLE TOKENS YEARLY REPORT 2020. https://observatorioblockchain.com/wp-content/uploads/2021/02/NFT-YEARLY-REPORT-2020-FREE-EN.pdf
- https://medium.com/building-the-metaverse/game-economics-part-1-the-attention-economy-efb64312ad6b
- https://medium.com/building-the-metaverse/the-metaverse-is-real-gamification-bc215fb4250b
- https://medium.com/building-the-metaverse/types-of-virtual-items-e12daa9580a2
- https://www.gamedeveloper.com/business/types-of-game-currencies-in-mobile-free-to-play
- https://medium.com/building-the-metaverse/when-the-virtual-became-real-4168809879f5
- https://digitalnative.substack.com/p/stay-for-who-you-can-be-avatars-in
- https://www.linkedin.com/pulse/how-brands-can-thrive-direct-avatar-economy-cathy-hackl/
- https://www.frontiersin.org/articles/10.3389/fbloc.2019.00028/full

- https://hackernoon.com/eli5-zero-knowledge-proof-78a276db9eff